I0020976

DATA SCIENCE CRASH COURSE FOR BEGINNERS

FUNDAMENTALS AND PRACTICES WITH PYTHON

AI PUBLISHING

© Copyright 2020 by AI Publishing
All rights reserved.
First Printing, 2020

Edited by AI Publishing
eBook Converted and Cover by Gazler Studio
Published by AI Publishing LLC

ISBN-13: 978-1-7347901-4-6

The contents of this book may not be copied, reproduced, duplicated, or transmitted without the direct written permission of the author. Under no circumstances whatsoever will any legal liability or blame be held against the publisher for any compensation, damages, or monetary loss due to the information contained herein, either directly or indirectly.

Legal Notice:
You are not permitted to amend, use, distribute, sell, quote, or paraphrase any part of the content within this book without the specific consent of the author.

Disclaimer Notice:
Kindly note that the information contained within this document is solely for educational and entertainment purposes. No warranties of any kind are indicated or expressed. Readers accept that the author is not providing any legal, professional, financial, or medical advice. Kindly consult a licensed professional before trying out any techniques explained in this book.

By reading this document, the reader consents that under no circumstances is the author liable for any losses, direct or indirect, that are incurred as a consequence of the use of the information contained within this document, including, but not restricted to, errors, omissions, or inaccuracies.

How to Contact Us

If you have any feedback, please let us know
by sending an email to contact@aipublishing.io.

Your feedback is immensely valued,
and we look forward to hearing from you.
It will be beneficial for us
to improve the quality of our books.

To get the Python codes and materials used in this book,
please click the link below:

www.aipublishing.io/book-data-science-python

The order number is required.

About the Publisher

At AI Publishing Company, we have established an international learning platform specifically for young students, beginners, small enterprises, startups, and managers who are new to data science and artificial intelligence.

Through our interactive, coherent, and practical books and courses, we help beginners learn skills that are crucial to developing AI and data science projects.

Our courses and books range from basic introduction courses to language programming and data science to advanced courses for machine learning, deep learning, computer vision, big data, and much more. The programming languages used include Python, R, and some data science and AI software.

AI Publishing's core focus is to enable our learners to create and try proactive solutions for digital problems by leveraging the power of AI and data science to the maximum extent.

Moreover, we offer specialized assistance in the form of our free online content and eBooks, providing up-to-date and useful insight into AI practices and data science subjects, along with eliminating the doubts and misconceptions about AI and programming.

Our experts have cautiously developed our online courses and kept them concise, short, and comprehensive so that you can understand everything clearly and effectively and start practicing the applications right away.

We also offer consultancy and corporate training in AI and data science for enterprises so that their staff can navigate through the workflow efficiently.

With AI Publishing, you can always stay closer to the innovative world of AI and data science.

If you are eager to learn the A to Z of AI and data science but have no clue where to start, AI Publishing is the finest place to go.

Please contact us by email at contact@aipublishing.io.

AI Publishing is Looking for Authors Like You

Interested in becoming an author for AI Publishing? Please contact us at author@aipublishing.io.

We are working with developers and AI tech professionals just like you, to help them share their insights with the global AI and Data Science lovers. You can share all your knowledge about hot topics in AI and Data Science.

Table of Contents

Preface

§ Who Is This Book For?

This book explains different data science fundamentals and applications using various data science libraries for Python. The book is aimed ideally at absolute beginners in Data Science and Machine Learning. Though a background in the Python programming language and data science can help speed up learning, the book contains a crash course on Python programming language in one chapter. Therefore, the only prerequisite to efficiently using this book is access to a computer with the internet. All the codes and datasets have been provided. However, to download data preparation libraries, you will need the internet.

§ How to Use This Book?

To get the best out of this book, I would suggest that you first get your feet wet with the Python programming language, especially the object-oriented programming concepts. To do so, you can take the crash course on Python in chapters 2 and 3 of this book. Also, try to read the chapters of this book in order since the concepts taught in subsequent chapters are based on previous chapters.

In each chapter, try to first understand the theoretical concepts behind different types of data science techniques and then try to execute the example code. I would again stress that rather than copying and pasting code, try to write code yourself, and in case of any error, you can match your code with the source code provided in the book as well as in the Python notebooks in the resources.

Finally, try to answer the questions asked in the exercises at the end of each chapter. The solutions to the exercises have been given at the end of the Book.

About the Author

M. Wasim Nawaz has a Ph.D. in Computer Engineering from the University of Wollongong, Australia. His main areas of research are Machine Learning, Data Science, Computer Vision, and Image Processing. Wasim has over eight years of teaching experience in Computer and Electrical Engineering. He has worked with both private and public sector organizations.

Get in Touch With Us

Feedback from our readers is always welcome.

For general feedback, please send us an email at contact@aipublishing.io and mention the book title in the subject line.

Although we have taken extraordinary care to ensure the accuracy of our content, errors do occur. If you have found an error in this book, we would be grateful if you could report this to us as soon as you can.

If you are interested in becoming an AI Publishing author and if you have expertise in a topic and you are interested in either writing or contributing to a book, please send us an email at author@aipublishing.io.

An Important Note to Our Valued Readers:

Download the Color Images

Our print edition books are available only in black & white at present. However, the digital edition of our books is available in color PDF.

We request you to download the PDF file containing the color images of the screenshots/diagrams used in this book here:

www.aipublishing.io/book-data-science-python

The typesetting and publishing costs for a color edition are prohibitive. These costs would push the final price of each book to $50, which would make the book less accessible for most beginners.

We are a small company, and we are negotiating with major publishers for a reduction in the publishing price. We are hopeful of a positive outcome sometime soon. In the meantime, we request you to help us with your wholehearted support, feedback, and review.

For the present, we have decided to print all of our books in black & white and provide access to the color version in PDF. This is a decision that would benefit the majority of our readers, as most of them are students. This would also allow beginners to afford our books.

Warning

In Python, indentation is very important. Python indentation is a way of telling a Python interpreter that the group of statements belongs to a particular code block. After each loop or if-condition, be sure to pay close attention to the intent.

Example

```
# Python program showing
# indentation

site = 'aisciences'

if site == 'aisciences':
    print('Logging to www.aisciences.io...')
else:
    print('retype the URL.')
print('All set !')
```

To avoid problems during execution, we advise you to download the codes available on Github by requesting access from the link below. Please have your order number ready for access:

www.aipublishing.io/book-data-science-python

1

Introduction to Data Science and Decision Making

This chapter provides a high-level introduction to natural language processing. The chapter explains natural language processing in great detail, some of the most common applications of natural language processing, and the basic approaches used for developing natural language processing applications.

1.1. Introduction

We are living in the age of data. Not only the amount of data we currently have is gigantic, but the pace of the data generation is also accelerating day by day. There are more than 4.5 billion active internet users at the time of writing this book, July 2020, which comprises about 60 percent of the global population. These internet users create large volumes of data by using social media such as Facebook, Twitter, Instagram, and Youtube.

The amount of mobile data is also blowing up. Furthermore, real-time data being produced by the Internet of Things (IoT) devices is seeing an unprecedented rate of growth. These mind-boggling statistics are growing at an exponential rate because of the digitization of the world.

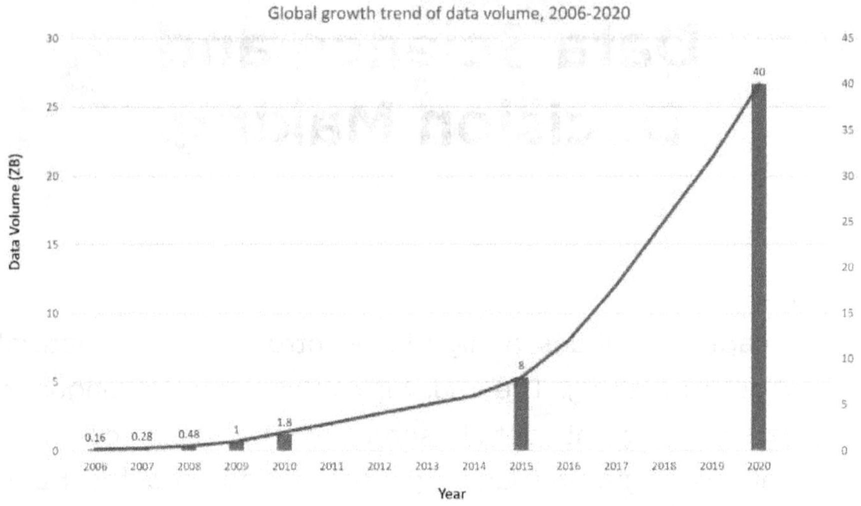

Figure 1.1: Global growth trend of data volume, 2006-2020.

Figure 1.1 shows the global growth trend of data volume from 2006-2020 based on "*The digital universe in 2020: big data, bigger digital shadows, and biggest growth in the far east.*" Note that the graph above is measured in zettabytes (ZB) or 10^{21} bytes - 1 ZB accounts for 1 trillion gigabytes (GB). This is a huge amount of data. The value associated with this data diminishes because the data is not processed and analyzed at the same rate. Thus, it is of utmost importance to extract knowledge from the data.

Data science applies scientific principles, methods, algorithms, and processes to extract knowledge, information and insights by collecting, processing and analyzing structured and unstructured data where the former type of data is obtained from a database management system such as MySQL, Oracle, MongoDB and the latter type of data comprise of text, audio, video, and documents.

Data science is a multidisciplinary field related to mathematics, statistics, programming, data mining, machine learning, deep learning, and big data. Data science uses machine learning (ML) algorithms and statistical methods to train the computer to make predictions from the data.

§ Applications of Data Science

Data science has a whole lot of applications in a diverse set of industries, including but not limited to the following business sectors.

- Financial companies use the data collected from their customers for fraud and risk detection.
- The healthcare sector receives great benefit from data science by analyzing medical images to detect tumors, artery stenosis, and organ delineation.
- Internet search engines such as Google use data science algorithms to provide us the best result for our searched query.
- Digital marketing strategies use data science algorithms to get insight into the preferences and needs of customers. Knowing the spending habits of people can help identify the customer base of a company.
- Internet giants like Amazon, LinkedIn, Twitter, Google, Netflix, and IMDb use recommendation systems to suggest relevant products to the users based upon

their previous searches, thereby improving the user experience.

- Social media websites use face recognition to suggest tags to your uploaded images.
- Speech recognition products such as Google Voice, Siri, Cortana, etc. convert speech to text and commands.
- Airline companies employ data science to identify the strategic areas of improvements such as flight delay prediction, route planning, and deciding the class of airplanes to buy for flight operation.
- Video games use data science and machine learning algorithms to analyze previous moves by players and progress the game accordingly. Sony, Nintendo, and EA Sports have changed gaming experience using data science.

§ What Is This Book About?

The main purpose of *Data Science Crash Course for Beginners with Python* is to demonstrate that:

- data science is an interesting field that can perform a variety of tasks;
- Python is an easy, user-friendly and versatile programming language with a simple syntax that makes data science quite doable;
- they can start applying data science to practical problems;
- how to answer data science problems and where to employ data science, thereby gaining a significant advantage over others, and increasing their chances

of getting a promotion or getting a new job in data science.

1.2. Python and Data Science

It is generally thought that one has to be a computer genius and expert in programming to perform complex tasks associated with data science, but this is far from reality. Python is an open-source, versatile, and flexible programming language with a simple syntax that makes data science tasks quite easy. Python offers numerous useful libraries that do all the tedious tasks for you in the background. Python offers libraries for data processing, analysis, modeling, and visualization that include:

- Numpy,
- Pandas,
- Scikit-Learn,
- Matplotlib.

NumPy ('Numeric Python') is a Python library used for fast mathematical computation on arrays and matrices. Pandas is one of the most widely-used Python libraries in data science. It provides high-performance, easy to use structures, and data analysis tools. Unlike the NumPy library, which provides objects for multi-dimensional arrays, Pandas provides a two-dimensional object called a DataFrame. It is like a spreadsheet with column names and row labels that makes the data analysis easy.

Matplotlib library is used to plot data from experiments. These packages and their uses are given in detail in this book. This book spends considerable time demonstrating to the readers that practical problems such as face recognition, which are considered very difficult problems by most beginners, can be solved quite easily using tools available in Python library Scikit-Learn.

The book emphasizes using the right tools to get started with data science. It starts with Anaconda, a free and open-source platform for Python. Anaconda accompanies several packages and utilities that help us work with data science, machine learning, and large-scale data processing and analytics. The Anaconda distribution includes data-science packages suitable for Windows, Linux, and macOS.

We use the Jupyter Notebook, which is part of the Anaconda installation. Jupyter Notebook is a fully interactive environment where we can mix presentation elements such as comments for better readability of the code, LaTeX document preparation, and even HTML code all in a single notebook.

To get started, the reader finds complete installation and setting up of the programming environment for Anaconda and a quick primer to the Python programming. The emphasis is on getting you familiar with Python as quickly as possible by presenting simple examples so that the programming does not become a bottleneck to learning. We discuss the installation and setup of Python in Chapter 2.

1.3. The Data Science Pipeline

The overall step by step process to collect, store, clean, preprocess, analyze, model, interpret, and visualize the data is known as a data science pipeline. The processes in the pipeline are followed in a particular order to make things work. The main steps of this pipeline are as follows:

- Data Acquisition,
- Data Preparation,
- Exploratory Data Analysis,
- Data Modeling and Evaluation, and
- Interpretation and Reporting of Findings.

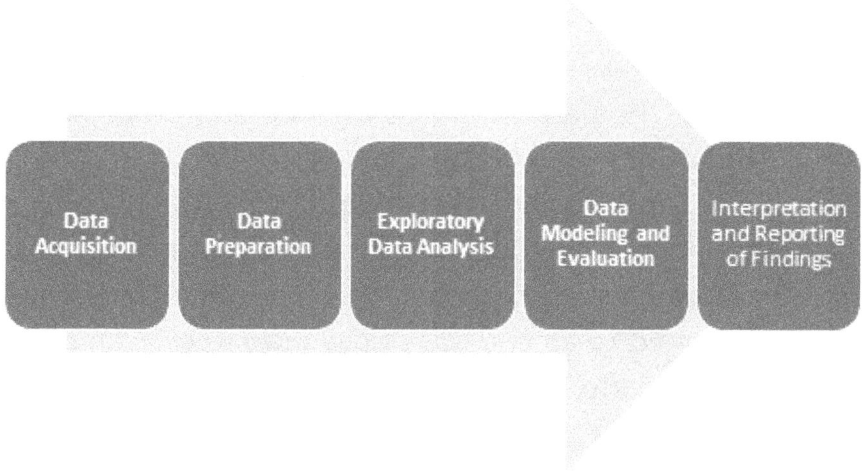

Figure 1.2: The data science pipeline

Understanding and following this pipeline enables us to:

- recognize patterns in the given data;
- extract useful information from the data;
- determine suitable models to describe the data;
- decide the best algorithms to be applied to the data;
- make appropriate decisions at different levels of a data science project.

Data Acquisition: We cannot perform any data science task without having data. The first step is to obtain data from either a database or from the internet. This data should be available in a usable format, for example, comma-separated values (CSV) and tab-separated values (TSV).

The data can be structured as obtained from a database management system: MySQL, Oracle, and MongoDB. Alternatively, it can be unstructured, for example, text, audio, video, and documents.

Data Preparation/cleaning/scrubbing: The data acquired from different sources is in a raw form, which is usually not used directly. The data has to be cleaned and prepared for further stages of the data science pipeline. The results from data science and machine learning projects greatly depend upon what input we give them, essentially *garbage in, garbage out.* Therefore, cleaning or scrubbing of the acquired data has to be performed to amend or remove incorrect, incomplete, improperly formatted, or duplicated data.

The clean data is sometimes transformed and mapped into a format more suitable for further processing than the original data. This process is called data wrangling or data munging.

Exploratory Data Analysis: In this phase, we apply different statistical tools to realize the range of values, important data variables and features, and data trends. We also extract significant features from the data by analyzing the cleaned data.

Data Modeling and Evaluation using Machine Learning: A model or a machine learning model is a set of assumptions about the underlying data. For example, to increase its sales, a company spends money on advertising its products. The company keeps a record of the dollars spent on advertisements at each of its stores and sales in dollars from the same store. It discovers that the relationship between the aforementioned variables is almost linear, as given in figure 1.3. Therefore, a model for this situation can be a linear relationship or a line between advertisement and sales. A good model, which makes accurate assumptions about the data, is necessary for the machine learning algorithm to give good results.

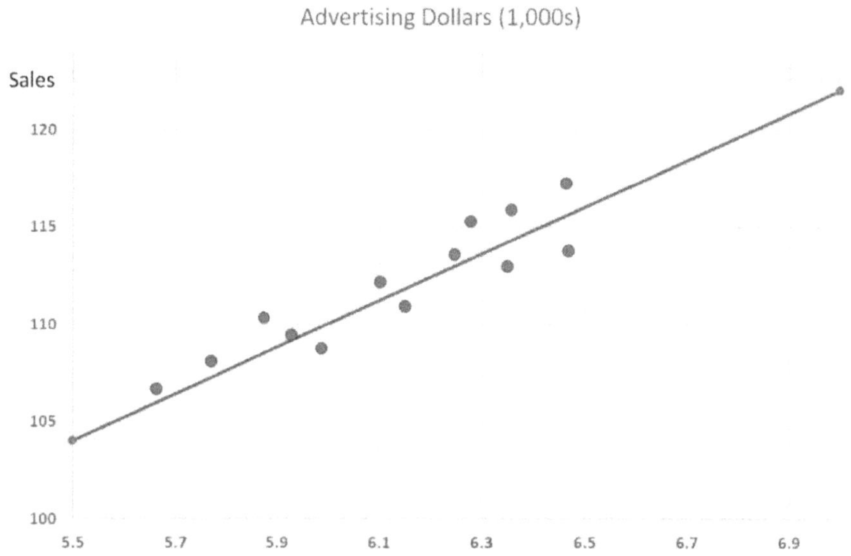

Figure 1.3: Relationship between dollars spent on advertisement and sales in dollars. Every point on the graph shows the data from one store. The line captures the overall trend of the data.

Machine learning algorithms typically build a mathematical model based on the given data, also known as the training data. Once a model is generated, it is used to make predictions or decisions on future test data. Often, when the model does not explain the underlying data, we revisit/update our model. Thus, it is a continuous process of making a model, assessing its performance, and updating the model if necessary, until a model of reasonable performance is obtained. The details of this process are given in Chapter 7.

A real-life example of predicting the future sale of products using machine learning models is by Walmart. The company records every purchase by the customer for future analysis. Data analysis by Walmart noticed a rise in the sales of toaster pastries, namely Pop-Tarts, whenever the National Weather Service (NWS) warned of a hurricane. Thus, store managers were instructed to put Pop-Tarts near store entrances during hurricane season. This move by the company saw a surge in the sale of Pop-Tarts. This story highlights the importance of machine learning models and their predictive powers.

Interpretation and Reporting of Findings: The next step in the data science pipeline is to interpret and explain our findings to others through communication. This can be achieved by connecting with and persuading people through interactive visualization and reporting to summarize the findings of a data science project.

1.4. Overview of the Contents

The book follows a very simple approach. It is divided into ten chapters.

Chapter 1 introduces the elementary concepts of data science and the processes to be followed to complete a data science project.

Chapter 2 lists the installation steps for Anaconda distribution of Python. It also introduces some of the datasets for data science projects.

Chapter 3 provides a crash course on Python for data science.

Chapter 4 utilizes Python commands and functions to acquire structured and unstructured data.

Chapter 5 uses Python commands, constructs, and functions to preprocess raw data for subsequent stages of a data science pipeline.

Chapter 6 explores the preprocessed data to analyze the behavior and trend of different features present in the data.

Chapter 7 employs machine learning and statistical techniques to create models from the given data for future predictions.

Chapter 8 presents techniques to measure the performance of a data science project.

Chapter 9 demonstrates the practical uses of data science through projects.

Chapter 10 concludes the book by giving key insights to the reader and possible further avenues.

In each chapter, several techniques have been explained theoretically as well as through practical examples. Each chapter contains exercise questions that can be used to evaluate the understanding of the concepts explained in the chapters. The Python Jupyter Notebooks and the datasets used in the book are provided in the resources.

Hands-on Time

It is time to check your understanding of the topic of this book through the exercise questions given in Section 1.5. The answers to these questions are given at the end of the book.

1.5. Exercises

Question 1:

What is the global growth trend of data volume in recent years?

A. Linearly increasing
B. Linearly decreasing
C. Exponentially increasing
D. Exponentially decreasing

Question 2:

Data science applies scientific principles, methods, algorithms, and processes to extract knowledge, information, and insights by:

A. collecting data
B. processing data
C. analyzing data
D. collecting, processing and analyzing data

Question 3:

Numpy, Pandas, Scikit-Learn and Matplotlib are popular

A. Programming languages
B. Inventors of Python
C. IT companies
D. Python libraries

Question 4:

In the list of following operations:

1. Exploratory Data Analysis
2. Data Preparation
3. Data Acquisition
4. Interpretation and Reporting of Findings
5. Data Modeling and Evaluation

What is the correct order of operations in a data science pipeline?

A. 12345

B. 54321

C. 32154

D. 13245

2

Python Installation and Libraries for Data Science

2.1. Introduction

Digital computers can understand instructions given to them in zeros and ones, where a one means turning ON a specific part of the central processing unit of a computer, and a zero means turning OFF that part. The computer instructions in the form of 0s and 1s are called machine language or machine code. It is very difficult for humans to understand and program the computer using machine language. Instead of using a low-level machine language, we use easily understandable higher-level languages that automatically translate high-level instructions into machine language.

There is a large pool of higher-level languages such as Java, C++, Visual Basic, MATLAB, etc. These languages are good for many tasks; however, these are not suitable for data science. On the contrary, Python provides a rich source of specialized libraries and packages that make it the right tool for data science.

This chapter provides the reader with a quick guide and a step-by-step process of installing and getting started with Python for data science. The chapter also introduces datasets. Moreover, the chapter introduces the reader with Python capabilities to handle data by furnishing Python libraries and packages. The details of Python coding are provided in Chapter 3.

2.2. Installation and Setup

There are different ways to download and install Python 3, the latest release of Python, which is widely used and supported by third-party libraries. One popular way is to download the software from the official website *Python Software Foundation* https://www.python.org/download. However, installing Python from the aforementioned link does not accompany many libraries and packages useful for data science tasks. These add-ons have to be installed separately. Therefore, we do not follow this method in this book.

Here, we use the Anaconda distribution of Python for data science and machine learning applications. Anaconda is a free and open-source distribution that includes data science libraries for Windows, Linux, and macOS operating systems. Since packages are included in this distribution, we should have high-speed internet and storage to download large installation files.

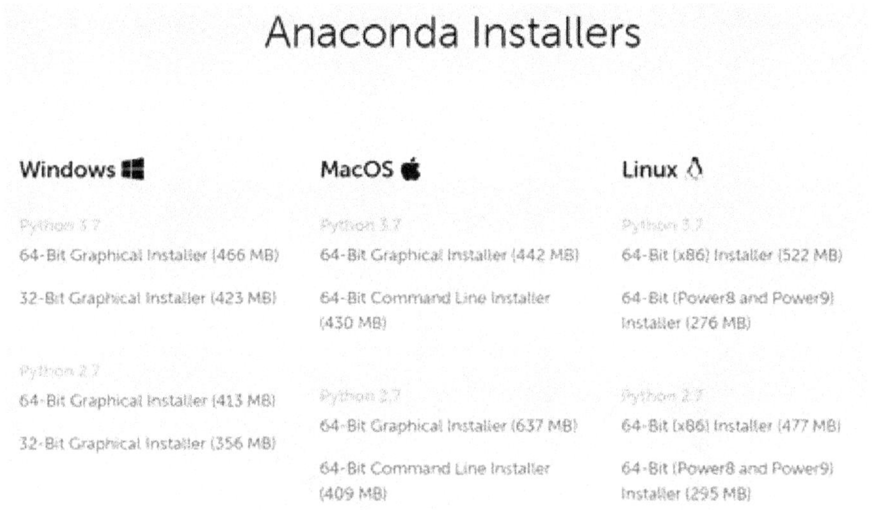

Figure 2.1: Anaconda Installers for Windows, MacOS, and Linux Individual Edition.

Anaconda Individual Edition can be downloaded from https://www.anaconda.com/products/individual, as shown in figure 2.1. We download the installation file by selecting the proper operating system and its version—either 32-bit or 64-bit—from the aforementioned link. We present a step-by-step installation guide for the installation and setup of Python using Anaconda.

2.2.1. Windows

1. Download the graphical Windows installer from https://www.anaconda.com/products/individual
2. Double-click the downloaded file. Then, click *Continue* to begin the installation.
3. Answer the following prompts: Introduction, Read Me, and License screens.
4. Next, click the *Install* button. Install Anaconda in a

specified directory (C:\Anaconda3_Python) given in the installation.

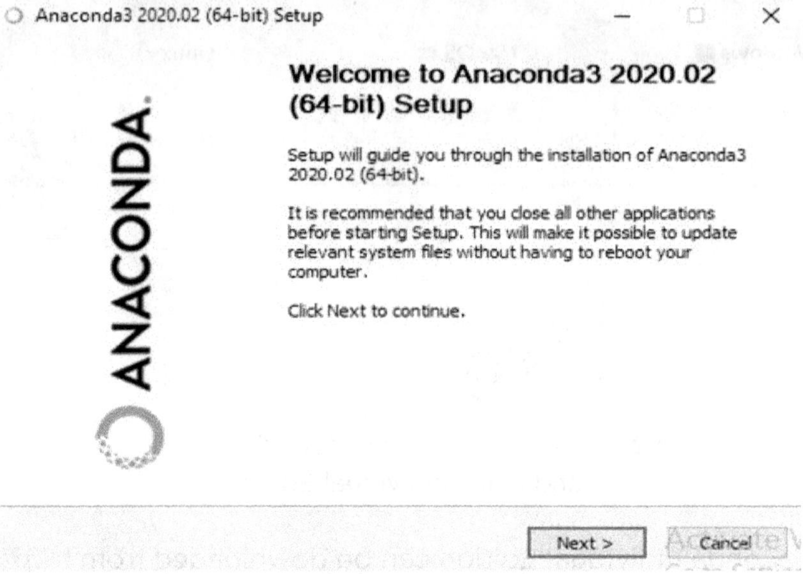

Figure 2.2: Anaconda Installation on Windows.

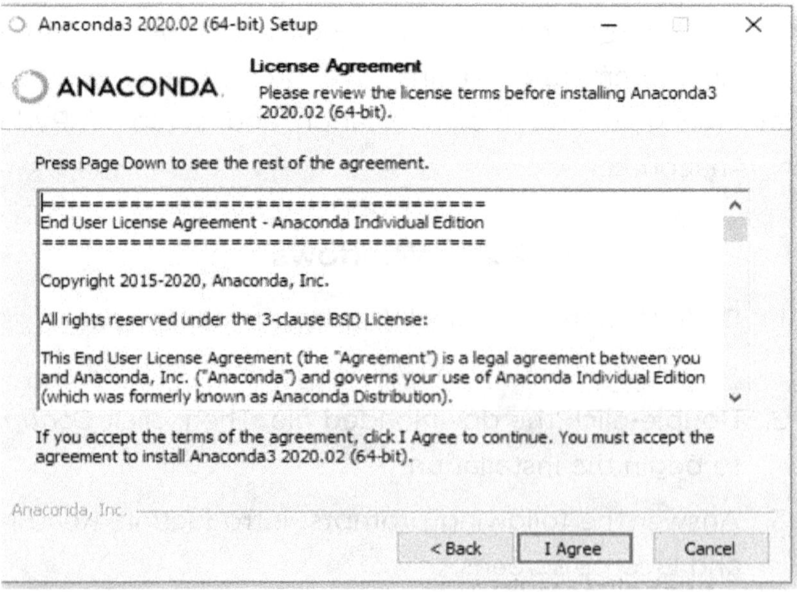

Figure 2.3: Anaconda Installation on Windows.

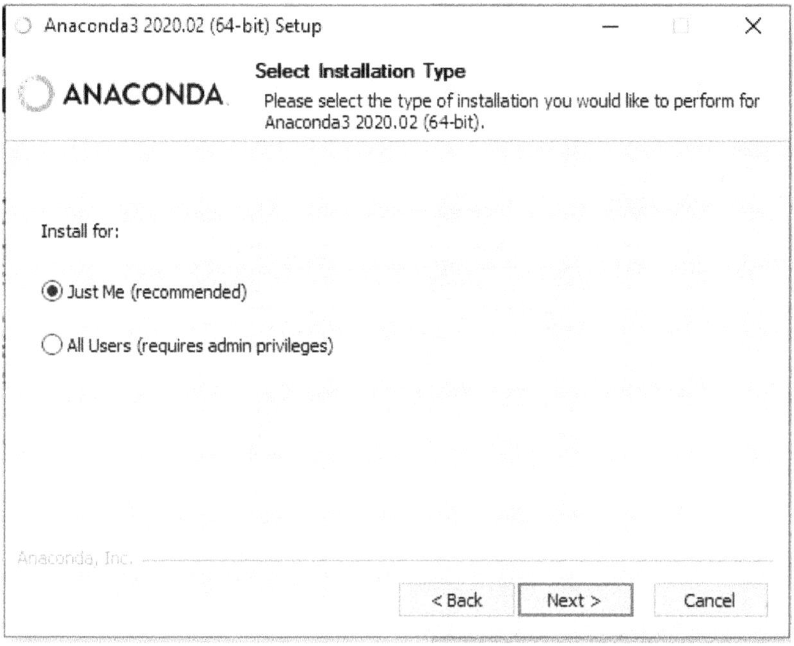

Figure 2.4: Anaconda Installation on Windows.

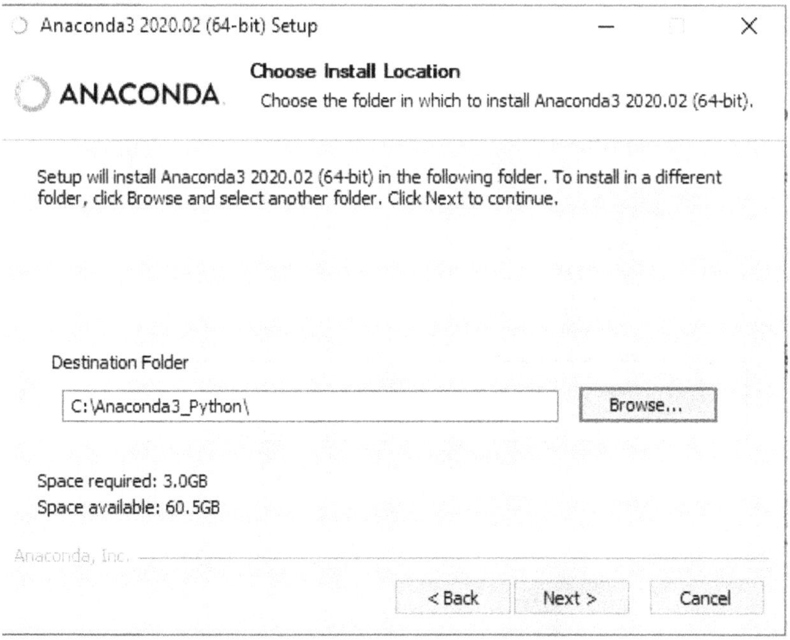

Figure 2.5: Anaconda Installation on Windows.

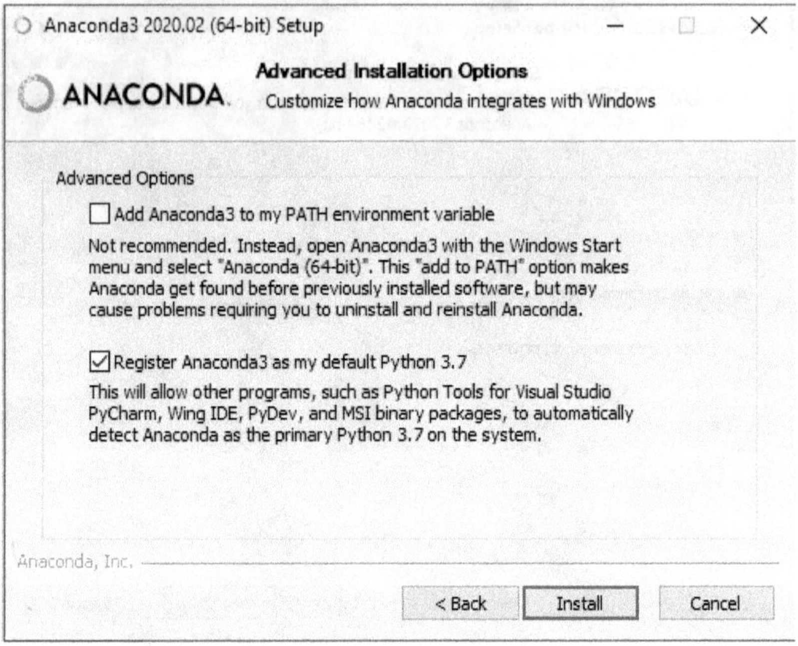

Figure 2.6: Anaconda Installation on Windows.

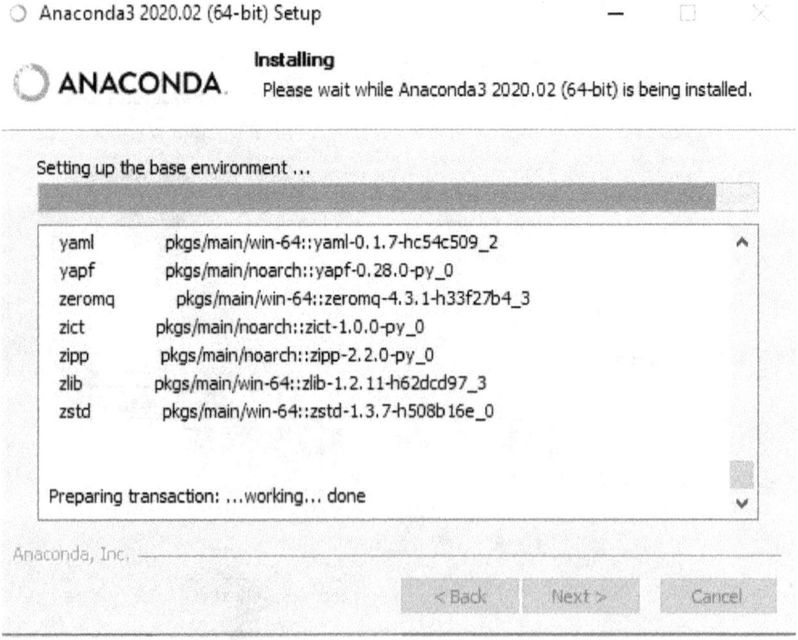

Figure 2.7: Anaconda Installation on Windows.

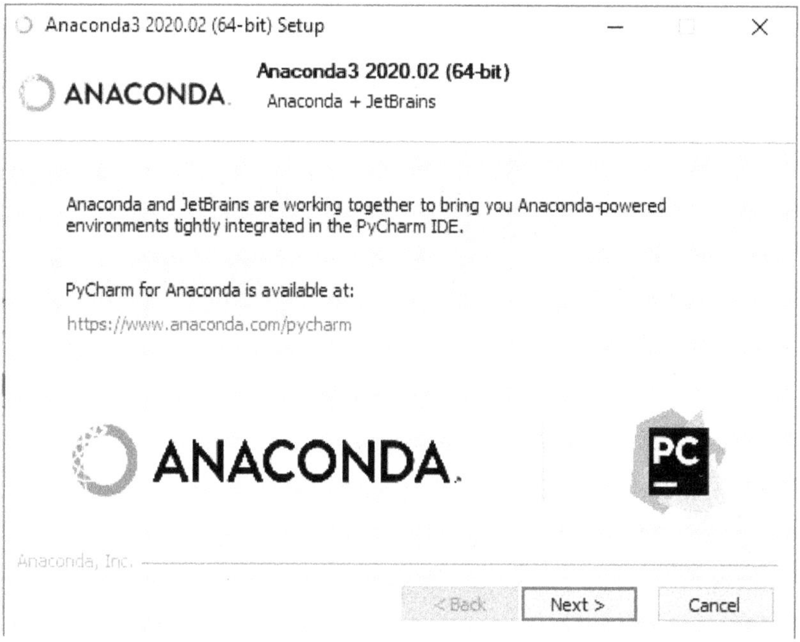

Figure 2.8: Anaconda Installation on Windows.

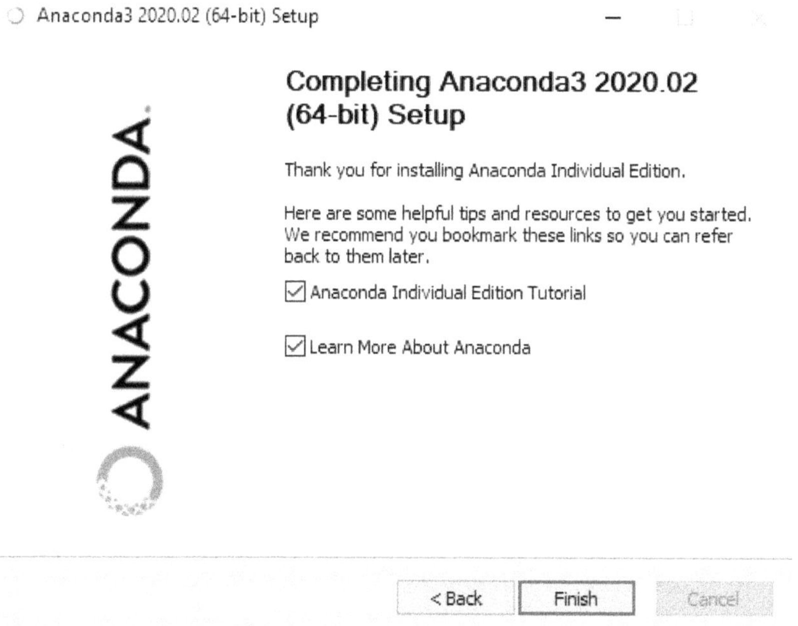

Figure 2.9: Anaconda Installation on Windows.

2.2.2. Apple OS X

1. Download the graphical MacOS installer from https://www.anaconda.com/products/individual
2. Double-click the downloaded file. Click *Continue* to begin the installation.
3. Next, click the Install button. Install Anaconda in the specified directory.

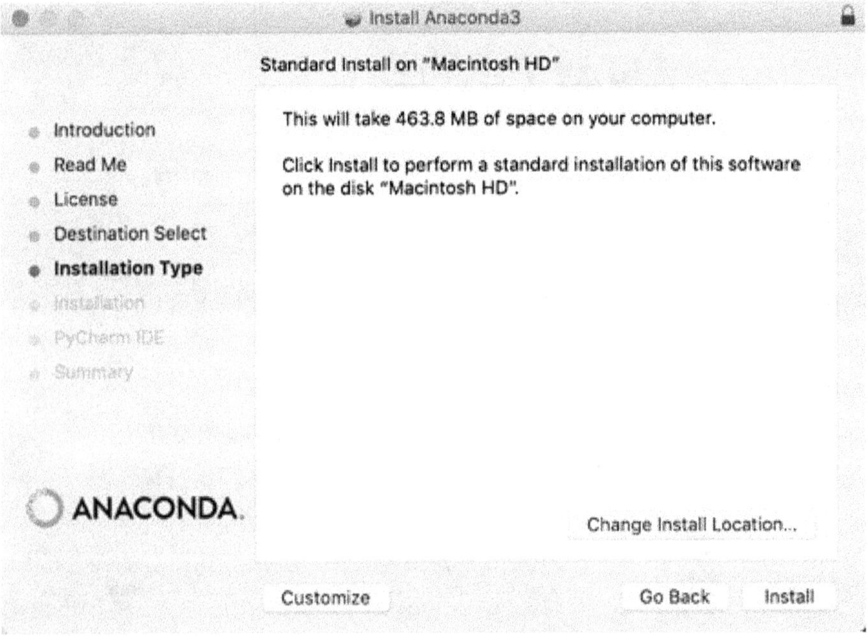

Figure 2.10: Anaconda Installation on Apple OS.

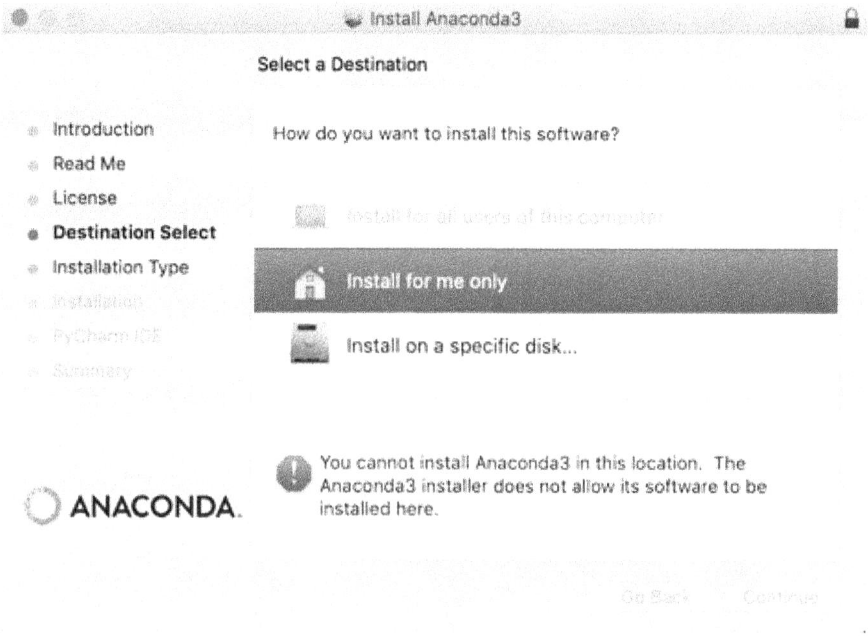

Figure 2.11: Anaconda Installation on Apple OS.

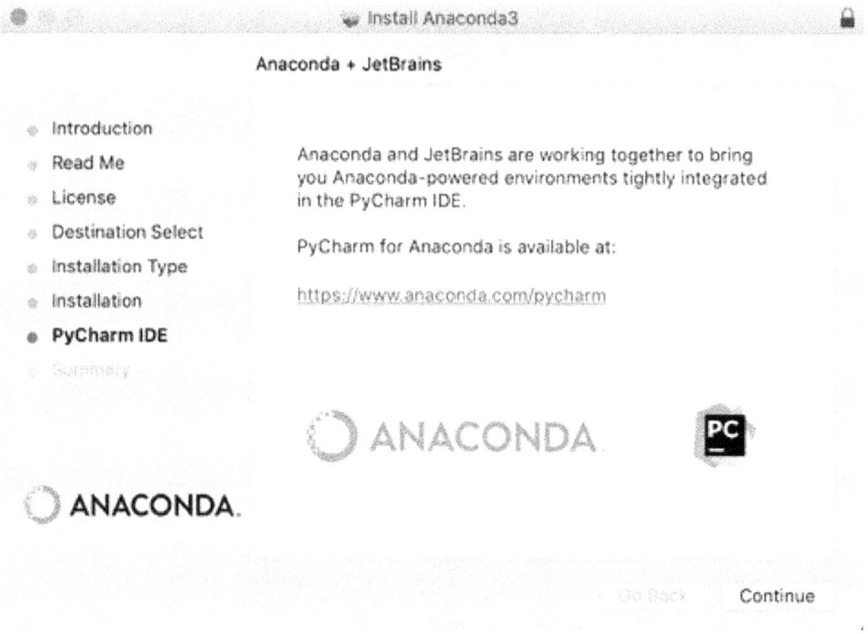

Figure 2.12: Anaconda Installation on Apple OS.

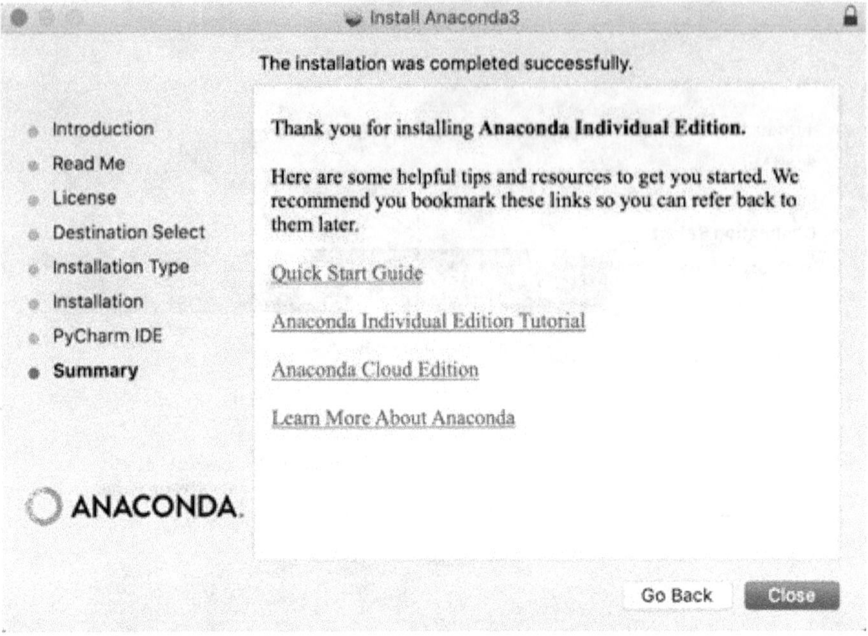

Figure 2.13: Anaconda Installation on Apple OS.

2.2.3. GNU/Linux

We use the command line to install Anaconda on Linux because there is no option for graphical installation. We download the copy of installation file from https://www.anaconda.com/products/individual first.

The following procedure should work on any Linux system, whether it is a 32-bit or 64-bit version of Anaconda.

1. Open a copy of Terminal on Linux.
2. Change directories to the downloaded copy of Anaconda on the system.
3. The name of the file normally appears as *Anaconda-3.7.0-Linux-x86.sh* for 32-bit systems and *Anaconda-3.7.0-Linuxx86_64.sh* for 64-bit systems. The version

number appears in the filename. In our case, the filename refers to version 3.7, which is the version used for this book.

4. Type

   bash ~/Downloads/Anaconda3-2020.02-Linux-x86.sh (for the 32-bit version) or

   bash ~/Downloads/Anaconda3-2020.02-Linux-x86_64.sh(for the 64-bit version), and press Enter.

5. An installation wizard opens up and asks you to accept the licensing terms for using Anaconda.
6. Accept the terms using the method required for the version of Linux.
7. Choose a location when the wizard requests you to provide an installation location for Anaconda. Then, click next.
8. The application extraction begins. A completion message pops up once the extraction is complete.

2.2.4. Creating and Using Notebooks

After the installation of Python is complete, it is time to explore the features of the language. To start working, we have to launch Jupyter Notebook accompanied with Anaconda installation. It can be launched by:

- the Anaconda Navigator by searching it in *Windows Search Box.* A new window will open, as shown in figure 2.14. Select and open the Jupyter Notebook from the top right side of the page.
- writing *Jupyter Notebook* in *Windows Search Box*, as shown in figure 2.15.

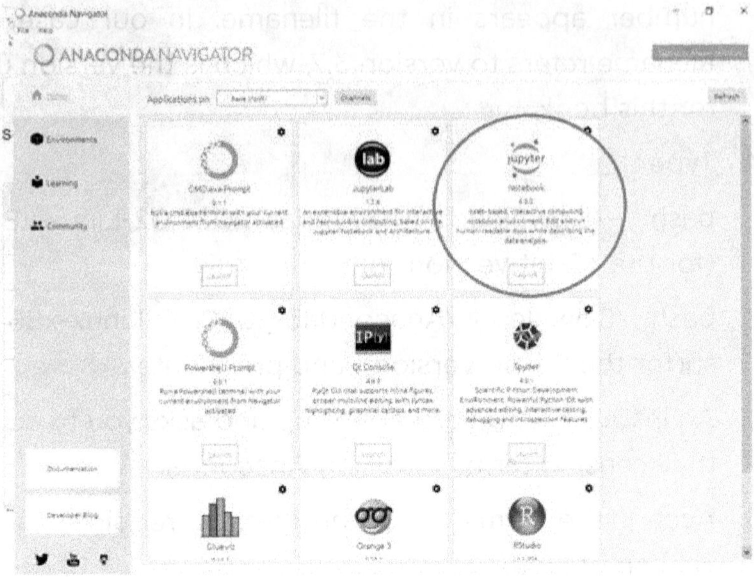

Figure 2.14: Launching Jupyter Notebook using Anaconda Navigator.

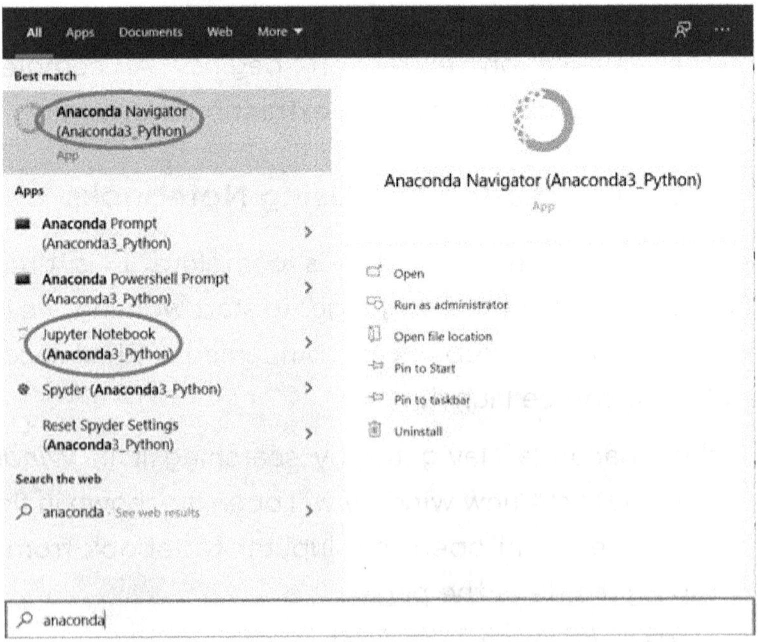

Figure 2.15: Launching Jupyter Notebook from the Windows search box.

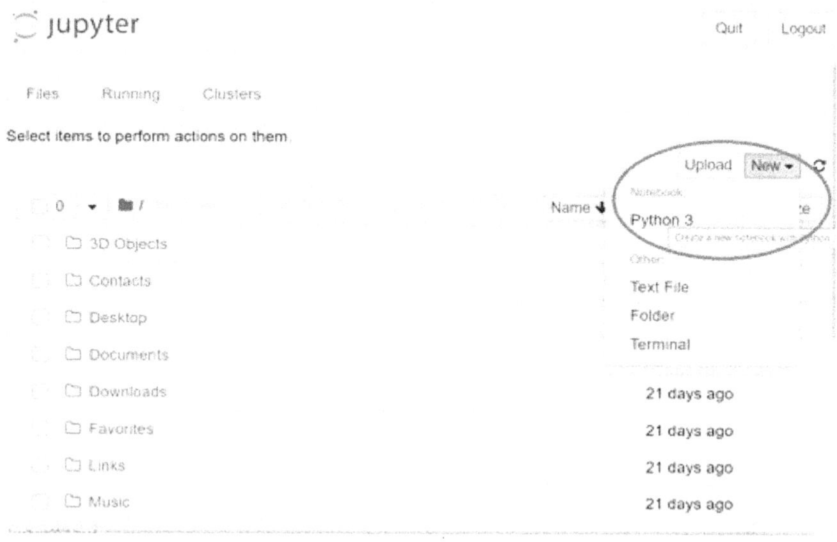

Figure 2.16: Creating a new Python 3 file in Jupyter Notebook.

A browser page will open, as shown in figure 2.16. To create a new notebook, go to *New* on the top right side of the page and select Python 3.

Note that the notebook contains a cell that is highlighted, indicating that we can begin typing code in it. The title of the notebook is Untitled1. We can rename our Notebook by clicking on Untitled1 next to the Jupyter icon in the top left corner of the Notebook. Make sure the highlighted box in the middle of figure 2.17 is selected to Code.

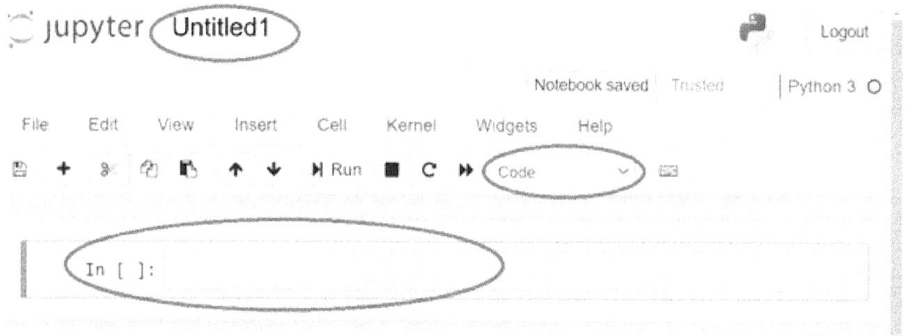

Figure 2.17: Start working with a Jupyter Notebook.

The box highlighted in the bottom of figure 2.17 has **In [ ]:** written next to it. This is the place where we write Python code. We are now ready to write our first program.

This Notebook doesn't contain anything yet. Place the cursor in the cell. Type print("Hello World"). Then, click on the *Run* button on the toolbar. The output of this line of code appears on the next line, as shown in figure 2.18.

```
In [1]: print("Hello World")

        Hello World
```

Figure 2.18: Output of the print statement in Python.

We can also hit shift+enter keys together to get the output of the aforementioned print command. The output is part of the same cell as the code. Visually, Notebook separates the output from the code. Notebook automatically creates a new cell for the next commands to be entered.

The cells in the Jupyter Notebook are used to enter either code or markdown. A markdown cell can be used to display text which can be formatted using a markdown language. A cell can be converted to a markdown cell from the cell menu, as shown in figure 2.19. The In [ ] prompt before the cell disappears, indicating that anything written in the cell will not run as Python code.

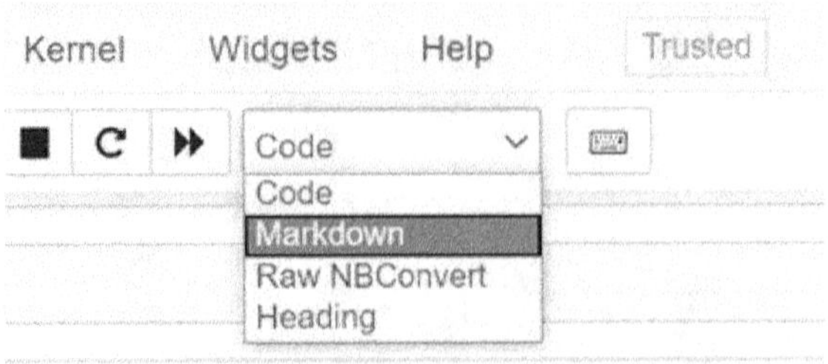

Figure 2.19: A markdown cell

When the Python code is run, it is executed on a line to line basis, i.e., the Python code is interpreted. This interpreter acts as a calculator. We can type an expression in the cell, and it will return us the output value.

This Notebook can be downloaded by going to the File drop-down menu, selecting *Download as* and clicking on *Notebook (.ipynb),* as shown in figure 2.20. Once the file is downloaded, it can be opened and used in the future by going to the File drop-down menu and clicking *open.*

The code we produce and use in this book will reside in a repository on the hard drive. A repository is a kind of filing cabinet or folder where we save our code. We can modify and run individual examples within the folder and add new examples.

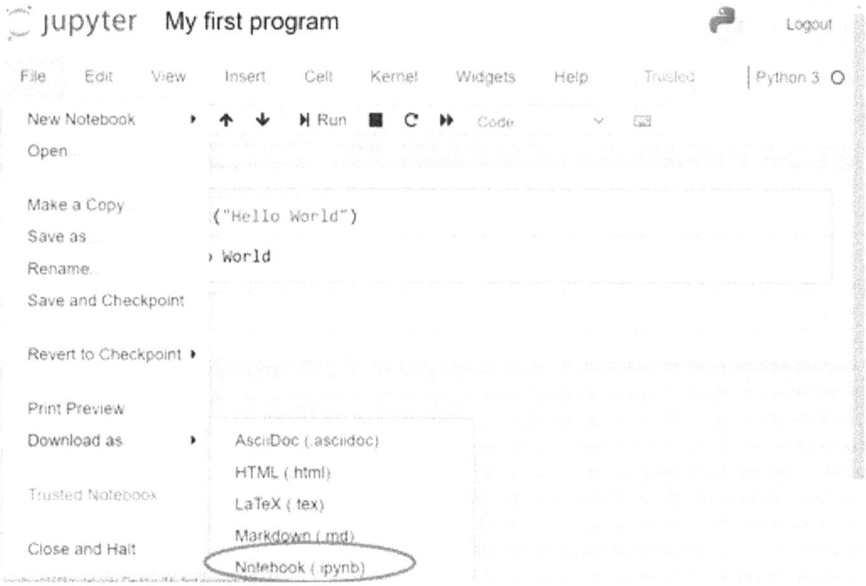

Figure 2.20: Saving a Jupyter Notebook for future use.

2.3. Datasets

Scikit-Learn, also called sklearn, is a free Python library for machine learning tasks such as classification, regression, and clustering. It is designed to work with the Python library NumPy that operates on numbers and is used to perform common arithmetic operations. The Scikit-Learn library comes with standard datasets that can be loaded using the Python functions.

A single Python command can load the dataset of our choice. For example,

from sklearn.datasets import load_boston

command loads the Boston house-prices dataset.

Table 2.1 shows some of the datasets available in the Scikit-Learn library.

Table 2.1: Scikit-Learn datasets for machine learning tasks.

Datasets	Description
load_boston(*[, return_X_y])	Load and return the Boston house-prices dataset (regression).
load_iris(*[, return_X_y, as_frame])	Load and return the iris dataset (classification).
load_diabetes(*[, return_X_y, as_frame])	Load and return the diabetes dataset (regression).
load_digits(*[, n_class, return_X_y, as_frame])	Load and return the digits dataset (classification).
load_linnerud(*[, return_X_y, as_frame])	Load and return the physical exercise linnerud dataset.
load_wine(*[, return_X_y, as_frame])	Load and return the wine dataset (classification).
load_breast_cancer(*[, return_X_y, as_frame])	Load and return the breast cancer Wisconsin dataset (classification).

We will use some of these datasets in the book. The details of some of these datasets and their usage are discussed in subsequent chapters of this book. Furthermore, publicly available datasets based on an opinion poll, analysis, politics, economics, and sports blogging can be downloaded from online resources such as Kaggle and FiveThirtyEight:

- https://www.kaggle.com/datasets
- https://fivethirtyeight.com/

2.4. Python Libraries for Data Science

Python has a rich source of open-source libraries that make data science tasks easy to perform. Here, we present the most important Python libraries for data preparation, processing, analysis, modeling, and visualization.

2.4.1. NumPy

NumPy (Numerical Python) is a core Python library for performing arithmetic and computing tasks. It offers multi-dimensional array objects for processing data. An array is a grid of values, as shown below:

$$x = [2 \quad 1 \quad 3.5 \quad -9 \quad 0.6],$$

where x is the name of an array object that stores five real numbers. Every value of the array has an associated index that can be used to access elements of the array. In Python, indices start from 0. A library must be imported in the Notebook to use its functions. The following command imports Numpy in the Notebook.

```
import numpy as np
```

np in this command is just the alias of Numpy. We call the functions of Numpy by using its alias. For example,

```
x = np.array([1, 2, 3])
```

creates an array, namely x that contains values [1, 2, 3]. To access an individual element of the array, we use x[index]. As an example, x[0] returns value 1, whereas x[2] returns value 3. Note that the name given to an array is case sensitive. Using X instead of x will return an error, as shown in figure 2.21.

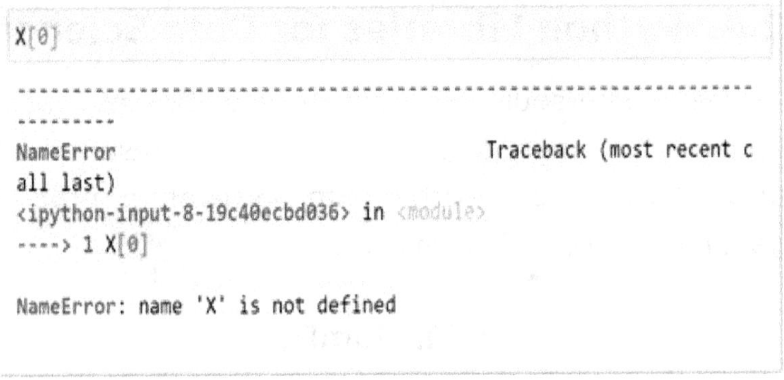
X[0]
NameError
Traceback (most recent c
all last)
<ipython-input-8-19c40ecbd036> in <module>
----> 1 X[0]
NameError: name 'X' is not defined

Figure 2.21: An error message indicating that the name we tried to use in the Notebook is undefined.

The library offers many handy features to perform operations on arrays and matrices in Python. The mathematical operations executed using NumPy arrays are fast. We shall give details of this and other libraries in subsequent chapters of the textbook.

2.4.2. Pandas

Pandas is a Python library for data cleaning manipulation and preprocessing. It is very handy to work with labeled data. Pandas allows importing data of various file formats such as comma-separated values (.csv) and excel. Pandas is based on two main data structures: *Series,* which is like a list of items, and DataFrames, which acts like a table with multiple columns. Pandas allows handling missing data and adding/deleting columns from a DataFrame. It allows data cleaning features such as replacing missing values, and operations such as groupby, join, and concatenation. Details of these operations are provided in Chapter 5.

2.4.3. Matplotlib

A picture is worth a thousand words. It is very convenient to discover patterns in the data by visualizing its important features. Matplotlib is a standard data science plotting library that helps us generate two-dimensional plots, graphs, and diagrams. Using one-liners to generate basic plots in Matplotlib is quite simple. For example, the following Python code generates a sine wave.

```
# Python Code to generate a Sine wave
import numpy as np
import matplotlib.pyplot as plt
#time values of wave
time = np.arange(0, 10, 0.1)
#Amplitude of wave
x = np.sin(time)
#Plotting the wave
plt.plot(time, x)
```

The first line starting from # is a comment, which is used for better readability of the code. Comments are not executed by Python and are ignored. The next two lines import Numpy and Matplotlib libraries. The next line time = np.arange(0,10,0.1) generates values from 0 to 10 with a step size of 0.1 between each value. x=np.sin(time) generates the sine wave using the built-in sine function in the Numpy library. The line plt.

plot(time, x) plots the values of a sine wave stored in x against independent variable time, as shown in figure 2.22.

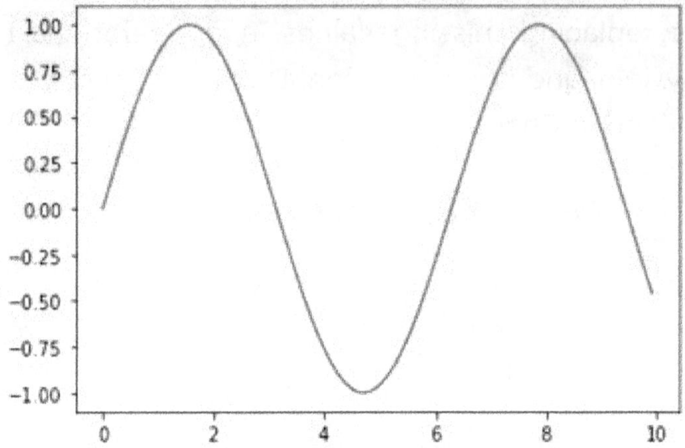

Figure 2.22: Sine wave generated from the code given above.

2.4.4. Scikit-Learn

Scikit-Learn is an open-source library in the SciPy Stack. The latter is a Python-based ecosystem of open-source software for mathematics, science, and engineering. Scikit-Learn uses the math operations of SciPy to implement machine learning algorithms for common data science tasks. These tasks include classification, regression, and clustering. The details of these tasks are provided in Chapter 7.

Further Reading

- Further reading related to the installation of Anaconda on Windows, MacOS, and Linux can be found at https://docs.anaconda.com/anaconda/install/.

Hands-on Time

It is time to check your understanding of the topic of this chapter through the exercise questions given in Section 2.5. The answers to these questions are given at the end of the book.

2.5. Exercise Questions

Question 1:

Anaconda is a free open source:

A. Python library for performing data science tasks
B. Python distribution that includes useful libraries
C. Synonym for Python
D. Data science pipeline

Question 2:

A Python Jupyter Notebook can contain:

A. Python code only
B. Python code, comments, plots, mathematical equations, and even HTML code
C. Python code with comments only
D. Python code, comments, and output of the code

Question 3:

Suppose we run the following commands in Jupyter Notebook

A. **import** numpy as np
B. x = np.array([1, 2, 3])
C. x[1]

What would be the output of this code?

A. 0

B. 1

C. 2

D. 3

Question 4:

Suppose we run the following commands in Jupyter Notebook

A. **import** matplotlib.pyplot as plt

B. time = [0, 1, 2, 3, 4, 5]

C. plt.plot(time)

D.

What would be the output of this code?

A. The plot of the current system time

B. The creation of the variable time

C. The plot of values specified in the variable time

D. None of the above.

Question 5:

Suppose we run the following commands in Jupyter Notebook

```
import numpy as np
  time = np.arange(0, 10, 0.1)  # time values of wave
  x = np.sin(time)              # Amplitude of wave
```

What would happen if we run this code?

A. The current system time would be stored

B. Variable named time is created

C. The plot of values specified in the variable time

D. Variables named time and x are created

3

Review of Python for Data Science

3.1. Introduction

Chapter 2 outlines the Python installation specific to data science. However, the installed Python can perform common tasks as well. This chapter provides a quick overview of the basic functionality of Python. If the reader is familiar with the basics of Python, this chapter can be skipped to directly move on to the next chapter. Nevertheless, it is recommended to briefly go through the material presented here and test some of the examples to review Python commands. The focus of this chapter is to provide an overview of the basic functionality of Python to solve data science problems.

3.2. Working with Numbers and Logic

A data scientist has to work with data from several categories, such as numbers and logical values. The former category of data includes integer and floating-point numbers, whereas the latter category consists of logical true and false values that are used to make decisions. For example, to find out whether two values are equal or whether one value is smaller than another value, we may use logical values. To this end, Python provides us with various types of numbers and logic values given below.

Integer: A whole number is an integer. 10 is a whole number; it is an integer. Conversely, 10.0 has a decimal part; it is not an integer. Integers are represented by the int data type in Python.

Float: A number that includes a decimal part is a floating-point number. For example, 4.5 is a floating-point number. Python stores floating-point values in the float data type.

Complex: A complex number has two parts: a real number and an imaginary number; both are paired together. The imaginary part of a complex number always appears with a *j*. If we create a complex number with 4 as the real part and 5 as the imaginary part, we make an assignment like this:

```
cmplx_no = 4 + 5j
```

Bool: Logical arguments require Boolean values represented as bool type in Python. A variable of type bool can either be True or False. Note that the first letter of both keywords is capital. We can assign a value by using the True or False keywords as,

```
1. a=True
2. type(a)   # it returns the type of a as bool.
```

Another way to define a bool variable is to create an expression that defines a logical idea. As an example,

```
bool_variable = 5 < 3
```

returns False because 5 is not smaller than 3.

3.2.1. Arithmetic Operators

Arithmetic operators +, -, * and / perform addition, subtraction, multiplication, and division, respectively. These operations can be grouped together using parentheses ( ). Arithmetic operators supported by Python are given in Table 3.1. To understand these operators, type the following code.

```
3+5-6

Output:
2

20-4*8

Output:
-12

(20-4*8)/3

Output:
-4

10/4
# division always returns a floating point number

Output:
2.5
```

The integer numbers, e.g., the number 20 has type int, whereas 2.5 has type float. To get an integer result from division by discarding the fractional part, we use the // operator.

```
50 // 8

Output:
6
```

To calculate the remainder, we use % operator.

```
50%8

Output:
2
```

To calculate powers in Python, we use ** operator.

```
2**5

Output:
32
```

Operations with mixed type operands return output that has float data type.

```
type(4*3.4)

Output:
float
```

Python has built-in support for complex numbers, and uses the j or J suffix to indicate the imaginary part. For example:

```
2+7j

Output:
(2+7j)
```

Table 3.1: Arithmetic operators supported by Python.

Operator and its Symbol	Description	Example

Addition
+
	Adds two values together.	`3+4`
		`Output:`
		`7`

Subtraction
–
	Subtracts the right-hand operand from the left operand.	`5-2`
		`Output:`
		`3`

Multiplication
*
	Multiplies the operands together	`5*2`
		`Output:`
		`10`

Division
/
	Divides the left-hand operand by the right operand.	`5/2`
		`Output:`
		`2.5`

Modulus
%
	Divides the left-hand operand by the right operand to return the remainder of division.	`15%6`
		`Output:`
		`3`

Exponent
**
	Calculates the exponential value of the right operand by the left operand.	`3**3`
		`Output:`
		`27`

Floor division
//
	Performs integer division of the left operand by the right operand to return the integer part of the result.	`20//3`
		`Output:`
		`6`

3.2.2. Assignment Operators

When working in a Python Notebook, we can store our results in what is known as variables. A *variable* is like a container that holds our information. We assign the data to a variable to store it by a number of assignment operators supported by Python and are given in Table 3.2. The equal sign (=) is used to assign a value to a variable.

```
1. height = 10
2. width = 3 * 4
3. width * height
Output:
120
```

If a variable is not assigned any value (not defined), we get an error when we try to use it:

```
Height

Output:
NameError: name 'Height' is not defined
```

The following code assigns 10 to my_variable, then adds value 10 to my_variable. Thus, the result stored in my_variable is 20.

```
1. my_variable = 10
2. my_variable+=10
3. my_variable
Output:
20
```

Try the following code.

```
1. my_variable1 = 10
2. my_variable2 = 3
3. my_variable1**=  my_variable2
4. my_variable1

Output:
1000
```

Table 3.2: Assignment Operators of Python.

Operator	Description	Example
=	Assigns the value of the right operand to the left operand.	my_variable = 10 assigns value 10 to the variable, namely my_variable.

+=	Adds the value of the right operand to the value of the left operand and stores the result in the left operand.	my_variable + = 10 adds 10 to the value stored in my_variable and assigns the sum to my_variable.
– =	Subtracts the value of the right operand from the value of the left operand and stores the result in the left operand.	my_variable - = 10 subtracts 10 from the value of my_variable and assigns the result to my_variable.
*=	Multiplies the value of the right operand by the value of the left operand and stores the result in the left operand.	my_variable * = 10 multiplies 10 with the previous value of my_variable and assigns the product to my_variable.
/=	Divides the value of the left operand by the value of the right operand and stores the result in the left operand.	my_variable /= 10 divides the value of my_variable by 10 and assigns the result to my_variable.
%=	Divides the value of the left operand by the value of the right operand and stores the remainder in the left operand.	my_variable %= 10 divides the value of my_variable by 10 and assigns the remainder to my_variable.
**=	Takes exponent of the left operand to the power given in the right operand and assigns the result to the left operand.	my_variable = 10 pow = 3 my_variable** = pow calculates the power of my_variable to the value given in pow and assigns the result to my_variable.

3.2.3. Bitwise Operators

Bitwise operators operate on individual bits of the operands. To understand bitwise operations, we need to understand the binary representation of the numbers in computers.

Every number is represented as a series of 0s and 1s in the computer. For example, decimal number 5 equals 0000 0101 in binary when we use 8 bits to represent a binary number in a computer.

Negative decimal numbers are represented in computers with a leading 1 on the left side instead of a leading 0. This procedure has two steps:

1. Invert individual bits of the number (this is called as taking 1's complement of the number). Operator ~ is used to take 1's complement.
2. Adding 1 to 1's complement (this is called taking 2's complement of the number).

For example, decimal −3 can be converted to binary by first taking 1's complement of 3 (0000 0011) that results in 1111 1100 in binary. Now adding a 1 to 1111 1100 results in 1111 1101 that is a binary representation of −3. To take negative of number 3 in Python, we may type:

```
~3+1
Output:
-3
```

Table 3.3: Bitwise Operators applied on operands x = 2 (0000 0010 in binary) and y = 5 (0000 0101 in binary).

<table>
<tr><th>Operator</th><th>Description</th><th>Example</th></tr>
<tr><td>Bitwise AND
&</td><td>For variables namely x and y, Bitwise AND, &, returns 1 if corresponding bits of x and y are 1; otherwise, it returns 0.</td><td>x & y

Output: 0</td></tr>
<tr><td>Bitwise OR
|</td><td>For variables namely x and y, Bitwise OR, |, returns 1 if any of the corresponding bit of x or y is 1; otherwise, it returns 0.</td><td>x | y

Output:
7</td></tr>
<tr><td>Bitwise NOT
~</td><td>For a variable namely x, ~x
returns -(x+1) which is 1's complement of x.</td><td>~x

Output:
-3</td></tr>
<tr><td>Bitwise XOR
^</td><td>For variables namely x and y, Bitwise XOR, ^, returns 1 if only one of the corresponding bits of x or y is 1; otherwise, it returns 0.</td><td>x ^ y

Output:
7</td></tr>
<tr><td>Bitwise right shift
>></td><td>Bitwise right shift, >>, shifts the bits of the operand by the amount specified in integers on the right side of the operator.
Specifying a float on the right side of >>, for example, y>>2.5, gives an error message.</td><td>y >> 2

Output:
1</td></tr>
<tr><td>Bitwise left shift
<<</td><td>Bitwise left shift, <<, shift the bits of the operand by the amount specified in integers on the left side of the operator.
Specifying a float on the right side of <<, for example, y<<2.5, gives an error message.</td><td>x << 2

Output:
8</td></tr>
</table>

3.2.4. Logical Operators

Logical operators work on the operands, which can take on one of two values: True and False. The logical operators used in Python are given in Table 3.4.

Table 3.4: Logical operators in Python.

Logical Operator	Description	Example

and	Returns True only when both the operands are true.	`x=True`
		`y=False`
		`x and y`
		
		Output:
		`False`

or	Returns True if either of the operands is true.	`x=True`
		`y=False`
		`x or y`
		
		Output:
		`True`

not	It complements the operand.	`x = True`
		`not x`
		
		Output:
		`False`

3.2.5. Comparison Operators

These operators are used to compare whether two values are equal or one value is greater than another value or vice versa. The result returned by these operators is either True or False. These operators are extensively used to make decisions in programming. Table 3.5 gives details of comparison operators.

Table 3.5: Comparison operators of Python for x = 8 and y = 3

Operator	Description	Example
Equal ==	Checks whether both operands x and y are equal.	x == y **Output:** False
Not equal !=	Checks whether both operands x and y are not equal.	x != y **Output:** True
Greater than >	Checks whether one operand is greater than the other operand.	x > y **Output:** True
Less than <	Checks whether one operand is smaller than the other operand.	x < y **Output:** False
Greater than or equal to >=	Checks whether one operand is greater than or equal to the other operand.	x >= y **Output:** True
Less than or equal to <=	Checks whether one operand is less than or equal to the other operand.	x <= y **Output:** False

3.2.6. Membership Operators

The membership operators are used to find whether a particular item or set of items are present in a collection or not. These operators are:

1. in
2. not in.

They are used to test whether a value or variable is found in a sequence such as string, list, tuple, set, and dictionary. These operators are used in the following example.

```
# x is a string of characters
x = 'Hello world'

# returns True if H is in x
print('H' in x)

# returns True if Hello is not present in x
print('Hello' not in x)
Output:
True
False
```

3.3. String Operations

A string is a data type used to represent text, including numbers, alphabets, spaces, and special characters such as comma, full stop, and colon. Python provides us with rich resources to manipulate strings.

The computer converts every character of the string into a number using a standard called Unicode and stores that number in memory. Unicode is used to encode and represent text as numbers. For example, the letter *a* is converted to its

Unicode 97. Type ord("a") in the Jupyter cell and press *Enter* to observe 97 as an output. Strings can be specified by:

- Enclosing characters in single quotes ('...') or
- Enclosing characters in double quotes ("...")

Type the following code to observe the output.

```
'A string enclosed in a single quote.'
Output:
'A string enclosed in a single quote.'

"Another way to specify a 'string'."
Output:
'Another way to specify a 'string'.'
```

We can specify multiple strings with the print statement. We use a comma to separate them out. These strings will be printed with a space in between.

```
print('apple', 'and banana', 'are fruits')


Output:
apple and banana are fruits
```

Trying to print a single quote within a string enclosed in single quotes or trying to print a double quote within a string enclosed in double quotes gives an error message as follows.

```
print('Are n't, you said this.')

Output:
File "<ipython-input-96-868ddf679a10>", line 1
       print('Are n't, you said this.')
       ^
SyntaxError: invalid syntax
```

To print such characters, we use backslash \, called the escape character.

```
print('Are n\'t, you said this.')

Output:
Are n't, you said this.
```

The print() function produces a readable output by omitting the enclosing quotes in the output. It can also perform special tasks by using escape characters. For example, \t generates a tab, and \n produces a new line within the print statement.

```
print('Are n\'t, \t you said this.')
Output:
Are n't,    you said this.

print('Are n\'t, \n you said this.')
Output:
Are n't,
you said this.
```

When we try to display the path of a directory such as C:\users\new_directory by using the following statement, we get an output like the one given below:

```
print('c:\new_directory')

Output:
c:
ew_directory
```

The reason is that \n is used to generate a new line. To avoid the new line, we use the letter *r* at the start of directory name as follows:

```
print('c:\new_directory')

Output:
c:\new_directory
```

Strings can be combined/concatenated together by using + operator.

```
str1 = 'Py'
str2 = 'thon'
str1 + str2

Output:
'Python'
```

Like other programming languages, Python considers a string as an array of bytes representing Unicode characters. A single character is a string with a length of 1.

§ Accessing Elements of a String

Python allows us to use positive as well as negative indices to access elements of a string. The indexing used by Python is shown in figure 3.1.

-11	-10	-9	-8	-7	-6	-5	-4	-3	-2	-1
H	E	l	l	o		w	o	r	l	d
0	1	2	3	4	5	6	7	8	9	10

Figure 3.1: Positive and negative indices to access elements of a string.

We use square brackets to access elements of a string. For example:

```
x = "Hello world"
print(x[0])

Output:
H
```

Remember, the indices start from 0 in Python. To access the last character of the string, we may write:

```
print(x[-1])
Output:
d
```

§ String Slicing

Python allows indexing the elements of a string to extract substrings. This is called string slicing. If x is a string, an expression of the form x[p1:p2] returns the portion of x from position p1 to the position just before p2. To access multiple characters of a string, we specify a range of indices as follows:

```
print(x[0:5])
```

which returns characters of x from index 0 to 4, i.e., Hello. Note that the last index 5 is not included. To print characters of string from a specific index to the last index, we may use:

```
print(x[6:len(x)])
```

to get the substring 'world' as the output.

When the first index is omitted, the slice starts at the beginning of the string: x[:p2] and x[0:p2] gives the same result. For an integer n $(0 \leq n \leq len(x),)$, x[:n] + x[n:] will be equal to x.

```
1. x = 'Hello world'
2. x[:6] + x[6:] == x
Output:
True
```

§ Stride (Step) in a String Slice

A stride or a step specifies the number of characters to jump after retrieving each character in the slice. When we add an additional colon in string indexing, we specify a stride. To retrieve every second character of string x starting from index 1 to index 7, we may add another colon and specify a step of 2 as follows:

```
x = 'Hello world'
x[1:8:2]
Output:
'el o'
```

We may specify a negative stride to step backward through the string. In this case, the first index should be greater than the second index:

```
x = 'Hello world'
x[10:0:-2]
Output:
'drwol'
```

Note that the first character of string x, H, is not displayed because we have specified a range of indices from 10 to 1 (0 is excluded from the second index). We get a different output when we write the following script.

```
x = 'Hello world'
x[10::-2]
Output:
'drwolH'
```

In this case, index 0 of the string corresponding to character H is included. If the first and second indices are omitted when we step backward in the string, the first index is set to the end of the string, and the second index is set to the beginning.

We can replicate a string multiple times by using * operator along with a specified integer value. To generate three copies of the string '123', type.

```
str = '123' * 3
str
Output:
'123123123'
```

The following command picks every third element of the string, str, starting from the last element and stepping backward.

```
1. str = '123' * 3
2. str[: : -3]
Output:
'333'
```

§ Built-in String Methods (Functions)

Python has a set of built-in methods (functions) that can be applied to strings. We give names and usage of these methods. The strip() method eliminates any whitespace from the beginning or the end.

```
1. str1 = "Hello world"
2. print(str1.strip())
Output:
Hello world
```

The method lower() returns the string in the lower case.

```
1. str2 = "Hello World"
2. print(str2.lower())
Output:
hello world
```

The method upper() returns the string in the upper case.

```
1. str3 = "Hello World"
2. print(str3.upper())
Output:
HELLO WORLD
```

The method replace() replaces a string with another string.

```
1. str4 = "I like apples"
2. print(str4.replace("apples", "pineapples"))
Output:
I like pineapples.
```

The method swapcase() returns a copy of the string with upper case alphabetic characters converted to lower case and vice versa.

```
'Hello, how are YOU doing?'.swapcase()

Output:
'hELLO, HOW ARE you DOING?'
```

The method split() breaks the string into substrings when it finds any instance of the separator specified in the input of the method:

```
1. str5 = 'Hello, how are YOU doing?'
2. print(str5.split(","))
Output:
['Hello', ' how are YOU doing?']
```

Table 3.6: Some commonly used Python string methods.

Method	Description	Example

capitalize()	Converts the first character to upper case.	`'hello'.capitalize()`
		Output:
		`'Hello'`

find()	Searches the string for a specified value and returns its position.	`'hello'.find('o')`
		
		Output:
		`4`

isalnum()	Returns True if all characters in the string are alphanumeric.	`'hello123'.isalnum()`
		Output:
		`True`
		
		`'hello*'.isalnum()`
		Output:
		`False.`

isdecimal()	Returns True if all characters in the string are decimals	`'2034'.isdecimal()`
		
		Output:
		`True`

islower()	Returns True if all characters in the string are lower case.	`"Python".islower()`
		
		Output:
		`False`

isupper()	Returns True if all characters in the string are upper case.	`"PYTHON".isupper()`
		
		Output:
		`True`

lower()	Converts a string into a lower case string.	`"PYTHON".lower()`
		
		Output:
		`'python'`

partition()	Returns a tuple, where the string is split into three parts.	`"python".partition('t')`
		
		Output:
		`('py', 't', 'hon')`

replace()	Returns a string, where a specified value is replaced with a specified value.	`"We learn ".replace('learn','have learned')`
		
		Output:
		`'We have learned'`

rfind()	Searches the string for a specified value and returns the position (index) of where it was found.	"Data Science". rfind('Sc') **Output:** 5
split()	Splits the string at the specified separator, and returns a list.	"Data Science". split(" ") **Output:** ['Data', 'Science']
splitlines()	Splits the string at line breaks and returns a list.	"""Learn Python for Data Science""". splitlines() **Output:** ['Learn Python', 'for Data Science']
startswith()	Returns True if the string starts with the specified value.	"Data Science". startswith("D") **Output:** True
strip()	Returns a trimmed version of the string by removing spaces in the start and end.	" Python ".strip() **Output:** 'Python'
swapcase()	Swaps cases, lower case becomes upper case and vice versa.	"Hello123". swapcase() **Output:** 'hELLO123'

title()	Converts the first character of each word to upper case.	`"python for data science".title()`
		
		Output:
		`'Python For Data Science'`

upper()	Converts a string into upper case.	`"python".upper()`
		
		Output:
		`'PYTHON'`

Further Readings

More information about Python and its commonly used functions can be found at

https://docs.python.org/3/tutorial/index.html

3.4. Dealing with Conditional Statements and Iterations

We have to control the flow of our program if we have to make decisions. We run a single line or a block of code if a condition is satisfied, and a different line or a block of code otherwise. To make decisions in Python, we have conditional statements given as:

1. if,
2. elif, and
3. else.

If statement can be used alone; however, both *elif* and *else* statements are accompanied by an *if* statement. The details of these statements and their usage are given in the following sections.

3.4.1. If, Elif, and Else Statements

If statement is the simplest example of a conditional statement. The syntax of this statement is:

```
if(condition):
    Statement1
```

Statement1 following the *if* statement is indented. We can have more indented statements after the Statement1. Statements indented the same amount after the colon (:) are run whenever the condition is True. When the condition is False, Statement1 and the following indented statements, if present, are not executed. The flowchart of an *if* statement is given in figure 3.2.

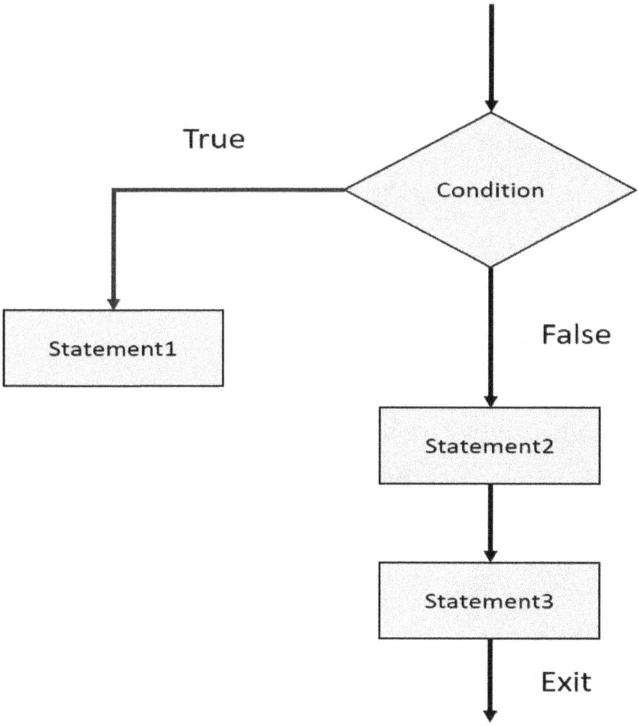

Figure 3.2: Flow chart of an *if* statement.

As an example, when we record marks obtained by students in a particular subject, total marks should not exceed 100. We shall display a warning or an error message when, due to some error, marks of a student exceed 100. Python script incorporating an *if* statement would be as follows:

```
obtained_marks = 80
if(obtained_marks > 100):
    print("Invalid marks.")
```

The colon (:) after if(obtained_marks>100) is important because it separates our condition from the statements to be run after the condition is evaluated. The condition inside if() is evaluated; it returns True if the condition is met, and False if the condition is not met. We can use conditional, arithmetic, and other operators to design a condition. We can also use the value of a variable input by a user to form a condition. For example, we can ask the user to enter the obtained_marks of a student.

```
print('Input marks of a student')
obtained_marks = int(input())
if(obtained_marks > 100):
    print("Invalid marks.")
```

Note that the input() function takes the input from the user and saves it as a string. We use int(input()) to convert the string to an integer. Now, if we run this program and enter any value greater than 100, we get a warning "Invalid marks." If the marks entered by a user are 100 or less, we do not get any warning message.

else Statement

The *else* statement is never used alone, it always comes with an associated if statement, i.e., if-else. The syntax of the if-else statements is given below.

if(condition):

Indented statement(s) when condition is True

else:

Indented statement(s) when condition is not True (False)

As an example, we want to display the message "Excellent," if the obtained_marks by a student are 80 or greater. We display the message "Not excellent," otherwise.

```
print('Input marks of a student')
obtained_marks = int(input())
if(obtained_marks >= 80):
    print("Excellent")
else:
    print("Not excellent")
```

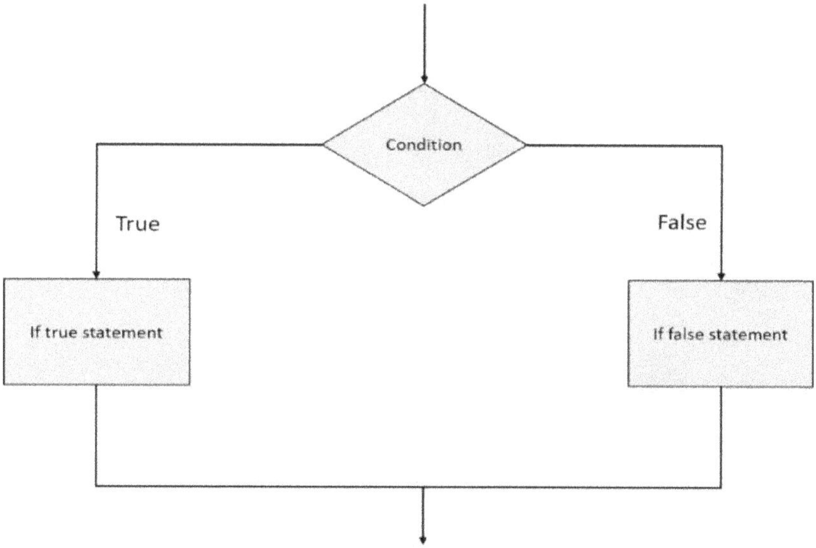

Figure 3.3: Flow chart of an *if-else* statement.

§ Nested Decisions

Multiple tests are to be performed to perform complex decisions. Python allows us to perform these tests via nested decisions. The Python statement to perform nested decisions is an *if-elif-else* statement. Suppose we want to display a warning if the marks of a student are greater than 100 or less than 0. Furthermore, we want to show the remarks as follows:

- Excellent: Marks are 80 or greater.
- Not excellent: Marks are less than 80.

```
print('Input marks of a student')
obtained_marks = int(input())
if(obtained_marks > 100 or obtained_marks < 0):
    print("Invalid marks.")
elif(obtained_marks >= 80):
    print("Excellent")
else:
    print("Not excellent")
```

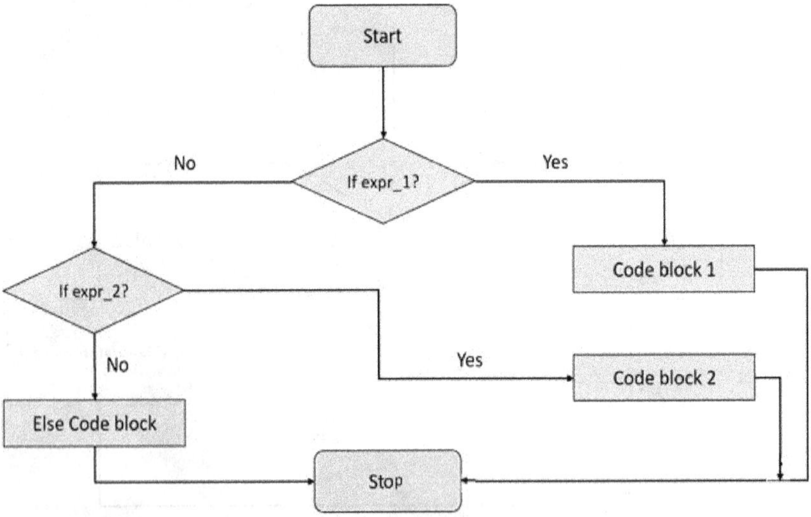

Figure 3.4: Flow chart of an *if-elif-else* statement.

Further Readings

More information about conditional statements can be found at
https://www.techbeamers.com/python-if-else/

3.4.2. Switch Statement

To make several decisions, we can use if, if-else, or if-elif-else statements. However, in this case, it is more convenient to use the switch statement. Its syntax is given as

```
switch = {
    case1: value1,
    case2: value2,
    case3: value3,
  ...
  }
switch.get(case)
```

As an example, if we want to display one of seven days of a week, we type the following.

```
switch = {
      1: 'Monday',
      2: 'Tuesday',
      3: 'Wednesday',
      4: 'Thursday',
      5: 'Friday',
      6: 'Saturday',
      7: 'Sunday'
      }
switch.get(5)
```

Output:

```
'Friday'
```

The output of the aforementioned Python script is 'Friday,' because case 5 corresponds to Friday. The aforementioned method to implement the switch case statement uses a dictionary. We shall go into the details of the dictionary, that is, a collection of multiple items in section 3.6 of this chapter.

3.4.3. For Loop

Sometimes, we need to perform a task more than once. To this end, we use iteration statements of Python. When we have to perform a task a specific number of times, we use a *for loop* statement. This loop has a definite beginning and end. The number of times a *for loop* executes depends upon the number of elements in the variable we provide as an input to the loop. The syntax of a *for loop* is as follows.

```
for loop_variable in input_variable:
        Statement(s) to be executed in the for loop
```

The flow chart of a *for loop* is given in figure 3.5.

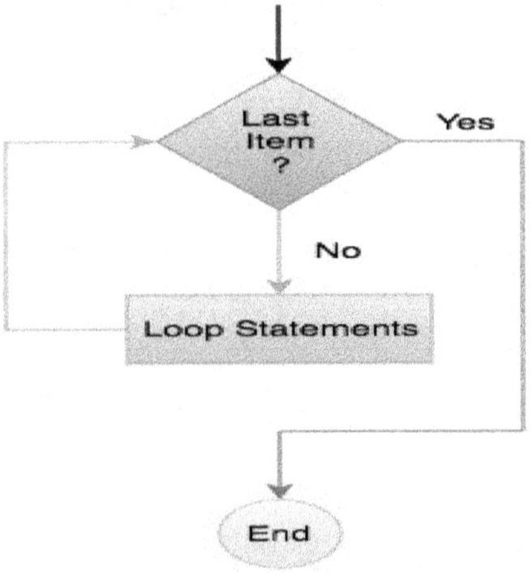

Figure 3.5: Flow chart of a *for loop.*

Note the Statement(s) to be executed in the body of the *for loop* are indented. The loop_variable used inside the *for loop* and the number of times the *for loop* runs depends upon the input_variable. To observe how the *for loop* works, type the following code:

```
fruits = ["pineapple", "orange", "banana"]
for k in fruits:
    print(k)
Output:
pineapple
orange
Banana
```

In this example, fruits is the input_variable to the *for* loop, which is a list of three fruit items. The loop runs for three iterations because the number of items stored in the variable fruits is three.

A useful function range() is used in a *for loop* that can generate a sequence of numbers. For example, range(10) will generate numbers from 0 to 9 (10 numbers). The following code generates the first 10 numbers.

```
for j in range(10):
    print(j)
Output:
0
1
2
3
4
5
6
7
8
9
```

Another example, where the step size is other than 1 is as follows:

```
for x in range(2, 10, 3):
    print(x)
Output:
2
5
8
```

In range(2, 10, 3), 3 is the step size. Two useful statements

1. break and
2. continue

are often used inside iteration statements. The former statement breaks the execution of the loop and forces the control to come out of the loop. The latter statement skips all the statements of the *for loop* following the keyword continue. Their usage is best illustrated by the following example:

```
fruits = ["pineapple", "orange", "banana", "melon",
"dates"]
for k in fruits:
    if k == "banana":
        continue
    print(k)
    if k == "melon":
        break
Output:
pineapple
orange
melon
```

The word banana is not printed by this code because the *continue* statement runs when the value of k equals banana. Note that print(k) statement is not in the body of if because it is not indented with *if* statement. Furthermore, when k equals melon, the code breaks right after it has printed the word melon. Interestingly, *for loop* can be used with *else* statement to indicate the end of the loop as in the following code:

```
numbers = [0, 1, 2, 3, 4, 5]
for i in numbers:
    print(i)
else:
    print("No items left.")
```

Output:

```
0
1
2
3
4
5
No items left.
```

3.4.4. While Loop

The second commonly used iteration statement is *while loop,* which iteratively executes a certain piece of code until a condition or multiple conditions are met. The syntax of the *while loop* is as follows.

while (condition):

Statement(s) to be executed in the while loop

As an example, we want to add natural numbers from 1 to 10. We may use a while loop as follows:

```
# Program to add natural numbers provided by the user.
n = int(input("Enter an integer = "))
# initialize sum to 0 and a variable k as a counter
sum = 0
k = 1
while k <= n:
    sum = sum + k
    k = k+1    # update counter
print("The sum of first", n, "natural number is=", sum)
```

When we run this program, we are asked to enter a natural number. We get a sum of 6 when we enter 3, and a sum of 55 if we enter 10. We get an error if the entered number is not of type int. For example,

```
Enter an integer = 10.5
---------------------------------------------------------------
-------------
ValueError                                    Traceback (most
recent call last)
<ipython-input-153-56101a25f19a> in <module>
      1# Program to add natural numbers provided by the user.
----> 2n = int(input("Enter an integer = "))
      3# initialize sum to 0 and a variable k as a counter
      4 sum =0
      5 k =1
ValueError: invalid literal for int() with base 10: '10.5'
```

Similar to a *for loop*, we can also use a break, continue, and else statements inside a *while loop*. The flow chart of a *while loop* is given in figure 3.6.

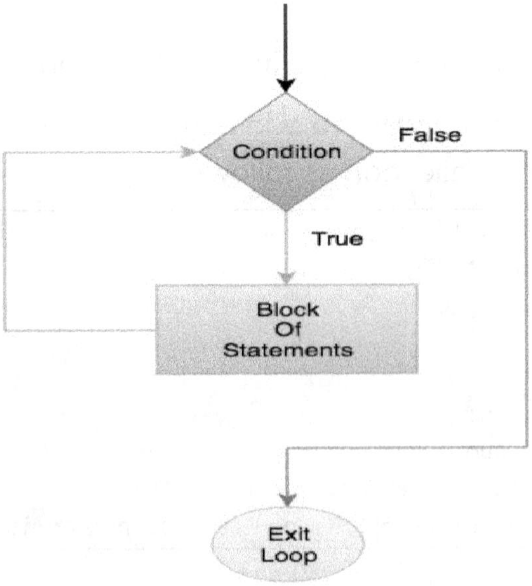

Figure 3.6: Flow chart of a *while loop*.

§ Nested Loops

Both *for* and *while* loops can be used inside each other. This is called nested loops, which are used to work in 2-dimensions. For example, if we have two variables, and we want to print all the combinations of these variables together, we may write the following program that uses two *for loops*, one nested inside another.

```
properties = ["red", "round", "tasty"]
fruits = ["apple", "orange", "banana"]
for j in properties:
      for k in fruits:
            print(j, k)
```

Output:

```
red apple
red orange
red banana
round apple
round orange
round banana
tasty apple
tasty orange
tasty banana
```

Further Readings

More information about conditional statements can be found at

https://bit.ly/3hQUFay

3.5. Creation and Use of Python Functions

In programming, a block of code that only runs when it is called is known as a function. A function performs a specific task. In Python, we can create/define a function using the keyword def. As an example, we may write the following two lines to define a function named my_function1:

```
def my_function1():
    print("This is my first Python function")
```

To run this function, we type its name.

```
my_function1()

Output:
This is my first Python function.
```

We can input data to a function, known as parameter or argument, passing into a function. For example, we can input a string to a function as given below:

```
def my_function2(str_in):
    print("This is " + str_in)

my_function2("Banana")
my_function2("Apple")
my_function2("Lemon")
Output:
This is Banana
This is Apple
This is Lemon
```

If we do not know beforehand the number of arguments that will be passed into our function, we add a * before the parameter name in the function definition. In this way, the function can receive multiple inputs/arguments, and can access the items accordingly. For example:

```
def my_function3(*fruits):
    print(fruits[2], "is the sweetest fruit.")
my_function3("Orange", "Apple", "Mango") # Giving 3 inputs.
Output:
Mango is the sweetest fruit.
my_function3("Orange", "Mango","Apple","dates")
  # Giving 4 inputs
Output:
Apple is the sweetest fruit.
```

A function can return data as a result. To get a return value from a function, use the return statement as follows.

```
def my_function4(x):
    return 100 * x
print(my_function4(2))
print(my_function4(8))
print(my_function4(100))
Output:
200
800
10000
```

To find the factorial of a number, we can use a *for* or a *while* loop to get the product of first N natural numbers. Another method to find the factorial is to use function recursion, which occurs when a function calls itself recursively. To illustrate this idea, we find the factorial of a function by recursion. The factorial of a number N is given as

$$N! = 1*2*3*...*(N-2)*(N-1)*N.$$

The factorial of 5 would be

$$5! = 1*2*3*4*5=120$$

Let us type the following program to implement the factorial using recursion.

```
def func_factorial(integer):
    if integer ==0:
        print("The factorial of 0 is 1")
    elif integer <0:
        print("The factorial of a negative number does
        not exist")
    elif integer ==1:
        return integer
    else:
     return integer*func_factorial(integer-1)
```

Note that the factorial of 0 is 1, and the factorial does not exist for negative numbers. Thus, we have incorporated these conditions using *if* and *elif* statements. The function checks whether the input is

1. Equal to 0
2. Smaller than 0
3. Equal to 1 or
4. Greater than 1.

To test the function func_factorial (), let us run the following lines of code.

```
print(func_factorial(5))
print(func_factorial(-5))
print(func_factorial(0))
Output:
120
The factorial of a negative number does not exist
None
The factorial of 0 is 1
None
```

None in the output means the function does not return any numeric value for 0 and negative inputs.

Python offers a small function, called a **lambda function,** that takes any number of input arguments, but has only one expression. To define a lambda function, we use

lambda *arguments* : *expression*

Using a lambda function, we can subtract 5 from each input number, for example, as follows.

```
x = lambda arg : arg - 5
print(x(10))
print(x(20))
print(x(30))
```

Output:

```
5
15
25
```

The lambda function is usually used anonymously inside another function. For example, we have a function that takes one input argument and multiplies that argument with an unknown number.

```
def my_lambda_func(n):
    return lambda arg : arg * n
```

We use this function definition my_lambda_func() to make another function that always triples the input number.

```
mytripler = my_lambda_func(3)
print(mytripler(2))
print(mytripler('A'))
print(mytripler(100))
```

Output:

```
6
AAA
300
```

3.6. Data Storage

Besides int, float, and str data types we have discussed earlier, Python provides collection data types to store a mix of multiple entries from alphabets, numbers, strings, alphanumeric, and special characters. The four collection data types of Python are given below.

- **List**: It is an ordered collection that is changeable. It allows duplicate entries.
- **Tuple**: It is an ordered collection that is unchangeable. It also allows duplicate entries.
- **Set**: It is an unordered and unindexed collection. It does not allow duplicate entries, just like real sets.
- **Dictionary**: It is an unordered, changeable, and indexed collection of entries. It does not allow duplicate entries.

We discuss these data types in the following sections.

3.6.1. Lists

A list is an ordered and changeable collection of elements. In Python, lists are written with square brackets. For example, to create a list named fruitlist, type the following code:

```
1. fruitlist = ["apple", "orange", "banana", "melon"]
2. print(fruitlist)
```

We can access the items/elements of a list by referring to the index number. For example, to print the second item, "orange," of the list, we type the following code:

```
print(fruitlist[1])
```

As discussed earlier, Python allows negative indexing. Index number −1 refers to the last item of the list, −2 pertains to the second last item, and so on. For example, to print the second last item, "banana" of the list, type the following code:

```
1. fruitlist = ["apple", "orange", "banana", "melon"]
2. print(fruitlist[-2])
```

To return the third and fourth element of the list, type:

```
1. # Elements at index 2 and 3 but not 4 are accessed.
2. print(fruitlist[2:4])
```

Try the following, and observe the output.

```
# returns list elements from the start to "banana"
print(fruitlist[:3])

# returns elements from "banana" to last element
print(fruitlist[2:])

# returns elements from index -3 to -1
print(fruitlist[-3:-1])
```

Since lists are mutable, we can change the value of a specific element by using its index. For example, to change the second element of the fruitlist, type the following:

```
fruitlist[1] = "dates"
print(fruitlist)
Output:
['apple', 'dates', 'banana', 'melon']
```

We can check if an element is present in the list by using the keyword *in* as follows:

```
if "apple" in fruitlist:
    print("apple is present in the list")
Output:
apple is present in the list
```

Table 3.7: Some useful methods for the list data type.

Method	Description	Example

append()	Adds an item to the end of the list	`fruitlist = ["apple", "orange", "banana", "melon"]`
		`fruitlist.append('watermelon')`
		`fruitlist`
		Output:
		`['apple', 'orange', 'banana', 'melon', 'watermelon']`

insert()	Adds an item at the specified index.	`fruitlist.insert(1, 'cherry')`
		`fruitlist`
		Output:
		`['apple', 'cherry', 'orange', 'banana', 'melon', 'watermelon']`

remove()	Removes the specified item.	`fruitlist.remove("banana")`
		`print(fruitlist)`
		Output:
		`['apple', 'cherry', 'orange', 'melon', 'watermelon']`

clear()	Empties the list.	`fruitlist.clear()`
		`print(fruitlist)`
		Output:
		`[]`

copy()	We cannot copy a list by typing fruitlist2 = fruitlist, because fruitlist2 is just a reference to fruitlist. Changes made to fruilist will be made to fruitlist2 automatically. One way to copy the elements of a list is to use the list method copy().	`fruitlist =  ["apple", "orange", "banana", "melon"]`
		`fruitlist2 = fruitlist.copy()`
		`print(fruitlist2)`
		
		Output:
		`['apple', 'orange', 'banana', 'melon']`

list()	It copies the elements of the list into another list.	`fruitlist =  ["apple", "orange", "banana", "melon"]`
		`fruitlist2 = list(fruitlist)`
		`print(fruitlist2)`
		Output:
		`['apple', 'orange', 'banana', 'melon']`

reverse()	Reverses the order of list elements.	fruitlist = ["apple", "orange", "banana", "melon"] fruitlist.reverse() fruitlist **Output:** ['melon', 'banana', 'orange', 'apple']
sort()	Sorts the list elements in an ascending order.	fruitlist = ["apple", "orange", "banana", "melon"] fruitlist.sort() fruitlist **Output:** ['apple', 'banana', 'melon', 'orange']

To completely remove a list, use keyword *del* as below.

```
del fruitlist     # removes fruitlist
fruitlist

Output:
NameError: name 'fruitlist' is not defined
```

Lists can be joined together using + operator as follows.

```
fruitlist =  ["apple", "orange", "banana", "melon"]
quantity = [10, 20, 30, 40]
fruit_quantity = fruitlist + quantity
print(fruit_quantity)
Output:
['apple', 'orange', 'banana', 'melon', 10, 20, 30, 40]
```

3.6.2. Tuples

A tuple is an ordered collection that is unchangeable. Tuples are written using round brackets () in Python. For example, to create a tuple, type:

```
mytuple = ("Python", "for", "Data Science")
print(mytuple)
Output:
('Python', 'for', 'Data Science')
```

Similar to a list, we can access the elements of a tuple using [ ]. For example:

```
print(mytuple[2])

Output:
Data Science
```

Negative indexing and a range of indexing can be used on tuples, the way we use them for the lists. We cannot change values present in a tuple once it is created because tuples are immutable. However, there is a workaround:

1. Convert the tuple into a list,
2. change the list, and
3. convert the list back into a tuple.

```
mytuple = ("Python", "for", "Data Science")
mylist = list(mytuple)
mylist[1] = "is handy for"
mytuple = tuple(mylist)
print(mytuple)
Output:
('Python', 'is handy for', 'Data Science')
```

Similar to lists, we can:

- loop through elements of a tuple by using a *for loop*;
- determine if a specified element is present in a tuple by using the keyword *in*;
- determine the number of elements of a tuple using the len() method; and
- join two or more tuples by using the + operator.

Once a tuple is created, we cannot add items to it. However, we can delete the tuple completely using *del mytuple*.

§ Tuple Methods

count() returns the number of times a specified value occurs in a tuple.

```
mytuple = ('Python', 'is handy for', 'Data Science')
print(mytuple.count('Data'))
print(mytuple.count('Data Science'))
Output:
0
1
```

index() searches the tuple for a specified value and returns the position where it is found. For example,

```
print(mytuple.index('Data Science'))
print(mytuple.index('Data'))
Output:
2
ValueError: tuple.index(x): x not in tuple
```

We get a ValueError if the specified value is not present in the tuple.

3.6.3. Sets

A set is an unordered and unindexed collection of elements. Sets are written with curly brackets { } in Python. For example,

```
myset = {"cat", "tiger", "dog", "cow"}
print(myset)
Output:
{"cat", "tiger", "dog", "cow"}
```

Since sets are unordered, there is no index associated with its elements. However, we can loop through the elements of a set using a *for loop*.

```
myset = {"cat", "tiger", "dog", "cow"}
for x in myset:
    print(x)
Output:
cow
dog
cat
tiger
```

Note there is no order in the printed output. We can also check if a specified value is present in a set by using the keyword *in*. For example,

```
print("tiger" in myset)
print("lion" in myset)
Output:
True
False
```

We cannot change elements of a set once it is created. However, we can add new items. We use the method **add()** to add one element to a set.

```
myset = {"cat", "tiger", "dog", "cow"}
myset.add("sheep")
print(myset)
Output:
{'cow', 'sheep', 'dog', 'cat', 'tiger'}
```

Note there is no order in the output. To add multiple elements, we use method **update()**.

```
myset = {"cat", "tiger", "dog", "cow"}
myset.update(["sheep", "goat", "sheep"])
print(myset)
Output:
{'cow', 'sheep', 'dog', 'cat', 'tiger', 'goat'}
```

Note that 'sheep' appears once in the output because duplicates are not allowed in sets. The method **len(myset)** gives the number of elements of a set.

We can use the **remove()** or the **discard()** method to remove an element in a set. For example, we remove "cow" by using the remove() method.

```
myset = {"cat", "tiger", "dog", "cow"}
myset.remove("cow")
print(myset)
Output:
{'tiger', 'dog', 'cat'}
```

We can use the **union()** method to join two or more sets in Python, or we can use the **update()** method that inserts all elements from one set into another. Type the following code:

```
myset1 = {"A", "B" , "C"}
myset2 = {1, 2, 3}
myset3 = myset1.union(myset2)
print(myset3)
Output:
{'B', 1, 2, 3, 'A', 'C'}
```

Furthermore, we can:

- remove the last item of a set by using the pop() method;
- empty the set by using the clear() method; and
- delete the set completely using the keyword *del*.

3.6.4. Dictionaries for Data Indexing

A dictionary is an unordered, changeable, and indexed collection of items. A Python dictionary has a key:value pair for every element. Dictionaries are optimized to retrieve values when the key is known. To create a dictionary in Python, we separate key:value element pairs by commas and place them inside curly braces { }. For instance, the following piece of code creates a dictionary named mydict.

```
mydict = {
"name": "Python",
"purpose": "Data science",
"year": 2020
}
print(mydict)

Output:
{'name': 'Python', 'purpose': 'Data science', 'year': 2020}
```

The values can repeat and they can be of any data type. However, keys must be a unique and immutable string, number, or tuple. We use **square brackets** to access a specified value of a dictionary by referring to its key name as follows.

```
# accesses value for key 'name'
print(mydict['name'])

# accesses value for key 'purpose'
print(mydict.get('purpose'))

Output:
Python
Data science
```

When we try to access a non-existent key, we get a message: None.

```
print(mydict.get('address'))

Output:
None
```

If we run print(mydict['address']), we get the following error:

KeyError: 'address'

This error indicates that the key 'address' does not exist. We can alter the value of a specific element by referring to its key name as follows:

```
mydict["year"] = 2019
mydict
Output:
{'name': 'Python', 'purpose': 'Data science', 'year': 2019}
```

We can loop through a dictionary by using a *for loop* that returns *keys* of the dictionary.

```
for k in mydict:
    print(k)
Output:
name
purpose
year
```

We can return the *values* as well.

```
for k in mydict:
    print(mydict[k])
Output:
Python
Data science
2019
```

We can get the same output if we use the following.

```
for k in mydict.values():
    print(k)
```

We can loop through a dictionary and access both keys and values by using the method items() as follows.

```
for x, y in mydict.items():
    print(x, y)

Output:
name Python
purpose Data science
year 2019
```

We can check whether a key is present in the dictionary by using a conditional *if* statement.

```
if "purpose" in mydict:
    print("'purpose' is one of the valid keys")
Output:
'purpose' is one of the valid keys
```

A new element can be added to the dictionary by using a new key and assigning a value to this key, as given below.

```
mydict["pages"] = 300
print(mydict)
Output:
{'name': 'Python', 'purpose': 'Data science', 'year': 2019,
'pages': 300}
```

The method pop() removes the element with the specified key name. The keyword *del* also does the same.

```
mydict.pop("year")
# or use del mydict["year"] to get same result
print(mydict)
Output:
{'name': 'Python', 'purpose': 'Data science', 'pages': 300}
```

The keyword *del* removes the whole dictionary when we use del mydict. The method clear() deletes all elements of a dictionary.

```
mydict.clear()
mydict
Output:
{ }
```

We can print the number of keys or values present in the dictionary by using len(dictionay_name).

```
mydict = {
"name": "Python",
"purpose": "Data science",
"year": 2020
}
print(len(mydict))
Output:
3
```

We cannot copy a dictionary by typing mydict2 = mydict because mydict2 is just a reference to the original dictionary mydict. Changes made to mydict will be made to mydict2 automatically. One way to copy the elements of a dictionary is to use the method copy() as given below.

```
mydict2 = mydict.copy()
print(mydict)
print(mydict2)
Output:
{'name': 'Python', 'purpose': 'Data science', 'year': 2020}
{'name': 'Python', 'purpose': 'Data science', 'year': 2020}
```

§ Nested Dictionaries

A dictionary inside another dictionary is called a nested dictionary. We can have multiple dictionaries inside a dictionary. For instance, the following code will create a dictionary family that contains three other dictionaries: child1, child2, and child3.

```
child1 = {
    "name" : "John",
    "dob" : 2004
}
child2 = {
     "name" : "Jack",
  "dob" : 2007
}
child3 = {
  "name" : "Tom",
  "dob" : 2011
}

family = {
  "child1" : child1,  # child1 is placed inside dictionary family
  "child2" : child2,  # child2 is placed inside dictionary family
  "child3" : child3   # child3 is placed inside dictionary family
}
family               # displays dictionary family
Output:
{'child1': {'name': 'John', 'dob': 2004},
 'child2': {'name': 'Jack', 'dob': 2007},
 'child3': {'name': 'Tom', 'dob': 2011} }
```

We can access the elements of a nested dictionary by using, for example:

```
family['child1'].items()

Output:
dict_items([('name', 'John'), ('dob', 2004)])
```

Further Readings

More detailed tutorials on Python can be found at https://bit.ly/2DqhAe5

3.7. Exercise Questions

Question 1:

Which statement is usually used when we have to make a decision based upon only one condition?

A. If Statement
B. else Statement
C. For Loop
D. Both A and B

Question 2:

Which statement is usually used when we need to iteratively execute a code fixed number of times?

A. If Statement
B. else Statement
C. For Loop
D. Both A and B

Question 3:

What will be the output if we type 19 / 3?

A. 6
B. 6.333333333333333
C. 1
D. Not given

Question 4:

What will be the output if we type 17 // 4?

A. 4

B. 1

C. 4.25

D. 68

Question 5:

What will be the output if we type 45 % 7?

A. 6

B. 3

C. 6.428571428571429

D. Not given

Question 6:

What will be the output if we type the following code?

word = 'Python'

word[1]

A. 'P'

B. 'p'

C. 'y'

D. 'Y'

Question 7:

What will be the output if we type the following code?

word = 'Python'

word[-2]

A. 'n'

B. 'o'

C. 'h'

D. 'P'

Question 8:

What will be the output if we enter 80 as student marks when we run the following code?

```
print('Input marks of a student')
obtained_marks = int(input())
if(obtained_marks > 100 or obtained_marks < 0):
    print("Invalid marks.")
elif(obtained_marks >= 80):
    print("Excellent")
else:
    print("Not excellent")
```

A. Nothing will be printed

B. Not excellent

C. Excellent

D. Invalid marks.

Question 9:

Suppose we have run the following piece of code.

```
mybirds =  ["Parrot", "Sparrow", "Crow", "Eagle"]
mybirds.insert(1,'Crow')
mybirds
```

What would be the result?

A. ['Parrot', 'Sparrow', 'Crow', 'Eagle']

B. ['Parrot', 'Sparrow', 'Crow', 'Crow', 'Eagle']

C. ['Parrot', 'Crow', 'Sparrow', 'Crow', 'Eagle']

D. ['Crow', 'Parrot', 'Sparrow', 'Crow', 'Eagle']

Question 10:

What would be the result if we have run the following piece of code?

```
mybirds =  ["Parrot", "Sparrow", "Crow", "Eagle"
mybirds.remove("Pigeon")
mybirds
```

A. ['Parrot', 'Sparrow', 'Crow', 'Eagle']

B. ['Parrot', 'Sparrow', 'Crow', 'Eagle', 'Pigeon']

C. An error message will be displayed

D. Not given

4

Data Acquisition

4.1. Introduction

As discussed earlier in Chapter 1, the process to collect, preprocess, clean, visualize, analyze, model, and interpret the data is called a data science pipeline. The main steps of this pipeline are as follows:

- Data Acquisition,
- Data Preparation,
- Exploratory Data Analysis,
- Data Modeling and Evaluation, and
- Interpretation and Reporting of Findings.

This chapter explains the data acquisition step in detail, along with practical Python examples. Subsequent chapters of the book explain the steps of the pipeline after the data acquisition. In the following sections, we describe different methods to acquire data.

4.2. Types of Data

Data is required for any data science application. The data is stored in different places, is in a variety of formats, and is usually unorganized. Furthermore, the same data can be interpreted in many different ways. Every organization stores data in a different manner and uses a different method to access and view data. Concisely, we should discover how to access the data in numerous forms before we can do any data science. Fortunately, Python provides us with a variety of functions to manipulate data when we acquire it from different sources.

Before we delve into the processes involved in data acquisition, we discuss the types of data. The data can be divided into four broad categories:

1. Nominal data,
2. Ordinal data,
3. Cardinal/Interval dat, and
4. Ratio data.

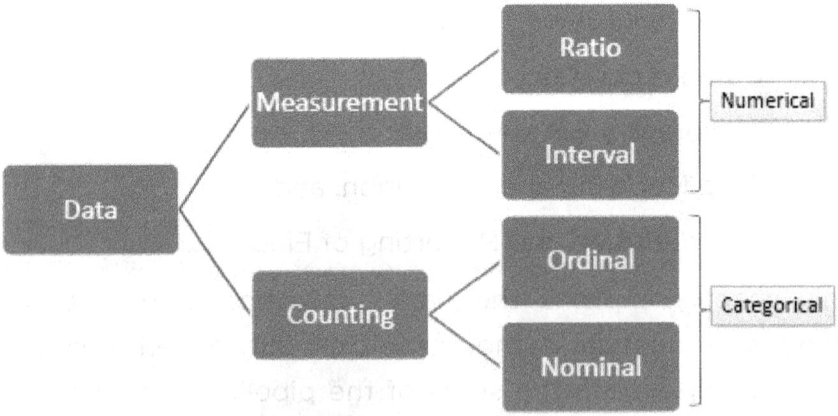

Figure 4.1: Types of data.

Nominal data can be organized into categories, for example, gender, type of pet, name of cities, etc. Nominal data is different from numerical data.

Ordinal data can be ordered or ranked by size, importance, or some other characteristic. For example, grades obtained by a student in an exam is ordinal data. If we assign A, B, C, and D grades to students, we rank them based upon their performance. Height of a person: tall, medium, or short is also ordinal data.

Interval (Cardinal) data refers to the data consisting of units/intervals. In this type of data, higher numbers are greater than lower numbers. Its examples include time measured using a clock. Time is a rotational measure that keeps restarting from zero. Moreover, the difference between 10 minutes and 20 minutes (any arbitrary interval) is the same as the difference between 20 minutes and 30 minutes (another interval). Calendar dates, IQ score, the temperature in Celsius or Fahrenheit, etc., are the other examples of interval data.

Ratio data, like interval data, have numeric values. However, unlike interval data where zero is arbitrary, in ratio data, zero is absolute. This means ratio data cannot have negative values. Height measured in centimeters, meters, inches, or feet is an example of ratio data because measured height is never negative. On the other hand, interval data such as temperature can be −25 degrees Celsius. However, when the temperature is measured in Kelvin, it becomes ratio data because zero is absolute in the Kelvin scale, there cannot be a temperature below zero degrees in Kelvin.

4.3. Loading Data into Memory

The data could be anywhere online or offline. We have to load the data into the memory of our computer system to access it. A dataset is usually arranged in columns and rows where the former represents features or variables, and the latter represents a collection of variables for a particular example (row) present in the dataset. Let us create a new text file, as shown below.

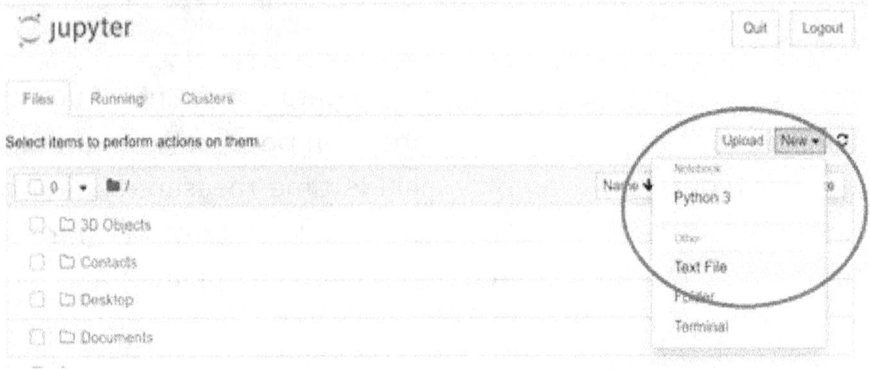

Figure 4.2: Creating a text file in Anaconda.

Suppose we have the following dataset that we store in a file and name the file days_of_week.txt.

Monday	1
Tuesday	2
Wednesday	3
Thursday	4
Friday	5
Saturday	6
Sunday	7

Figure 4.2 shows how to create a new text file. In Python, the method open() is used to open files. Type the following lines of code to load days_of_week.txt directly into memory.

```
myfile = open("days_of_week.txt", "r")
print(myfile.read())
Output:
Monday          1
Tuesday         2
Wednesday    3
Thursday        4
Friday          5
Saturday        6
Sunday          7
```

The method open() takes two parameters, filename and mode to obtain a file object named *myfile*. In our case, the access mode is r: read. The next line uses the method read() on the file object myfile to read all the data in the file until the End Of File (EOF). If we specify a size as part of read(), such as read(21), the method reads the number of characters we specify.

When we load a file containing some data, the entire dataset is available to us. Type the following to observe the output.

```
myfile = open("days_of_week.txt", "r")
print(myfile.read(21))
Output:
Monday      1
Tuesday     2
```

We can also read individual observations from our dataset one at a time. Type the following code.

```
myfile = open("days_of_week.txt")
for k in myfile:
    print ('Reading Observations from the Dataset: ' + k)
Output:
Reading observations from our dataset: Monday       1
Reading observations from our dataset: Tuesday      2
Reading observations from our dataset: Wednesday    3
Reading observations from our dataset: Thursday     4
Reading observations from our dataset: Friday       5
Reading observations from our dataset: Saturday     6
Reading observations from our dataset: Sunday       7
```

The process of loading a dataset into memory may fail if the system lacks sufficient memory to load the dataset. We resort to streaming or sampling data when our dataset is large, and we do not have sufficient memory to load it. Normally, we do not experience any problems when we work with small datasets.

4.4. Sampling Data

Loading data into the memory obtains all the columns and rows of the dataset. When we need only a few examples (rows), we sample the data. This means retrieving a few rows or records such as every third row or selecting random rows as samples of the data. The following code retrieves every third row from the days_of_week.txt file.

```
n = 3
myfile = open("days_of_week.txt")
for k, observation in enumerate(myfile):
    if k % n==0:
        print('Sampling rows: ' + str(k) + ', Retrieved data ' + observation)
Output:
Sampling rows: 0, Retrieved data Monday     1
Sampling rows: 3, Retrieved data Thursday   4
Sampling rows: 6, Retrieved data Sunday     7
```

The aforementioned code uses a built-in function enumerate() that keeps a count of iterations by adding a counter to its input that is called as an iterable. In our case, myfile is iterable. The function enumerate() returns its input in the form of an enumerate object. The enumerate object is used directly in for loops to access the elements of a dataset.

4.5. Reading from Files

Microsoft Excel and other MS Office applications store formatted data. The trigonometirc_functions.xls file used for this example provides a listing of sine, cosine, and tangent values against angles in degrees, as shown in figure 4.3. We store it on the main page of the Jupyter Notebook by following the procedure in figure 4.2.

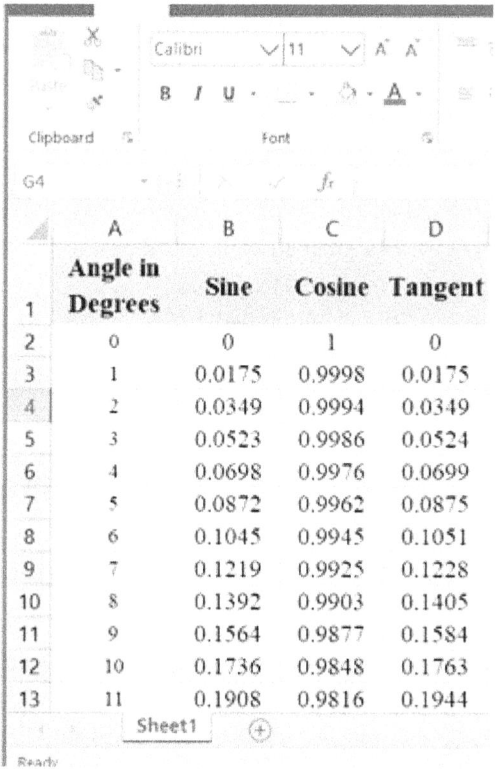

Angle in Degrees	Sine	Cosine	Tangent
0	0	1	0
1	0.0175	0.9998	0.0175
2	0.0349	0.9994	0.0349
3	0.0523	0.9986	0.0524
4	0.0698	0.9976	0.0699
5	0.0872	0.9962	0.0875
6	0.1045	0.9945	0.1051
7	0.1219	0.9925	0.1228
8	0.1392	0.9903	0.1405
9	0.1564	0.9877	0.1584
10	0.1736	0.9848	0.1763
11	0.1908	0.9816	0.1944

Figure 4.3: Data table for trigonometric identities sine, cosine, and tangent stored in an MS Excel file trigonometirc_functions.xls.

An MS Excel file can contain more than one worksheet; we have to tell Python library Pandas the name of the worksheet to process. We upload the trigonometirc_functions.xls file by clicking the upload button next to the *New* button, as shown in figure 4.2. To read values from an MS Excel file's Sheet1, we import Python library Pandas. Type the following code.

```
1. import pandas as pd
2. xl_file = pd.ExcelFile("trigonometric_functions.xlsx")
3. trig_values = xl_file.parse('Sheet1')
4. print(trig_values)

Output:
     Degrees     Sine  Cosine  Tangent
0          0        0       1        0
1          1   0.0175  0.9998   0.0175
2          2   0.0349  0.9994   0.0349
3          3   0.0523  0.9986   0.0524
4          4   0.0698  0.9976   0.0699
..       ...      ...     ...      ...
356      356  -0.0698  0.9976  -0.0699
357      357  -0.0523  0.9986  -0.0524
358      358  -0.0349  0.9994  -0.0349
359      359  -0.0175  0.9998  -0.0175
360      360        0       1        0

[361 rows x 4 columns]
```

The built-in Pandas constructor class ExcelFile() creates a pointer to the MS Excel file trigonometric_functions.xlsx. The Python parser parse() takes the Excel sheet as an input. Finally, the print command prints the contents of the specified sheet along with the number of rows and columns.

A comma separated values (CSV) file is a popular data storage file format. It is a type of plain text file that uses specific structuring to arrange tabular data. Since it is a text file, it contains text data as ASCII or Unicode characters only. Usually, a CSV file uses a comma to separate each specific data value. An example of a CSV file structure is given below.

column 1 name,column 2 name, column 3 name

first row data 1,first row data 2,first row data 3

second row data 1,second row data 2,second row data 3

Generally, the first line identifies the name of a data column. Every subsequent line represents the examples present in the dataset. The separator character is called a *delimiter*. Other than the comma, a delimiter can be the tab (\t), the colon (:), or the semicolon (;). Parsing a CSV file requires us to know which delimiter is being used.

A CSV file is a convenient way to export data from spreadsheets and databases. Since Python supports text file input and string manipulation, it is convenient to work with CSV files directly. We create an example CSV file with the following content and save it as example_csv.csv by following the procedure given in figure 4.2.

```
name,age,designation
John,50,Manager
Julia,40,Assistant Manager
Tom,30,Programmer
Sophia,25,Accountant
```

Type the following code to read the contents of this file.

```
import csv
csv_file = open('example_csv.csv')
csv_reader = csv.reader(csv_file, delimiter=',')
line_count = 0
for row in csv_reader:
    if line_count == 0:
        print(f'Column names are {", ".join(row)}')
        line_count += 1
    else:
        print(f'\
t{row[0]} is {row[1]} year old, and works as {row[2]}.')
        line_count += 1
print(f'Processed {line_count} lines.')
```

```
Output:
Column names are name, age, designation
John is 50 years olds and works as Manager.
Julia is 40 years old and works as Assistant Manager.
Tom is 30 years old and works as Programmer.
Sophia is 25 years old and works as Accountant.
Processed 5 lines.
```

The join() method takes all items in its input argument and connects them into one string. {", ".join(row)} connects all row values together using a comma.

To embed Python expressions inside string literals with formatting, we use F-strings. When a prefix f is placed at the start of a string, an F-string is created. Both *if* and *else* statements use the F-string to print values of the variable row.

The aforementioned method to read a CSV file seems quite complicated. We can use the Pandas library to process CSV files easily as follows.

```
1. import pandas as pd
2. data1 = pd.read_csv("example_csv.csv")
3. data1.head()
```

Output:

	name	age	designation
0	John	50	Manager
1	Julia	40	Assistant Manager
2	Tom	30	Programmer
3	Sophia	25	Accountant

The read_csv("example_csv.csv") function reads the CSV file, whereas head() function returns the first five rows of the data. If we specify an integer as the input to the head() function, it returns the number of lines specified by the integer input.

4.6. Getting Data from the Web

A markup language is used to annotate and format the text in computer-based text processing systems. Hypertext Markup Language (HTML) and Extensible Markup Language (XML) are the two most widely used markup languages in websites that make each web page a structured document. A huge amount of data resides on web pages; thus, it is quite useful to obtain data from them.

Normally, data on websites is not present in a convenient format, such as CSV. We have to get data from the web in a format useful to us while at the same time, we need to preserve the structure of the data. To this end, we perform **web scraping,** the practice of using a computer program to scan web pages and acquire the data we need.

Python's **lxml** library provides us with resources to parse XML and HTML documents very quickly. We import the following to handle requests to HTML documents.

```
from lxml import html
import requests
```

We use **requests.get()** to get the web page with the retrieved data. Next, we parse it using the html module and save the results in a tree, mytree.

```
page = requests.get('http://econpy.pythonanywhere.com/
ex/001.html')
tree = html.fromstring(page.content)
```

The whole HTML file is now stored in a structure mytree that is processed using XPath that provides a way of locating information in HTML/XML documents.

We can right-click on the specified web page and select inspect to get the HTML code given on the right side of figure 4.4.

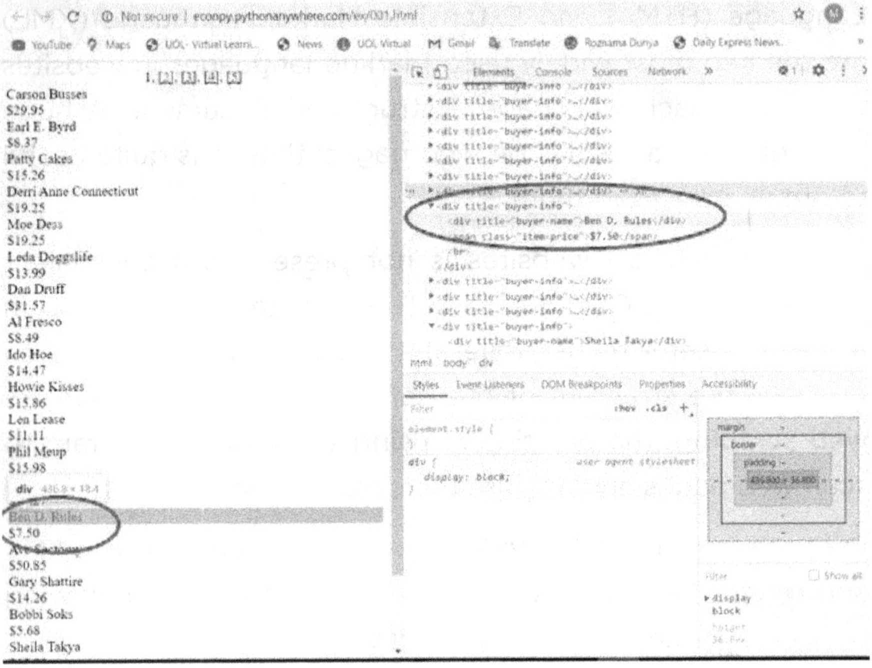

Figure 4.4: Getting HTML code from a web page by right-clicking anywhere on the page and selecting inspect.

A quick analysis of the HTML code reveals that the data is stored in two elements in the specified page : the 'buyer-name' and 'item-price'.

```
<div title="buyer-name">Carson Busses</div>

<span class="item-price">$29.95</span>
```

Now, we are able to create the correct **XPath** query and use the **lxml xpath** function as given below.

```
# Creates a list of buyers
buyers = tree.xpath('//div[@title="buyer-name"]/text()')
# Create a list of prices
prices = tree.xpath('//span[@class="item-price"]/text()')
print ('Buyers: ', buyers)
print ('Prices: ', prices)

Output:
Buyers:  ['Carson Busses', 'Earl E. Byrd', 'Patty Cakes',
    'Derri Anne Connecticut', 'Moe Dess', 'Leda Doggslife',
    'Dan Druff', 'Al Fresco', 'Ido Hoe', 'Howie Kisses', 'Len
    Lease', 'Phil Meup', 'Ira Pent', 'Ben D. Rules', 'Ave
    Sectomy', 'Gary Shattire', 'Bobbi Soks', 'Sheila Takya',
    'Rose Tattoo', 'Moe Tell']

Prices:  ['$29.95', '$8.37', '$15.26', '$19.25', '$19.25',
    '$13.99', '$31.57', '$8.49', '$14.47', '$15.86', '$11.11',
    '$15.98', '$16.27', '$7.50', '$50.85', '$14.26', '$5.68',
    '$15.00', '$114.07', '$10.09']
```

We have been successful in scraping all the needed data from a web page by using lxml and requests. This data is stored as two lists in memory. Now, we can analyze it using Python, or we can save it for future use.

Suppose we have an XML file present on https://www.w3schools.com/xml/books.xml, as shown in figure 4.5.

```
▼<bookstore>
  ▼<book category="cooking">
      <title lang="en">Everyday Italian</title>
      <author>Giada De Laurentiis</author>
      <year>2005</year>
      <price>30.00</price>
    </book>
  ▼<book category="children">
      <title lang="en">Harry Potter</title>
      <author>J K. Rowling</author>
      <year>2005</year>
      <price>29.99</price>
    </book>
  ▼<book category="web">
      <title lang="en">XQuery Kick Start</title>
      <author>James McGovern</author>
      <author>Per Bothner</author>
      <author>Kurt Cagle</author>
      <author>James Linn</author>
      <author>Vaidyanathan Nagarajan</author>
      <year>2003</year>
      <price>49.99</price>
    </book>
  ▼<book category="web" cover="paperback">
      <title lang="en">Learning XML</title>
      <author>Erik T. Ray</author>
      <year>2003</year>
      <price>39.95</price>
    </book>
  </bookstore>
```

Figure 4.5: An XML file.

To read data from this XML file, we type the following code:

```
from lxml import objectify
my_xml = objectify.parse('books.xml')
my_xml
Output:
<lxml.etree._ElementTree at 0x1de253ed488>
```

To find the root element, which in this case is bookstore, we type:

```
1.  root = my_xml.getroot()
2.  root
Output:
<Element bookstore at 0x1de2678b588>
```

Next, we access the name of the author.

```
root.book.author

Output:
'Giada De Laurentiis'
```

To retrieve the year of publication of the book, we type:

```
root.book.year

Output:
2005
```

We can find the children of the root element of the XML page.

```
root.getchildren()

Output:
[<Element book at 0x1de26789808>,
 <Element book at 0x1de26789a48>,
 <Element book at 0x1de26789a88>,
 <Element book at 0x1de26789ac8>]
```

To find XML tags of child elements, we type:

```
[child.tag for child in root.book.getchildren()]

Output:
['title', 'author', 'year', 'price']
```

Finally, to access the text stored in the child of the root element, we type:

```
[child.text for child in root.book.getchildren()]

Output:
['Everyday Italian', 'Giada De Laurentiis', '2005', '30.00']
```

Hands-on Time

It is time to check your understanding of the topic of this chapter through the exercise questions given in Section 4.7. The answers to these questions are given at the end of the book.

4.7. Exercise Questions

Question 1: Suppose we get data of students ranked as "First," "Second," "Third," and so on. What type of data is this?

A. Nominal

B. Ordinal

C. Cardinal

D. Ratio

Question 2: Suppose we gather some data on hair color such as "Black," "Brown," "Gray," and so on. What type of data is this?

A. Nominal

B. Ordinal

C. Cardinal

D. Ratio

Question 3: "Height" and "Weight" are examples of _____ data?

A. Nominal

B. Ordinal

C. Cardinal

D. Ratio

Question 4: Suppose we have data stored in a file named "days_of_week.txt" containing seven records (rows). We type the following code.

```
n = 4
myfile = open("days_of_week.txt")
for k, observation in enumerate(myfile):
    if k % n==0:
        print('Sampling rows: ' + str(k) + ', Retrieved data ' + observation)
```

How many records (row) will be displayed?

A. 1

B. 2

C. 3

D. 4

Question 5: Which function is used to retrieve the data from a web page?

A. read_csv()

B. tree.xpath()

C. requests.get()

D. All of the above

5

Data Preparation (Preprocessing)

5.1. Introduction

Data preparation is the process of constructing a clean dataset from one or more sources such that the data can be fed into subsequent stages of a data science pipeline. Common data preparation tasks include handling missing values, outlier detection, feature/variable scaling, and feature encoding. Data preparation is often a time-consuming process.

Python provides us with a specialized library, Pandas, for data preparation and analysis. Thus, understanding the functions of this library is of the utmost importance for those who are beginners in data science. In this chapter, we shall mostly be using Pandas along with Numpy and Matplotlib.

5.2. Pandas for Data Preparation

Pandas is a specialized library that makes the tedious tasks of data preparation and analysis easy. Pandas uses two data structures called Series and DataFrame. These data structures are designed to work with labeled or relational data and are suitable to manage data stored in a tabular format such as in databases, Excel spreadsheets, and CSV files.

Since we shall be working with Numpy and Pandas, we import both. The general practice for importing these libraries is as follows:

```
import pandas as pd
import numpy as np
```

Thus, each time we see pd and np, we are making reference to an object or method referring to these two libraries.

5.3. Pandas Data Structures

All operations for data preprocessing and analysis are centralized on two data structures:

- Series,
- DataFrame.

The Series data structure is designed to store a sequence of one-dimensional data, whereas the DataFrame data structure is designed to handle data having several dimensions.

5.3.1. The Series

The Series data structure, similar to a Numpy array, is used to handle one-dimensional data. It provides features not provided by simple Numpy arrays. To create a series object, we use the Series () constructor.

```
1. myseries = pd.Series([1, -3, 5, -20])
   # note capital S in Series
2. myseries
Output:
0    1
1   -3
2    5
3  -20
dtype: int64
```

dtype: int64 means the data type of values in a Series is an integer of 64 bits.

The structure of a Series object is simple. It consists of two arrays, index and value, associated with each other. The first array (column) stores the index of the data, whereas the second array (column) stores the actual values.

Pandas assigns numerical indices starting from 0 onward if we do not specify any index. It is sometimes preferable to create a Series object using descriptive and meaningful labels. In this case, we can assign indices during the constructor call as follows:

```
1. myseries2 = pd.Series([1, -3, 5, 20], index =
   ['a', 'b', 'c', 'd'])
2. myseries2
Output:
a     1
b    -3
c     5
d    20
dtype: int64
```

Two attributes of the Series data structure index and values can be used to view the values and index separately.

```
1. myseries2.values
Output:
array([ 1, -3,  5, 20], dtype=int64)
1. myseries2.index
Output:
Index(['a', 'b', 'c', 'd'], dtype='object')
```

The elements of a Series can be accessed in the same way we access the array elements. Type the following to understand this process.

```
1. myseries2[2]
Output:
C    5
1. myseries2[0:2]
Output:
a    1
b   -3
dtype: int64
1. myseries2['b']
Output:
b    -3
1. myseries2[['b','c']]
Output:
b   -3
c    5
dtype: int64
```

Note double brackets in the aforementioned indexing that uses the list of labels within an array. We can select the value by index or label, and assign a different value to it, for example:

```
1. myseries2['c'] = 10
2. myseries2
Output:
a     1
b    -3
c    10
d    20
dtype: int64
```

We can create a Series object from an existing array as follows:

```
1. myarray = np.array([1,2,3,4])
2. myseries3 = pd.Series(myarray)
3. myseries3
Output:
0    1
1    2
2    3
3    4
dtype: int32
```

Most operations performed on simple Numpy arrays are valid on a Series data structure. Additional functions are provided for Series data structure to facilitate data processing. We can use conditional operators to filter or select values. For example, to get values greater than 2, we may use:

```
myseries3[myseries3 >2]

Output:
2    3
3    4
dtype: int32
```

Mathematical operations can be performed on the data stored in a Series. For example, to take the logarithm of values stored in myseries3, we enter the following command that uses the log function defined in the Numpy library.

```
np.log(myseries3)

Output:
0    0.000000
1    0.693147
2    1.098612
3    1.386294
dtype: float64
```

Note that the logarithm of a negative number is undefined; it is returned as a NaN, standing for Not a Number. Thus, Python throws the following warning:

```
C:\Anaconda3_Python\lib\site-packages\pandas\core\series.
py:679: RuntimeWarning: invalid value encountered in log

result = getattr(ufunc, method)(*inputs, **kwargs)
```

NaN values are used to indicate an empty field or an undefinable quantity. We can define NaN values by typing np.NaN. The isnull( ) and notnull( ) functions of Pandas are useful to identify the indices without a value or NaN.

We create a Series, mycolors, to perform some common operations that can be applied to a Series.

```
1. mycolors = pd.Series ([1,2,3,4,5,4,3,2],
   index=['white','black','blue','green','green','yellow',
   'black', 'red'])
2. mycolors

Output:
white     1
black     2
blue      3
green     4
green     5
yellow    4
black     3
red       2
dtype: int64
```

The Series, mycolor, contains some duplicate values. We can get unique values from the Series by typing:

```
mycolors.unique()

Output:
array([1, 2, 3, 4, 5], dtype=int64)
```

Another useful function value_counts() returns how many times the values are present in a Series.

```
mycolors.value_counts()

Output:
4    2
3    2
2    2
5    1
1    1
dtype: int64
```

This output indicates that the values 2, 3, and 4 are present twice each, whereas values 1 and 5 are present once only.

To find a particular value contained in a Series data structure, we use isin( ) function that evaluates the membership. It returns the Boolean value True or False, which can be used to filter the data present in a Series. For example, we search for values 5 and 7 in the Series mycolors by typing.

```
mycolors.isin([5,7])

Output:
white     False
black     False
blue      False
green     False
green      True
yellow    False
black     False
red       False
dtype: bool
```

We can use the Boolean values returned by mycolors.isin([5,7]) as indices to the Series mycolors to get the filtered Series.

```
mycolors[mycolors.isin([5,7])]

Output:
green    5
dtype: int64
```

A Series can be created from an already defined dictionary.

```
1. mydict = {'White': 1000, 'Black': 500, 'Red': 200,
   'Green': 1000}
2. myseries = pd.Series(mydict)
3. myseries
Output:
White     1000
Black     500
Red        200
Green     1000
dtype: int64
```

5.3.2. The DataFrame

The DataFrame, a tabular data structure, is very similar to an Excel Spreadsheet. It can be considered an extension of a Series to multiple dimensions. The DataFrame consists of an ordered group of columns. Every column contains values of numeric, string, or Boolean, etc. types.

A DataFrame can be created by passing a dictionary object to the DataFrame() constructor. This dictionary object contains a key for each column with a corresponding array of values for each of them.

```
mydata = {'Employee Name' : ['Ashley','Tom','Jack','John',
'Alicia'],
'Specialization' : ['Python','Data Science','Data
preparation','Data Analysis','Machine Learning'],
'Experience (years)' : [3,5,8,2,4]}
myframe = pd.DataFrame(mydata)   # note capital D and F
in DataFrame() constructor.
myframe
```

Output:

	Employee Name	Specialization	Experience (years)
0	Ashley	Python	3
1	Tom	Data Science	5
2	Jack	Data preparation	8
3	John	Data Analysis	2
4	Alicia	Machine Learning	4

We can select a few columns from the DataFrame in any arbitrary order, using the columns option. The columns will always be created in the order we specify irrespective of how they are stored within the dictionary object. For example,

```
myframe2 = pd.DataFrame(mydata, columns = ['Experience
(years)', 'Employee Name'])
myframe2
```

Output:

	Experience (years)	Employee Name
0	3	Ashley
1	5	Tom
2	8	Jack
3	2	John
4	4	Alicia

If we use the index option, we can specify indices of our choice to the DataFrame.

```
1. myframe3 = pd.DataFrame(mydata, index=['zero','one','two',
   'three','four'])
2. myframe3
Output:
```

	Employee Name	Specialization	Experience (years)
zero	Ashley	Python	3
one	Tom	Data Science	5
two	Jack	Data preparation	8
three	John	Data Analysis	2
four	Alicia	Machine Learning	4

An alternative way to create a DataFrame is to pass input arguments to the DataFrame() constructor in the following order:

1. a data matrix,
2. an array of the labels for the indices (index option),
3. an array containing the column names (columns option).

We can use np.arange() to create an array. To convert this array to a matrix, we use reshape() function. For example, we type the following command.

```
np.arange(15).reshape((3,5))

Output:
array([[ 0,  1,  2,  3,  4],
       [ 5,  6,  7,  8,  9],
       [10, 11, 12, 13, 14]])
```

This is a 2-dimensional array or a matrix of size three rows and five columns (3x5). To create the DataFrame, myframe4, from this matrix, we type:

```
1. myframe4 = pd.DataFrame(np.arange(15).reshape((3,5)),
   index=['row0','row1','row2'], columns=['col0','col1',
   'col2','col3', 'col4'])
2. myframe4
```

Output:

	col0	col1	col2	col3	col4
row0	0	1	2	3	4
row1	5	6	7	8	9
row2	10	11	12	13	14

5.4. Putting Data Together

Once we have our data in a DataFrame, it is ready to be manipulated for preparation so that the data can be effortlessly analyzed and visualized. We illustrate several operations that can be performed using the Pandas library to carry out data preparation. The data contained in a Series or a DataFrame object can be put together in the following ways:

- **Concatenating**: pandas.concat() function concatenates the objects along an axis.
- **Merging**: pandas.merge( ) function connects the rows in a DataFrame based on one or more keys by implementing join operations.
- **Combining**: pandas.DataFrame.combine_first( ) function allows us to connect overlapped data to fill in missing values in a data structure.

5.4.1. Concatenating Data

The concatenation is a process of linking together two or more separate data structures and placing them next to each other to make a single entity. Similar to Numpy's concatenate () function, Pandas provides concat () function to perform concatenation. Type the following commands to generate two Series of five randomly generated numbers each.

```
1. myseries1 = pd.Series(np.random.rand(5), index=[0,1,2,3,4])
2. myseries1
Output:
0     0.865165
1     0.305467
2     0.692341
3     0.859180
4     0.004683
dtype: float64
```

```
1. myseries2 = pd.Series(np.random.rand(5), index=[5,6,7,8,9])
2. myseries2
Output:
5     0.670931
6     0.762998
7     0.200184
8     0.266258
9     0.296408
dtype: float64
```

To concatenate myseries1 and myseries2, type the following command:

```
pd.concat([myseries1,myseries2])

Output:
0     0.865165
1     0.305467
2     0.692341
3     0.859180
4     0.004683
5     0.670931
6     0.762998
7     0.200184
8     0.266258
9     0.296408
dtype: float64
```

The concat() function works on axis = 0 (rows), by default, to return a Series. If we set axis = 1 (columns), then the result will be a DataFrame.

```
pd.concat([myseries1, myseries2],axis=1)

Output:
```

	0	1
0	0.865165	NaN
1	0.305467	NaN
2	0.692341	NaN
3	0.859180	NaN
4	0.004683	NaN
5	NaN	0.670931
6	NaN	0.762998
7	NaN	0.200184
8	NaN	0.266258
9	NaN	0.296408

If we use the option **keys,** along the axis = 1, the provided keys become the column names of the DataFrame.

```
pd.concat([myseries1, myseries2],axis=1, keys=['series1',
    'series2'])
```

Output:

	series1	series2
0	0.865165	NaN
1	0.305467	NaN
2	0.692341	NaN
3	0.859180	NaN
4	0.004683	NaN
5	NaN	0.670931
6	NaN	0.762998
7	NaN	0.200184
8	NaN	0.266258
9	NaN	0.296408

The function concat () is applicable to a DataFrame as well. Let us create two data frames as follows.

```
1. myframe1 = pd.DataFrame({'Student Name': ['A','B','C'],
   'Sex':['M','F','M'], 'Age': [10, 16, 17], 'School':
   ['Primary','High', 'High']})
2. myframe1
```

Output:

	Student Name	Sex	Age	School
0	A	M	10	Primary
1	B	F	16	High
2	C	M	17	High

```
1. myframe2 = pd.DataFrame({'Student Name': ['D','E','A'],
   'Class':[9,10,5], 'School': ['High', 'High', 'Primary']})
2. myframe2
```

Output:

	Student Name	Class	School
0	D	9	High
1	E	10	High
2	A	5	Primary

We concatenate these two data frames as follows.

```
pd.concat([myframe1, myframe2])
```

Output:

	Student Name	Sex	Age	School	Class
0	A	M	10.0	Primary	NaN
1	B	F	16.0	High	NaN
2	C	M	17.0	High	NaN
0	D	NaN	NaN	High	9.0
1	E	NaN	NaN	High	10.0
2	A	NaN	NaN	Primary	5.0

Note the NaN values have been placed in those columns whose information is not present in individual data frames.

5.4.2. Merging Data

The process of merging consists of combining data through the connection of rows using one or more keys. The keys are common columns in the DataFrames to be merged. Based on the keys, it is possible to obtain new data in a tabular form. The merge() function performs this kind of operation. We may merge myframe1 and myframe2 by typing the following command.

```
pd.merge(myframe1, myframe2)
```

Output:

	Student Name	Sex	Age	School	Class
0	A	M	10	Primary	5

Note the difference between the outputs of concat () and merge (). The merge operation merges only those columns together for which the key entries, Student Name and Class, are the same. However, the concat () operation returns all the rows even with NaN values.

Consider the case when we have multiple key columns, and we want to merge on the basis of only one column. In this case, we can use the option **"on"** to specify the key for merging the data.

```
pd.merge(myframe1, myframe2,on='School')
```

Output:

	Student Name_x	Sex	Age	School	Student Name_y	Class
0	A	M	10	Primary	A	5
1	B	F	16	High	D	9
2	B	F	16	High	E	10
3	C	M	17	High	D	9
4	C	M	17	High	E	10

In this case, the merge operation renames those key attributes, which are common to both data frames but not used for merging. These are Student Name_x and Student Name_y. If we merge on the basis of Student Name, we get a completely different result.

```
pd.merge(myframe1, myframe2,on='Student Name')
```

Output:

	Student Name	Sex	Age	School_x	Class	School_y
0	A	M	10	Primary	5	Primary

Thus, it is important to consider the columns for merging different data frames together.

We can merge on the basis of indices using "**join.**" For this purpose, neither of the data frames should have the same column names. Thus, we rename columns of one of the data frames and merge both together using the following commands.

```
1. myframe2.columns = ['Student Name2','Class','School2']
2. myframe1.join(myframe2)
```

Output:

	Student Name	Sex	Age	School	Student Name2	Class	School2
0	A	M	10	Primary	D	9	High
1	B	F	16	High	E	10	High
2	C	M	17	High	A	5	Primary

5.4.3. Combining Data

Consider the case in which we have two datasets with overlapping indices. We want to keep values from one of the datasets if an overlapping index comes during combining these datasets. If the index is not overlapping, then its value is kept. This cannot be obtained either by merging or with concatenation. The combine_first () function provided by the Pandas library is able to perform this kind of operation. Let us create two Series data structures.

```
1. myseries1 =  pd.
   Series([50, 40, 30, 20, 10], index=[1,2,3,4,5])
2. myseries1
Output:
1    50
2    40
3    30
4    20
5    10
dtype: int64
```

```
1. myseries2 = pd.
   Series([100, 200, 300, 400] ,index=[3,4,5,6])
2. myseries2
Output:
3    100
4    200
5    300
6    400
dtype: int64
```

To keep the values from myseries1, we combine both series as given below:

```
myseries1.combine_first(myseries2)

Output:
1     50.0
2     40.0
3     30.0
4     20.0
5     10.0
6    400.0
dtype: float64
```

To keep the values from myseries2, we combine both series as given below:

```
myseries2.combine_first(myseries1)

Output:
1     50.0
2     40.0
3    100.0
4    200.0
5    300.0
6    400.0
dtype: float64
```

5.5. Data Transformation

The process of data transformation involves the removal or replacement of duplicate or invalid values, respectively. It aims to handle outliers and missing values, as well. We discuss various data transformation techniques in the following sections.

5.5.1. Removing Unwanted Data and Duplicates

To remove an unwanted column, we use del command, and to remove an unwanted row, we use drop() function. Let us apply these commands on a DataFrame.

```
myframe5 = pd.DataFrame({'Student Name': ['A','B','C'],
'Sex':['M','F','M'], 'Age': [10, 16, 17], 'School':
['Primary','High', 'High']})

del myframe5['School']
myframe5
Output:
```

	Student Name	Sex	Age
0	A	M	10
1	B	F	16
2	C	M	17

To remove the row indexed 1, we use:

```
myframe5.drop(1)
```

Output:

	Student Name	Sex	Age
0	A	M	10
2	C	M	17

Duplicate rows in a dataset do not convey extra information. These rows consume extra memory and are redundant. Furthermore, processing these extra records adds to the cost of computations. Thus, it is desirable to remove duplicate rows from the data. Let us create a DataFrame with duplicate rows.

```
1. item_frame = pd.
   DataFrame({'Items':['Ball','Bat','Hockey','Football',
   'Ball'],'Color':['White','Gray','White', 'Red','White'],
   'Price':[100,500,700,200,100]})
2. item_frame
```

Output:

	Items	Color	Price
0	Ball	White	100
1	Bat	Gray	500
2	Hockey	White	700
3	Football	Red	200
4	Ball	White	100

We note that the rows indexed 0 and 4 are duplicate. To detect duplicate rows, we use the duplicated () function.

```
item_frame.duplicated()

Output:
0    False
1    False
2    False
3    False
4     True
dtype: bool
```

To display the duplicate entries only, we can use the item_frame.duplicated() as the index to the DataFrame item_frame.

```
item_frame[item_frame.duplicated()]

Output:
```

	Items	Color	Price
4	Ball	White	100

To remove the duplicate entries, we use the following command:

```
item_frame.drop_duplicates()

Output:
```

	Items	Color	Price
0	Ball	White	100
1	Bat	Gray	500
2	Hockey	White	700
3	Football	Red	200

5.5.2. Handling Outliers

Outliers are values outside the expected range of a feature. Common causes of outliers include:

- Human errors during data entry;

- Measurement (instrument) errors;
- Experimental errors during data extraction or manipulation; and
- Intentional errors to test the accuracy of outlier detection methods.

During the data preparation and analysis, we have to detect the presence of unexpected values within a data structure. For instance, let us create a DataFrame myframe1.

```
1. student_frame = pd.DataFrame({'Student Name':
   ['A','B','C', 'D','E','F','G'], 'Sex':['M','F','M','F','F'
   ,'M','M'], 'Age': [10, 14, 60, 15, 16, 15, 11], 'School':
   ['Primary','High', 'High', 'High', 'High','High',
   'Primary']})
2. student_frame
```

Output:

	Student Name	Sex	Age	School
0	A	M	10	Primary
1	B	F	14	High
2	C	M	60	High
3	D	F	15	High
4	E	F	16	High
5	F	M	15	High
6	G	M	11	Primary

We find the age of student C to be an expected value, i.e., 60 years. This is deliberately entered wrong, and is considered as an outlier. We describe important statistics of student_frame by using the **describe ()** function.

```
student_frame.describe()

Output:
```

	Age
count	7.000000
mean	20.142857
std	17.714670
min	10.000000
25%	12.500000
50%	15.000000
75%	15.500000
max	60.000000

Note that the statistics of numeric columns is calculated and displayed. In our case, **Age** is the only numeric column in the student_frame.

The statistic count gives the number of elements in the column, mean gives the average value, std provides standard deviation, which is the average deviation of data points from the mean of the data, min is the minimum value, max is the maximum value, 25%, 50%, and 75% give the 25th percentile (the first quartile - Q1), the 50th percentile (the median - Q2), and the 75th percentile (the third quartile - Q3) of the values.

The presence of outliers shifts the statistics. We expect the mean or the average age of students to be around 15 years. However, the average age of students is 20.142857 due to the presence of the outlier, i.e., 60 years.

There are different ways to detect outliers. For example, if the difference between the mean and median values is too high, it can indicate the presence of outliers. A better approach to detect numeric outliers is to use InterQuartile Range (IQR). In IQR, we divide our data into four quarters after we sort it in ascending order.

Any data point that lies outside some small multiple of the difference between the third and the first quartiles is considered as an outlier. This difference is IQR. For example,

$$IQR = Q3 - Q1 = 15.5 - 12.5 = 3$$

Using a typical interquartile multiplier value k=1.5, we can find the lower and upper values beyond which data points can be considered as outliers.

$$IQR \times 1.5 = 4.5$$

We subtract this value, 4.5, from the Q1 to find the lower limit, and add 4.5 to the Q3 to find the upper limit. Thus,

$$\text{Lower limit} = Q1 - 4.5 = 8$$

$$\text{Upper limit} = Q3 + 4.5 = 20$$

Now any value lesser than 8 or greater than 20 can be treated as an outlier. A popular plot that shows these quartiles is known as a Box and Whisker plot shown in figure 5.1.

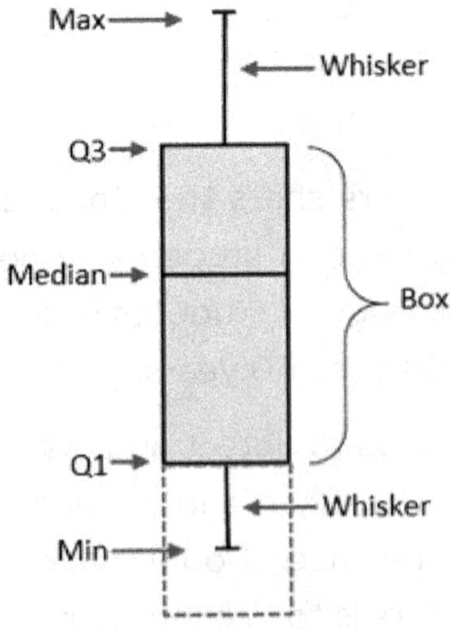

Figure 5.1: A Box and Whisker plot.
The length of the box represents IQR.

To calculate lower and upper limits, we can enter the following script:

```
Q1 = student_frame.quantile(0.25)   # 25% (quartile 1)
Q3 = student_frame.quantile(0.75)       # 75% (quartile 3)

IQR = Q3 - Q1                     #InterQuartile Range (IQR)
IQR_mult = IQR*1.5

lower= Q1 - IQR_mult
upper= Q3 + IQR_mult

print("The lower limit is = ", lower)
print("The upper limit is = ", upper)
```

Output:

```
The lower limit is =  Age   8.0
dtype: float64
The upper limit is =  Age   20.0
dtype: float64
```

Now, we are able to filter our DataFrame, student_frame, to remove outliers. We access the column **Age** using student_frame['Age'], and compare it with int(lower). The result is used as indices to student_frame. Finally, student_frame is updated by making an assignment as follows:

```
student_frame = student_frame[student_frame['Age'] > int(lower)]
student_frame = student_frame[student_frame['Age'] < int(upper)]
student_frame
```

Output:

	Student Name	Sex	Age	School
0	A	M	10	Primary
1	B	F	14	High
3	D	F	15	High
4	E	F	16	High
5	F	M	15	High
6	G	M	11	Primary

5.5.3. Handling Missing or Invalid Data

It is often the case that the data we receive has missing information in some columns. For instance, some customer's data might be missing their age. If the data has a large number of missing entries, the result of data analysis may be unpredictable or even wrong. Missing values in a dataset can be either

- Ignored,
- Filled-in, or
- Removed or dropped.

Ignoring the missing values is often not a good solution because it leads to erroneous results. Let us create a Series object with missing values.

```
1. myseries4 = pd.Series([10, 20, 30, None, 40, 50, np.
   NaN], index=[0,1,2,3,4,5,6])
2. print (myseries4.isnull())
3. myseries4
Output:
0     False
1     False
2     False
3      True
4     False
5     False
6      True
dtype: bool

0    10.0
1    20.0
2    30.0
3     NaN
4    40.0
5    50.0
6     NaN
dtype: float64
```

To get the indices where values are missing, we may type:

```
myseries4[myseries4.isnull()]

Output:
3    NaN
6    NaN
dtype: float64
```

We can drop the missing values by using the function **dropna ( )**.

```
1. myseries4_dropped = myseries4.dropna()
2. myseries4_dropped
Output:
0     10.0
1     20.0
2     30.0
4     40.0
5     50.0
dtype: float64
```

The process in which the missing values are filled-in is called **"data imputation."** One of the widely used techniques is mean value imputation, where we impute the missing values by the average value of that particular column in which the value is missing.

```
1. myseries4_filled = myseries4.fillna(myseries4.mean())
2. myseries4_filled
Output:
0     10.0
1     20.0
2     30.0
3     30.0
4     40.0
5     50.0
6     30.0
dtype: float64
```

Here, the values at indices 3 and 6 are filled-in by the mean or average of the rest of the valid values. The mean is calculated as

$$\text{Mean} = (10+20+30+40+50)/5 = 30.$$

Besides mean, we can impute the missing data using the median by typing myseries4.median () in place of myseries4. mean ().

5.5.4. Data Mapping

The Pandas library provides useful data mapping functions to perform numerous operations. The mapping is the creation of a list of matches between two values. To define a mapping, we can use dictionary objects.

```
mymap = {
'label1' : 'value1,
'label2' : 'value2,
...
}
```

The following functions accept a dictionary object as an argument to perform mapping:

- **replace()** function replaces values;
- **map()** function creates a new column;
- **rename()** function replaces the index values.

The replace function replaces the matches with the desired new values. To illustrate this idea, let us create a DataFrame.

```
data = {'color' : ['blue','green','yellow','red','white'],
'object' : ['ball','pen','pencil','paper','mug'],
'price' : [1.2,1.0,0.6,0.9,1.7]}
myframe = pd.DataFrame(data)
myframe
```

Output:

	color	object	price
0	blue	ball	1.2
1	green	pen	1.0
2	yellow	pencil	0.6
3	red	paper	0.9
4	white	mug	1.7

We create a dictionary to perform mapping.

```
mymap = {'blue':'dark blue', 'green': 'light green'}
```

Next, this dictionary is provided as an input argument to the replace () function.

```
myframe.replace(mymap)
```

Output:

	color	object	price
0	dark blue	ball	1.2
1	light green	pen	1.0
2	yellow	pencil	0.6
3	red	paper	0.9
4	white	mug	1.7

Note, the original colors blue and green have been replaced by dark blue and light green as mapped inside the dictionary mymap. The function **replace ()** can also be used to replace NaN values contained inside a data structure.

```
1. myseries = pd.Series([1,2,np.nan,4,5,np.nan])
2. myseries.replace(np.nan,0)
Output:
0    1.0
1    2.0
2    0.0
3    4.0
4    5.0
5    0.0
dtype: float64
```

To add a new column to an existing DataFrame, we again create a dictionary object that serves as a map.

```
1. mymap2 = {'ball':'round', 'pencil':'long', 'pen': 'long',
   'mug': 'cylindrical', 'paper':'rectangular'}
2. myframe['shape']=myframe['object'].map(mymap2)
3. myframe
Output:
```

	color	object	price	shape
0	blue	ball	1.2	round
1	green	pen	1.0	long
2	yellow	pencil	0.6	long
3	red	paper	0.9	rectangular
4	white	mug	1.7	cylindrical

We use **map ()** function that takes the dictionary as its input argument, and maps a particular column of the DataFrame to create a new column. In our case, the column named **object** is used for the mapping.

Finally, we can rename the indices of a DataFrame using the function rename (). We create new indices using a dictionary.

```
reindex = { 0: 'first', 1: 'second', 2: 'third', 3: 'fourth',
   4: 'fifth'}
   myframe=myframe.rename(reindex)
   myframe
```

Output:

	color	object	price	shape
first	blue	ball	1.2	round
second	green	pen	1.0	long
third	yellow	pencil	0.6	long
fourth	red	paper	0.9	rectangular
fifth	white	mug	1.7	cylindrical

Note that we rename the indices, and assign the result of the right-hand side to myframe to update it. If this assignment operation is not performed, myframe will not be updated.

5.5.5. Discretization and Binning

Occasionally, when we have a large amount of data, we want to transform this into discrete categories to facilitate the analysis. For instance, we can divide the range of values of the data into relatively smaller intervals or categories to discover the statistics within each interval. Suppose we gather data from an experimental study and store it in a list.

```
1. readings = [34, 39, 82, 75, 16, 17, 15, 74, 37, 68, 22, 92,
   99, 54, 39, 96, 17, 36, 91, 86]
```

We find that the range of data values is 0 to 100. Thus, we can uniformly divide this interval, suppose, into four equal parts (bins):

- the first bin contains the values between 0 and 25,
- the second between 26 and 50,

- the third between 51 and 75, and
- the last between 76 and 100.

```
1. bins = [0, 25, 50, 75, 100]
```

We pass these readings and bins to the function **cut ()**.

```
1. mycategory = pd.cut(readings, bins)
2. mycategory
Output:
[(25, 50], (25, 50], (75, 100], (50, 75], (0, 25], ..., (75,
   100], (0, 25], (25, 50], (75, 100], (75, 100]]

Length: 20

Categories (4, interval[int64]): [(0, 25] < (25, 50] < (50,
   75] < (75, 100]]
```

We get four categories or intervals when we run the function cut (), i.e., [(0, 25] < (25, 50] < (50, 75] < (75, 100]]. Note that each category has a lower limit with parenthesis and the upper limit with a bracket. This is consistent with mathematical notation used to indicate the intervals. In the case of a square bracket, the number belongs to the range, and if it is a parenthesis, the number does not belong to the interval. In (0,25], 0 is excluded, whereas 25 is included. To count the number of elements in each bin, we may write:

```
pd.value_counts(mycategory)

Output:
(75, 100]    6
(25, 50]     5
(0, 25]      5
(50, 75]    4
dtype: int64
```

In place of numbers, we can give meaningful names to the bins.

```
bin_names = ['Poor','Below Average','Average','Good']
pd.cut(readings, bins, labels=bin_names)
Output:
[Below Average, Below Average, Good, Average, Poor, ..., Good,
   Poor, Below Average, Good, Good]

Length: 20
Categories (4, object): [Poor < Below Average < Average <
   Good]
```

The Pandas library provides the function **qcut()** that divides the data into quantiles. qcut() ensures that the number of occurrences for each bin is equal, but the ranges of each bin may vary.

```
pd.qcut(readings, 4)

Output:
[(31.0, 46.5], (31.0, 46.5], (46.5, 83.0], (46.5, 83.0],
   (14.999, 31.0], ..., (83.0, 99.0], (14.999, 31.0], (31.0,
   46.5], (83.0, 99.0], (83.0, 99.0]]

Length: 20
Categories (4, interval[float64]): [(14.999, 31.0] < (31.0,
   46.5] < (46.5, 83.0] < (83.0, 99.0]]
```

To check the number of elements in each bin, we type:

```
pd.value_counts(pd.qcut(readings,4))

Output:
(83.0, 99.0]        5
(46.5, 83.0]        5
(31.0, 46.5]        5
(14.999, 31.0]    5
dtype: int64
```

5.5.6. Aggregating Data

Aggregation is the process of grouping data together into a list or any other data structure. The aggregation uses statistical functions such as mean, median, count, or sum to combine several rows together. The combined data resulting from data aggregation is easier to analyze. It protects the privacy of an individual and can be matched with other sources of data. Let us create a DataFrame to understand the concept of grouping or aggregation.

```
data = {'color' : ['blue','white','red','red','white'],
'object' : ['ball','pen','pencil','paper','mug'],
'price' : [1.2,1.0,0.6,0.9,1.7]}

myframe = pd.DataFrame(data)
myframe
```

Output:

	color	object	price
0	blue	ball	1.2
1	white	pen	1.0
2	red	pencil	0.6
3	red	paper	0.9
4	white	mug	1.7

Note that the column **color** has two entries for both white and red. If we want to group the data based upon the column color, for example, we may type:

```
mygroup = myframe['price'].groupby(myframe['color'])
mygroup.groups
```

Output:

```
{'blue': Int64Index([0], dtype='int64'),
 'red': Int64Index([2, 3], dtype='int64'),
 'white': Int64Index([1, 4], dtype='int64')}
```

Thus, we get three distinct groups, blue, red, and white, by invoking the attribute **groups.** We can find the average value and sum of numeric features for each group as well.

```
1. mygroup.mean()
Output:
color
blue      1.20
red       0.75
white    1.35
Name: price, dtype: float64

1. mygroup.sum()
Output:
color
blue     1.2
red       1.5
white    2.7
Name: price, dtype: float64
```

The data aggregation can be performed using more than one column. For instance, we may group data by both color and object. It is called hierarchical grouping. We may type the following commands.

```
1. mygroup2 = myframe['price'].
   groupby([myframe['color'],myframe['object']])

2. mygroup2.groups
Output:
{('blue', 'ball'): Int64Index([0], dtype='int64'),
 ('red', 'paper'): Int64Index([3], dtype='int64'),
 ('red', 'pencil'): Int64Index([2], dtype='int64'),
 ('white', 'mug'): Int64Index([4], dtype='int64'),
 ('white', 'pen'): Int64Index([1], dtype='int64')}
```

Let us create a new dataframe **myframe2** that is the same as **myframe** except for an extra entry ['red','pencil',0.8] at index 5.

```
1. myframe2 = myframe
2. myframe2.loc[5]=['red','pencil',0.8]
3. myframe2
Output:
```

	color	object	price
0	blue	ball	1.2
1	white	pen	1.0
2	red	pencil	0.6
3	red	paper	0.9
4	white	mug	1.7
5	red	pencil	0.8

Now, we group myframe2 by color as well as by object.

```
1. mygroup2 = myframe2['price'].
   groupby([myframe2['color'],myframe2['object']])
2. mygroup2.groups
Output:
{('blue', 'ball'): Int64Index([0], dtype='int64'),
 ('red', 'paper'): Int64Index([3], dtype='int64'),
 ('red', 'pencil'): Int64Index([2, 5], dtype='int64'),
 ('white', 'mug'): Int64Index([4], dtype='int64'),
 ('white', 'pen'): Int64Index([1], dtype='int64')}
```

We find the average value and sum of numeric features for each group.

```
1. mygroup2.mean()
Output:
color         object
blue          ball          1.2
red           paper         0.9
pencil        0.7
white         mug
       1.7

       pen           1.0
Name: price, dtype: float64
1. mygroup2.sum()
Output:
color         object
blue          ball
       1.2
red           paper         0.9
          pencil            1.4
white         mug
       1.7
              pen           1.0
Name: price, dtype: float64
```

5.6. Selection of Data

Sometimes, we have to work with a subset of a dataset. In this case, we select data of interest from the dataset. Let us work on an already created DataFrame, myframe4.

```
1. myframe4.columns
Output:
Index(['col0', 'col1', 'col2', 'col3', 'col4'],
   dtype='object')
myframe4.index

Output:
Index(['row0', 'row1', 'row2'], dtype='object')
1. myframe4.values
Output:
array([[ 0,  1,  2,  3,  4],
       [ 5,  6,  7,  8,  9],
       [10, 11, 12, 13, 14]])
```

We can select a single column.

```
myframe4['col2']

Output:
row0     2
row1     7
row2    12
Name: col2, dtype: int32
```

Alternatively, we can use the column name as an attribute of our DataFrame.

```
myframe4.col2

Output:
row0     2
row1     7
row2    12
Name: col2, dtype: int32
```

It is possible to extract or select a few rows from the DataFrame. To extract rows with index 1 and 2 (3 excluded), type the following command.

```
myframe4[1:3]

Output:
```

	col0	col1	col2	col3	col4
row1	5	6	7	8	9
row2	10	11	12	13	14

The attribute **loc** accesses rows by the names of their indices.

```
myframe4.loc['row1']

Output:
col0    5
col1    6
col2    7
col3    8
col4    9
Name: row1, dtype: int32
```

The rows and columns of a DataFrame can be given meaningful names.

```
1. myframe4.index.name = 'Rows'
2. myframe4.columns.name = 'Columns'
3. myframe4
Output:
```

Columns	col0	col1	col2	col3	col4
Rows					
row0	0	1	2	3	4
row1	5	6	7	8	9
row2	10	11	12	13	14

We can add columns to the existing DataFrame by using a new column name and assigning value(s) to this column.

```
1. myframe4['col5'] = np.random.randint(100,  size = 3)
2. myframe4
```

Output:

Columns	col0	col1	col2	col3	col4	col5
Rows						
row0	0	1	2	3	4	11
row1	5	6	7	8	9	99
row2	10	11	12	13	14	70

In the aforementioned example, we have used Numpy's random module to generate an array of three random numbers from 0 (inclusive) to 100 (exclusive).

Finally, we can change a single value by selecting that element and updating it. For example, to update element 1 of col1, we write:

```
1. myframe4['col1'][1] = 1000
2. myframe4
```

Output:

Columns	col0	col1	col2	col3	col4	col5
Rows						
row0	0	1	2	3	4	11
row1	5	1000	7	8	9	99
row2	10	11	12	13	14	70

Similar to the Series, we use the function isin() to check the membership of a set of values. For instance,

```
myframe4.isin([1,4,99])

Output:
```

Columns	col0	col1	col2	col3	col4	col5
Rows						
row0	False	True	False	False	True	False
row1	False	False	False	False	False	True
row2	False	False	False	False	False	False

If we use the Boolean values returned by myframe4.isin([1,4,99]) as indices to the DataFrame, we get NaN values at locations where our specified values are not present.

```
myframe4[myframe4.isin([1,4,99])]

Output:
```

Columns	col0	col1	col2	col3	col4	col5
Rows						
row0	NaN	1.0	NaN	NaN	4.0	NaN
row1	NaN	NaN	NaN	NaN	NaN	99.0
row2	NaN	NaN	NaN	NaN	NaN	NaN

To delete a column from the existing DataFrame, use the keyword del.

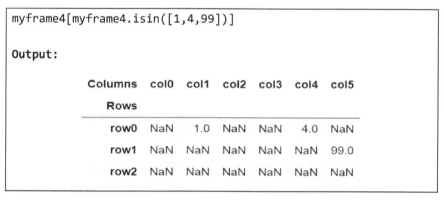

```
1. del myframe4['col5']
2. myframe4
Output:
```

Columns	col0	col1	col2	col3	col4
Rows					
row0	0	1	2	3	4
row1	5	1000	7	8	9
row2	10	11	12	13	14

Let us display the already created DataFrame **myframe3**.

```
3. myframe3
Output:
```

	Employee Name	Specialization	Experience (years)
zero	Ashley	Python	3
one	Tom	Data Science	5
two	Jack	Data preparation	8
three	John	Data Analysis	2
four	Alicia	Machine Learning	4

We can select a single row or multiple rows from a DataFrame. Suppose we are interested in those employees having more than four years of experience. We use the following command for the selection.

```
1. myframe3[myframe3['Experience (years)']>4]
Output:
```

	Employee Name	Specialization	Experience (years)
one	Tom	Data Science	5
two	Jack	Data preparation	8

In the aforementioned example, myframe3['Experience (years)']>4 returns values that are used as indices to myframe3 to display only those employees who have an experience of more than four years. Finally, to transpose any DataFrame, we use:

```
2. myframe3.T
```

Output:

	zero	one	two	three	four
Employee Name	Ashley	Tom	Jack	John	Alicia
Specialization	Python	Data Science	Data preparation	Data Analysis	Machine Learning
Experience (years)	3	5	8	2	4

Hands-on Time

It is time to check your understanding of the topic of this chapter through the exercise questions given in Section 5.7. The answers to these questions are given at the end of the book.

5.7. Exercise Questions

Question 1: Let us write the following commands:

```
1. myseries2 = pd.Series([1, -3, 5, 20], index =
   ['a', 'b', 'c', 'd'])
2. myseries2[2:3]
```

What will be the output?

A. c 5

B. b -3

   c 5

C. c 5

   d 20

D. 5 c

Question 2: Let us write the following commands:

```
1. mycolors = pd.Series([1,2,3,4,5,4,3,2], index=['white',
   'black','blue','green','green','yellow', 'black', 'red'])
2. mycolors.unique()
```

What will be the output?

A. ['white','black','blue','green','yellow', 'red'])

B. array([1, 2, 3, 4, 5], dtype=int64)

C. ['True','False','True','False','False', 'True','False','True'])

D. Not given

Question 3: We link together two or more separate data structures and place them next to each other using?

A. pandas.DataFrame.combine_first( )
B. pandas.merge( )
C. pandas.concat( )
D. All of the above.

Question 4: We combine the data through the connection of rows using one or more keys by typing?

A. pandas.DataFrame.combine_first( )
B. pandas.merge( )
C. pandas.concat( )
D. All of the above.

Question 5: We combine the data in such a way that we keep values from one of the datasets if an overlapping index comes during combining the datasets. If the index is not overlapping, then its value is kept. For this purpose, we use?

A. pandas.DataFrame.combine_first( )
B. pandas.merge( )
C. pandas.concat( )
D. All of the above.

6

Exploratory Data Analysis

6.1. Introduction

In the previous chapter, we have seen that data preprocessing is an important step in the data science pipeline. Once we get the preprocessed data, we have to choose suitable machine learning algorithms to model the data. However, before applying machine learning, we have to answer the following questions:

- How to find the structure of the data?
- How to test assumptions about the data?
- How to select the features that can be used for machine learning methods?
- How to choose suitable machine learning algorithms to model our dataset?

Exploratory Data Analysis (EDA) is a process to get familiar with the structure and important features of a dataset. EDA helps us answer the aforementioned questions by providing us with a good understanding of what the data contains. EDA explores the preprocessed data using suitable visualization tools to find the structure of the data, its salient features, and important patterns.

EDA is also intended to define and refine the selection of important features. Once EDA is complete, we can perform more complex modeling and machine learning tasks on the selected features such as clustering, regression, and classification.

The goal of EDA is to make sure that the dataset is ready to be deployed in a machine learning algorithm. EDA is a valuable step in a data science project, validating the results, and making the interpretation of the results simpler in the desired context. In the ensuing sections, we explain the process of exploratory data analysis along with practical Python examples.

6.2. Revealing Structure of Data

Knowing the underlying structure of our data enables us to use appropriate machine learning methods for data modeling and future predictions using these models. In EDA, several techniques are employed to reveal the structure of the data. These include:

Univariate visualization is used to generate summary statistics for each feature or variable in a dataset. We summarize our dataset through descriptive statistics that uses a variety of statistical measurements to better understand the dataset. It is also known as **data profiling.** The goal of univariate visualization is to have a solid understanding of the data so we can start querying and visualizing our data in various ways. It uses visualization tools such as bar plots and histograms to reveal the structure of the data.

Bivariate visualization is carried out to find the relationship between two variables in a given dataset, where one of the two variables can be the target variable of interest. It uses correlations, scatter, and line plots to reveal the structure of the data.

Multivariate visualization is employed to understand interactions between different fields in the dataset. It uses line plots, scatter plots, and matrices with multiple colors to understand the relationship between various features of a dataset.

Revealing the underlying structure of data enables us to discover patterns, spot anomalies such as missing values and outliers, and check assumptions about the data.

We first download a real-world dataset to reveal its underlying structure. Suppose we want to foretell the price of a house based upon already available data of houses in a particular city or country. Fortunately, we have a dataset of house prices in the United States of America: USA_Housing dataset. This dataset can be downloaded from either

https://www.kaggle.com/aariyan101/usa-housingcsv

Or

https://raw.githubusercontent.com/bcbarsness/machine-learning/master/USA_Housing.csv

The USA_Housing dataset contains the following columns or variables:

1. **Avg. Area Income**: It shows the average income of the residents of the city.
2. **Avg. Area House Age**: It shows the average age of houses located in the same city.
3. **Avg. Area Number of Rooms**: It shows the average number of rooms for the houses located in the same city.

4. **Avg. Area Number of Bedrooms**: It shows the average number of bedrooms for the houses located in the same city.
5. **Area Population**: It shows the average population of the city where the house is located.
6. **Price**: It shows the price that the house is sold at.
7. **Address**: It shows the address of the house.

Let us start to explore this dataset. We import necessary libraries first by typing the following commands.

```
import numpy as np
import pandas as pd
import matplotlib.pyplot as plt
import seaborn as sns
```

We have imported Matplotlib, a commonly used Python library for data visualization. Advanced data visualization library Seaborn is based upon Matplotlib. We use both libraries for the plotting and visualization of our dataset.

Further Readings -Anaconda, Jupyter, and Matplotlib

The Python scripts have been executed using the Jupyter notebook. Thus, we should have the Jupyter notebook installed. Since Jupyter notebook has Matplotlib, Numpy, and Pandas libraries, we do not need to install them separately.

Hands-on Time – Source Codes

The Jupyter notebook containing the source code given in this chapter can be found in Resources/Chapter 6.ipynb. We suggest that the reader writes all the code given in this chapter to verify the outputs mentioned in this chapter.

6.3. Plots and Charts

6.3.1. Line Plot

Line plots are predominantly useful for conveying changes over space or time. Line plots are mostly used to plot data along a scale divided into equal intervals, for example, time. Let us generate a simple line plot.

```
import matplotlib.pyplot as plt
x1 = [1,2,3]
y1 = [2,4,1]
plt.plot(x1, y1, label = "line 1")
plt.show()
```

Output:

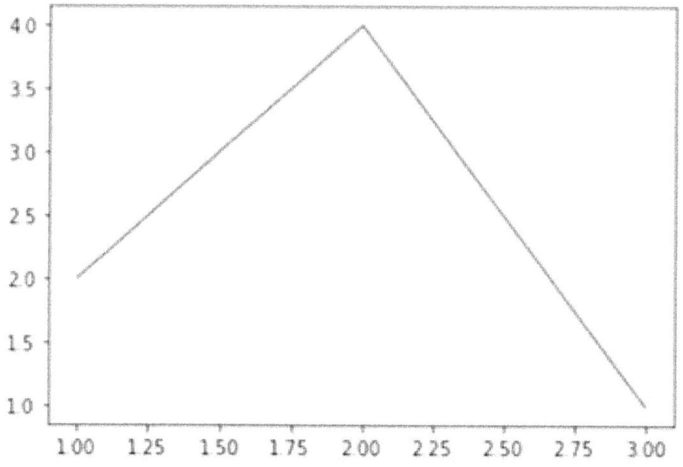

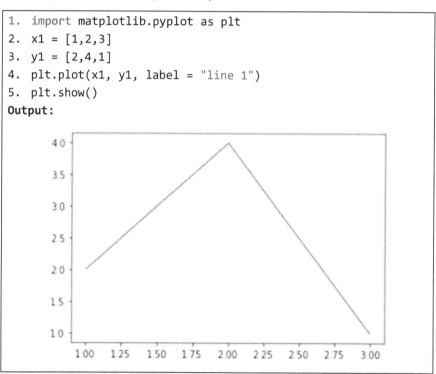

In this graph, we generate three values of variable x1 and y1. To generate a line plot via the pyplot module, we call the function plot(), pass it the values for the x and y axes. It is important to mention that we are using plt as an alias for pyplot.

We can add titles, labels, and legends to the generated plots. To add titles, labels, and legend to a plot, we use the title, xlabel, ylabel, and legend methods of the pyplot module, respectively. We pass string values to these methods, which appear on the plots, as shown below.

```
x1 = [1,2,3]
y1 = [2,4,1]

plt.plot(x1, y1, label = "line 1")

# naming the x axis
plt.xlabel('x - axis')
# naming the y axis
plt.ylabel('y - axis')
# giving a title to my graph
plt.title('My first line plot')
plt.legend()
plt.show()
```

Output:

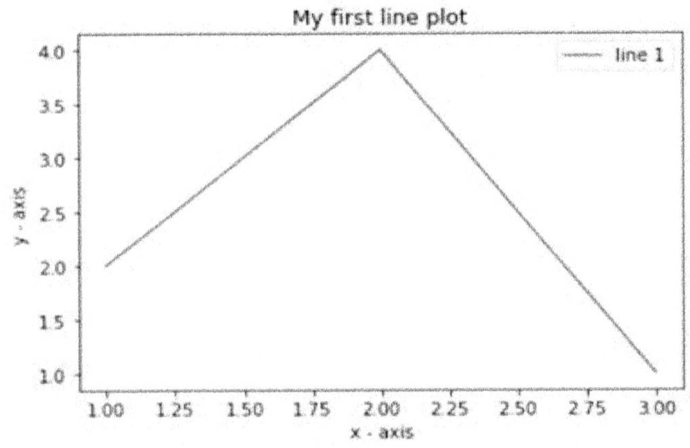

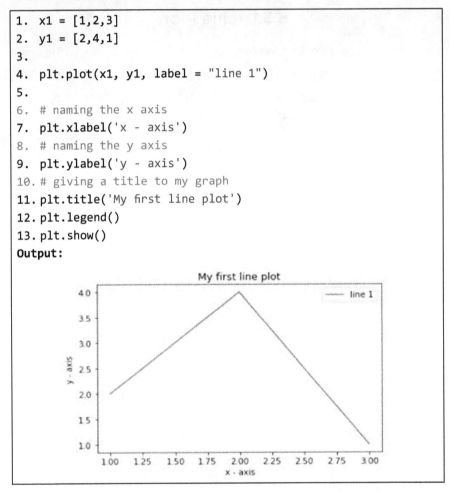

Multiple plots can be drawn on the same figure, as shown in the Python script given below.

```
# Generating x and y points to plot
x1= np.arange(0, 10*(np.pi), 0.1)
y1 = np.cos(x1)     # cosine function from Numpy library

# potting the points
plt.plot(x1, y1, label = 'cosine')

plt.legend()               # shows the legend with labels
plt.xlabel('Angle')        # naming the x axis
plt.ylabel('Amplitude')    # naming the y axis

# Generating x and y points for the second plot
x2= np.arange(0, 10*(np.pi), 0.1)
# decaying cosine function
y2 = np.cos(x2)*0.1*np.arange(10*(np.pi),0,-0.1)
# potting the points
plt.plot(x2, y2, label = 'Decaying cosine')
# show a legend on the plot
plt.legend()
# gives a title to the plot
plt.title('Two functions on the same graph')
# shows the graph, and removes the text output.
plt.show()
```

Output:

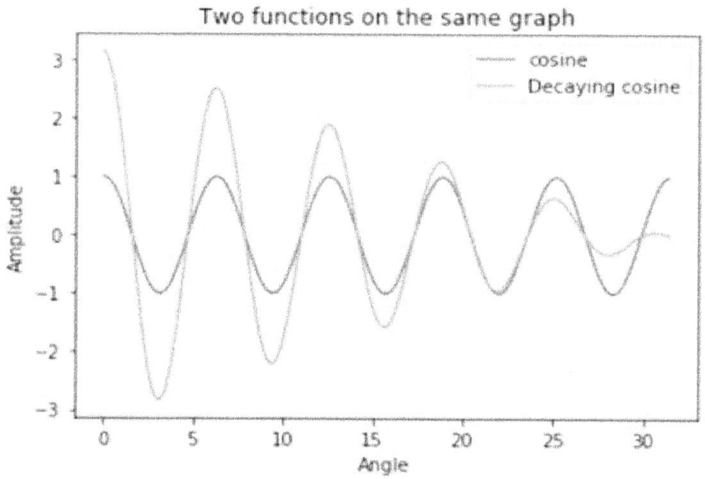

Let us plot **Avg. Area Income** against **Price** from US_Housing dataset.

```
#The database is available here https://www.kaggle.com/faressayah/linear-regression-house-price-prediction

housing_price = pd.read_csv(USA_Housing.csv')
housing_price.head()
```

```
# Plotting Avg. Area Income vs Price
plt.plot(housing_price['Avg. Area Income'], housing_price['Price'], color='red', marker='o')

# Giving title and label names
plt.title('Avg. Area Income Vs Price', fontsize=14)
plt.xlabel('Avg. Area Income', fontsize=14)
plt.ylabel('Price', fontsize=14)
plt.grid(True)

plt.show()
```

Output:

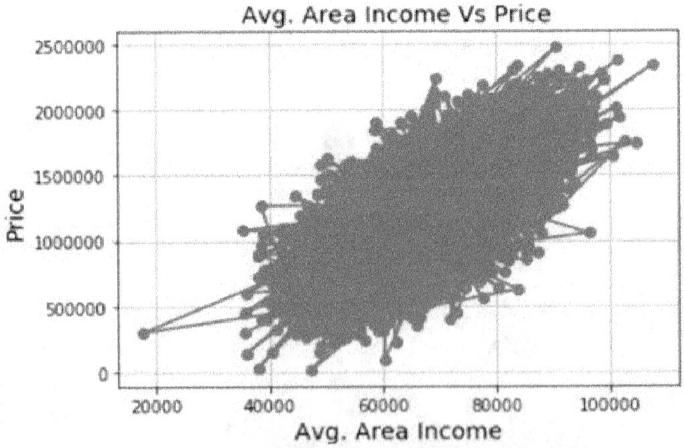

Since there are 5000 observations, it is evident that a line plot does not give us a clear picture of what is the relationship between these two variables.

6.3.2. Scatter Plot

A scatter plot is used to visualize any two variables from a given dataset in two dimensions. It uses dots or marks to plot values of two variables, one along the x-axis and the other along the y-axis.

Scatter plots allow us to observe the relationship between the variables. If an increase in one variable causes an increase in another variable and vice versa, we can infer there is a positive linear relationship between two variables. However, if increasing the first variable reveals a decrease in the second variable, we say that there is a negative linear relationship between both variables. For example, let us generate a scatter plot between **Avg. Area Income** and **Price.**

```
# Adjusting the figure size using rcParams function
plt.rcParams['figure.figsize'] = [12,8]

# Scatter plot
plt.scatter(housing_price['Avg. Area Income'], housing_price['Price'], color='red', marker='o')

# Giving title and label names
plt.title('Avg. Area Income Vs Price', fontsize=14)
plt.xlabel('Avg. Area Income', fontsize=14)
plt.ylabel('Price', fontsize=14)
plt.grid(True)
plt.show()
```

Output:

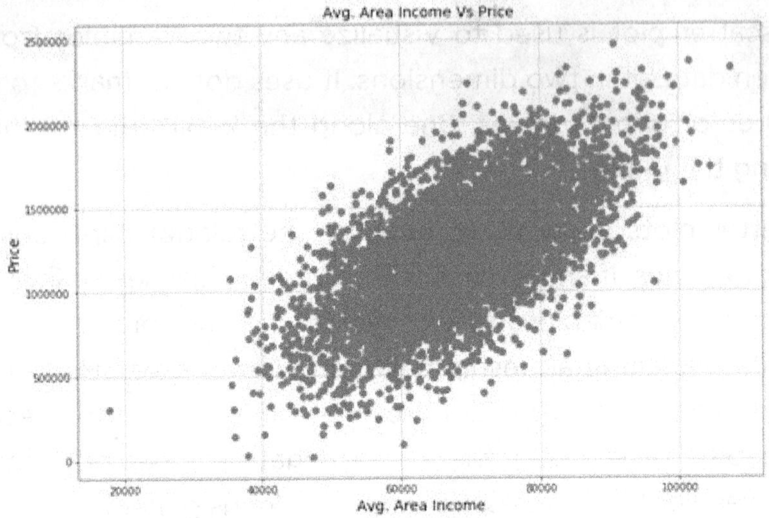

This plot shows that there is a positive linear relationship between variables **Avg. Area Income** and **Price.** To increase the size of plot for better readability, we have used **rcParams** option of pyplot module.

plt.rcParams['figure.figsize'] = [12,8]

If the points or dots are color-coded in a scatter plot, additional variables can be shown in two-dimensions. For example, let us create the **Avg. Area Income** against **Price** and **Avg. Population** against **Price** by color-coding the plots on the same figure.

```
1. plt.scatter(housing_price['Avg. Area Income'], housing_
   price['Price'], color='red', marker='o', label =
   'Avg. Area Income')
2.
3. # Scatter plot
4. plt.scatter(housing_price['Area Population'], housing_
   price['Price'], color='blue', marker='x', label =
   'Area Population')
5.
```

```
# Giving title and label names
plt.title('Avg. Area Income Vs Price', fontsize=14)
plt.xlabel('Avg. Area Income (Red),
Area Population (blue)',  fontsize=14)
plt.ylabel('Price', fontsize=14)
plt.legend()
plt.grid(True)
plt.show()
```

Output:

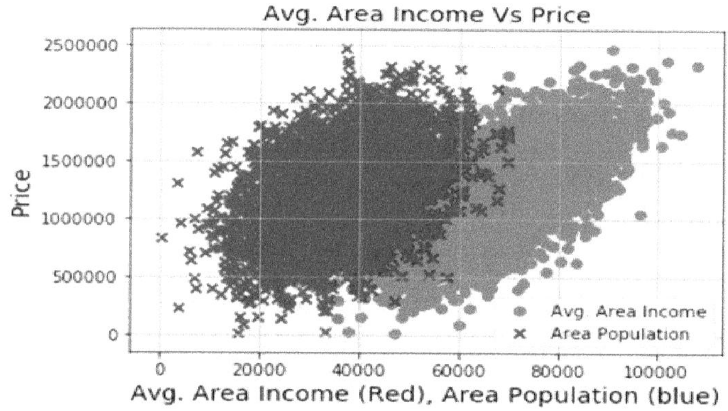

6.3.3. Box Plots

A box plot, also called a box and whisker plot displays the summary of a dataset or its subset as five numbers. These five numbers are

1. The minimum value excluding any outlier,
2. The first quartile,
3. The second quartile or median,
4. The third quartile, and
5. The maximum value excluding any outlier.

The outliers are shown beyond the minimum and maximum points. A box and whisker plot is shown in figure 6.1.

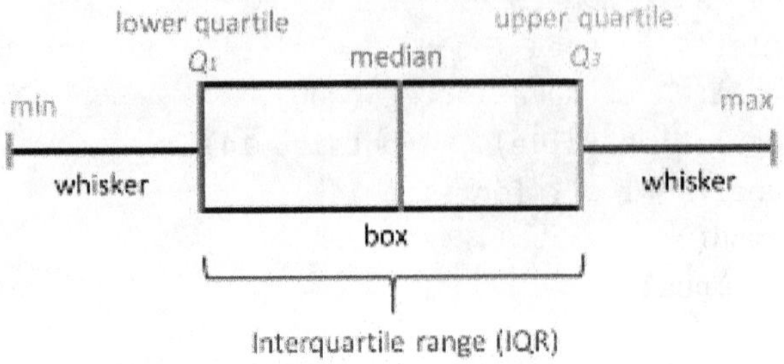

Figure 6.1: A box and whisker plot.

We can generate a box plot using either Matplotlib, Pandas, or Seaborn. To create a box plot using Matplotlib, we can type the following lines of code:

```
1. plt.boxplot([0, 1, 10, 15, 4, -6, -15 -2, 30, 40, -20, 11])
2. plt.show()
```

Output:

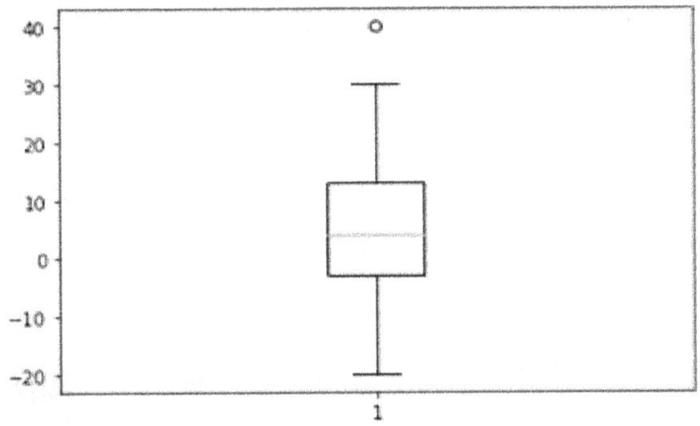

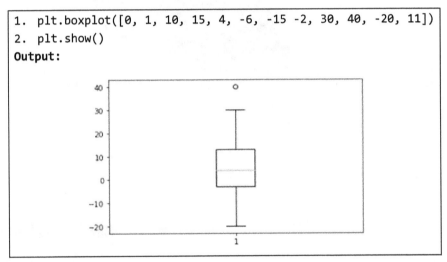

We can generate multiple box plots on the same figure. Let us produce the data for the box plots by using the **numpy.random.randn()** function. This function takes two input arguments: the number of arrays to be created and the number of values within each array.

```
1. myframe = pd.DataFrame(np.random.
   randn(10, 3), columns=['Col1', 'Col2', 'Col3'])
2. boxplot = myframe.boxplot(column=['Col1', 'Col2', 'Col3'])
```

Output:

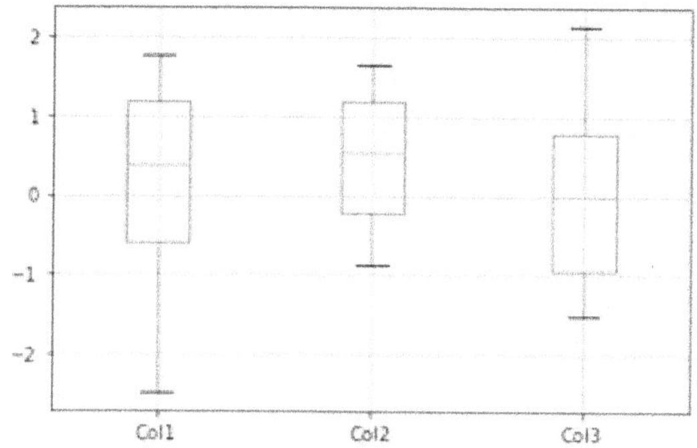

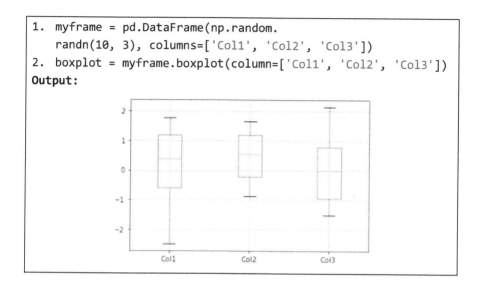

6.3.4. Histogram

A histogram is a plot that indicates the frequency distribution or shape of a numeric feature in a dataset. This allows us to discover the underlying distribution of the data by visual inspection. To plot a histogram, we pass a collection of numeric values to the method hist (). For example, the following histogram plots the distribution of values in the price column of the USA_Housing dataset.

```
plt.hist(housing_price['Price'])
plt.show()
```

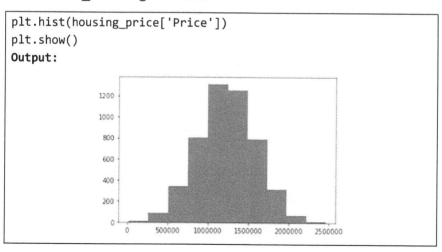

Output:

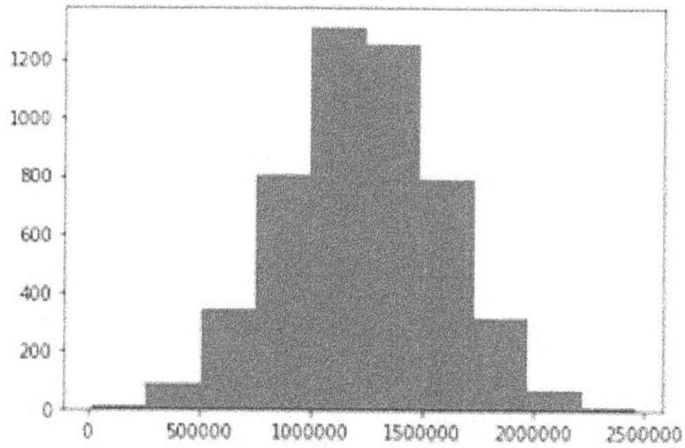

This plot shows that more than 1,200 houses, out of 5,000, have a price of around $ 1,000,000. A few houses have prices less than $ 500,000 and greater than $ 2,000,000. By default, the method hist () uses 10 bins or groups to plot the distribution of the data. We can change the number of bins by using the option **bins**.

```
plt.hist(housing_price['Price'], bins = 100)
plt.show()
```

Output:

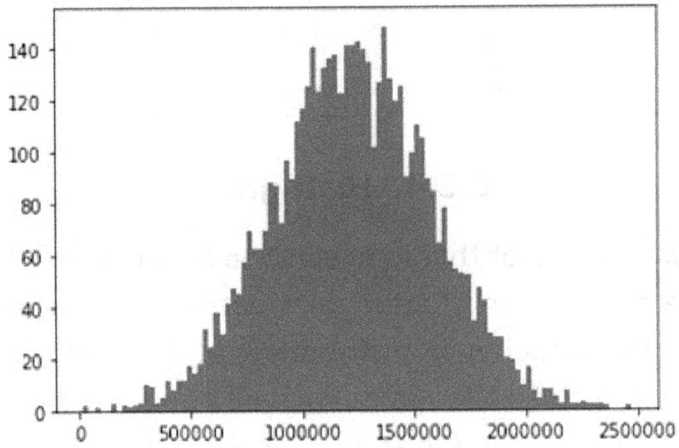

From this plot, it can be observed that the house price follows a Normal or a Gaussian distribution that is a bell curve. It is important to know that many machine learning algorithms assume Gaussian distribution of features. Thus, it is better for a feature to follow this distribution.

6.3.5. Bar Chart

If we have categorical or discrete data that can take one of a small set of values, we use bar charts to show the values of categories as rectangular bars whose lengths are proportional to the values. Since the **USA_Housing dataset** has a continuous range of prices for houses, it is not suitable to draw bar charts for this dataset. We import the **"Iris"** dataset that contains three species of Iris plant: Iris-setosa, Iris-virginica, and Iris-versicolor.

```
iris_data = pd.read_csv('iris_dataset.csv')
iris_data.info()
```

Output:

```
<class 'pandas.core.frame.DataFrame'>
RangeIndex: 150 entries, 0 to 149
Data columns (total 6 columns):
#   Column         Non-Null Count  Dtype
---  ------         --------------  -----
 0   Id             150 non-null   int64
 1   SepalLengthCm  150 non-null   float64
2   SepalWidthCm    150 non-null   float64
3   PetalLengthCm   150 non-null   float64
4   PetalWidthCm    150 non-null   float64
5   Species    150 non-null object
dtypes: float64(4), int64(1), object(1)
memory usage: 7.2+ KB
```

To make a bar chart of **SepalLengthCm**, we may write the following Python script.

```
# Generating a bar chart
plt.bar(iris_data['Species'], iris_data['SepalLengthCm'])

# Giving title and label names
plt.title('SepalLengthCm Vs Species', fontsize=14)
plt.xlabel('Species', fontsize=14)
plt.ylabel('SepalLengthCm', fontsize=14)

plt.show()
```

Output:

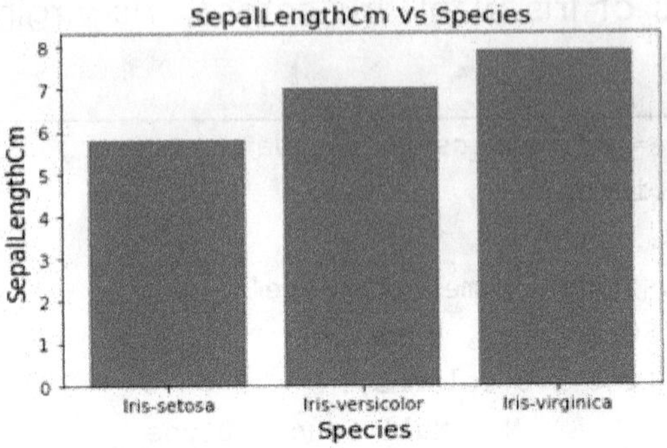

Similarly, we generate bar charts for SepalWidthCm, PetalLengthCm and PetalWidthCm.

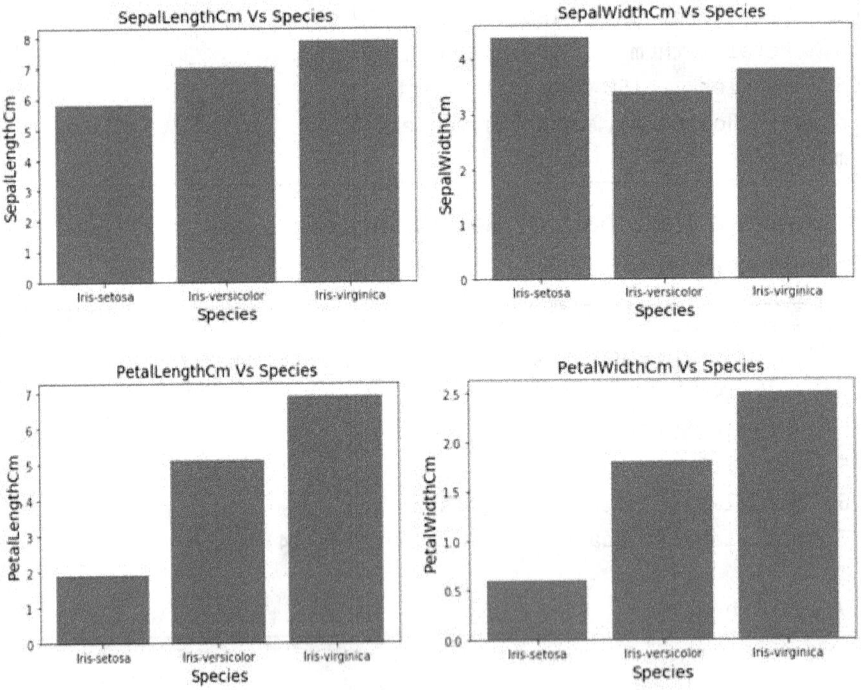

For the bar charts given above, we observe that species Iris-virginica has the highest petal length, petal width, and sepal length. Species Iris-setosa has the smallest petal length, petal width, and sepal length. However, there is a deviation from the trend; Iris-setosa shows the highest sepal width, followed by virginica and versicolor.

6.3.6. Pie Charts

A pie chart, a circular statistical chart, is used to display the percentage distribution of categorical variables. The area of the entire chart represents 100 percent or the whole data. The area of each pie in the chart denotes the percentage of share of data.

Pie charts are popular in business communications because they give a quick summary of the various activities such as sales and operations. Pie charts are also used to summarize survey results, resource usage diagrams, and memory usage in a computer system.

To draw a pie chart, we use the function pie() in the pyplot module. The following Python code draws a pie chart showing the world population by continents.

```
cont_pop = {'Asia': 4641054775, 'Africa':1340598147,
 'Europe': 747636026, 'North America': 592072212,
 'South America': 430759766, 'Australia/Oceania': 42677813}
explode = (0.05, 0.05, 0.05, 0.05, 0.05, 0.05)

# Generating a pie plot
plt.pie(cont_pop.values(), explode, labels=cont_pop.
 keys(), autopct='%1.1f%%', shadow=True)
plt.show()
```

Output:

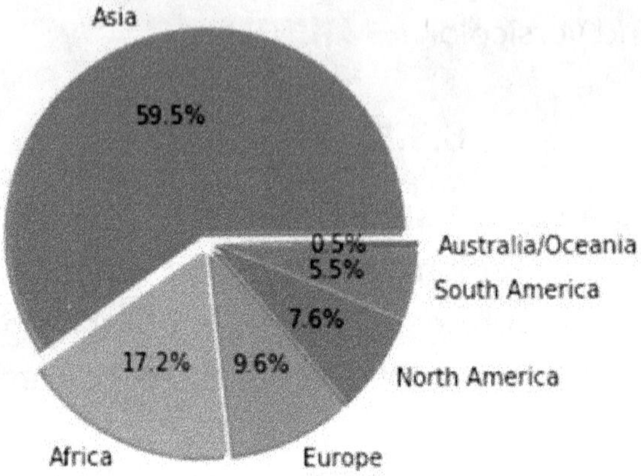

The explode option is used to generate some distance from the center of the plot. The ***autopct***='%.1f%%' string formatting is used for the formatting of how the percentages appear on the pie chart.

Further Readings - Matplotlib Plots

To study more about Matplotlib plots, please check Matplotlib's official documentation for plots:

https://matplotlib.org/tutorials/introductory/pyplot.html#sphx-glr-tutorials-introductory-pyplot-py

You can explore more features of Matplotlib by searching and reading this documentation.

6.4. Testing Assumptions about Data

Statistical and machine learning models work best if the data follows some assumptions. These assumptions can be the:

- Independence of features;
- Linear or quadratic dependency of features with the target variable; and

· Normal or Gaussian distribution of features.

One of the major objectives of the EDA is to test these assumptions. To check these assumptions, we work with the USA_Housing dataset. We download the USA_Housing dataset and store it on the desktop. We can display the first five observations of the dataset by using the function head().

```
housing_price = pd.read_csv(USA_housing.csv.csv')
housing_price.head()
```

Output:

	Avg. Area Income	Avg. Area House Age	Avg. Area Number of Rooms	Avg. Area Number of Bedrooms	Area Population	Price	Address
0	79545.45857	5.682861	7.009188	4.09	23086.80050	1.059034e+06	208 Michael Ferry Apt 674\nLaurabury, NE 3701...
1	79248.64245	6.002900	6.730821	3.09	40173.07217	1.505891e+06	188 Johnson Views Suite U/9\nLake Kathleen, CA...
2	61287.06718	5.865890	8.512727	5.13	36882.15940	1.058988e+06	9127 Elizabeth Stravenue\nDanieltown, WI 06482...
3	63345.24005	7.188236	5.586729	3.26	34310.24283	1.260617e+06	USS Barnett\nFPO AP 44820
4	59982.19723	5.040555	7.839388	4.23	26354.10947	6.309435e+05	USNS Raymond\nFPO AE 09386

In place of 'c:/.../dataset_housing.csv', specify the complete path where the dataset is stored.

The output shows that the dataset has seven variables or features. The last five observations of the dataset can be viewed using the function tail().

```
housing_price.tail()
```

Output:

	Avg. Area Income	Avg. Area House Age	Avg. Area Number of Rooms	Avg. Area Number of Bedrooms	Area Population	Price	Address
4995	60567.94414	7.830362	6.137356	3.46	22837.36103	1060193.786	USNS Williams\nFPO AP 30153-7653
4996	78491.27543	6.999135	6.576763	4.02	25616.11549	1482617.729	PSC 9258, Box 8489\nAPO AA 42991-3352
4997	63390.68689	7.250591	4.805081	2.13	33266.14549	1030729.583	4215 Tracy Garden Suite 076\nJoshualand, VA 01...
4998	68001.33124	5.534388	7.130144	5.44	42625.62016	1198656.872	USS Wallace\nFPO AE 73316
4999	65510.58180	5.992305	6.792336	4.07	46501.28380	1298950.480	37778 George Ridges Apt. 509\nEast Holly, NV 2...

It shows that the dataset has 5,000 observations. To confirm this finding, type:

```
housing_price.shape

Output:
(5000, 7)
```

Information on the dataset can be found by the use of the info () function.

```
housing_price.info()

Output:
<class 'pandas.core.frame.DataFrame'>
RangeIndex: 5000 entries, 0 to 4999
Data columns (total 7 columns):
 #   Column          Count  Non-NullDtype
---  ------      ------------  -----
 0   Avg. Area Income     5000 non-null   float64
 1   Avg. Area House Age  5000 non-null   float64
 2   Avg. Area Number of Rooms 5000 non-null   float64
 3   Avg. Area Number of Bedrooms 5000 non-null float64
 4   Area Population             5000 non-null   float64
 5   Price                      5000 non-null   float64
 6   Address                            5000 non-null   object
dtypes: float64(6), object(1)
memory usage: 273.6+ KB
```

We can find out important statistics of the dataset by the function describe().

```
housing_price.describe()
```

Output:

	Avg. Area Income	Avg. Area House Age	Avg. Area Number of Rooms	Avg. Area Number of Bedrooms	Area Population	Price
count	5000.000000	5000.000000	5000.000000	5000.000000	5000.000000	5.000000e+03
mean	68583.108984	5.977222	6.987792	3.981330	36163.516039	1.232073e+06
std	10657.991214	0.991456	1.005833	1.234137	9925.650114	3.531176e+05
min	17796.631190	2.644304	3.236194	2.000000	172.610686	1.593866e+04
25%	61480.562390	5.322283	6.299250	3.140000	29403.928700	9.975771e+05
50%	68804.286405	5.970429	7.002902	4.050000	36199.406690	1.232669e+06
75%	75783.338665	6.650808	7.665871	4.490000	42861.290770	1.471210e+06
max	107701.748400	9.519088	10.759588	6.500000	69621.713380	2.469066e+06

We observe that some statistics are given in floating points. For example, in **Avg. Area Number of Rooms,** min equals 3.236194, and max shows 10.759588. This is because these statistics report the minimum and maximum values of the average number of rooms in an area. Let us find the number of null or missing values in our dataset.

```
housing_price.isnull().sum()

Output:
Avg. Area Income                0
Avg. Area House Age             0
Avg. Area Number of Rooms      0
Avg. Area Number of Bedrooms 0
Area Population                         0
Price                                   0
Address                                 0
dtype: int64
```

Since there are 5,000 observations, we resort to plotting and visualization to explore the dataset. The following section reports a number of visualization plots and tools to understand the data better.

§ Checking Assumption of Normal Distribution of Features

Many machine learning models assume a Normal or Gaussian distribution of features. We can check whether the features in our dataset are normally distributed by just plotting the histogram of features.

```
# Plotting histogram of all the features
plt.hist(housing_price['Avg. Area Income'], bins = 100,
label = 'Avg. Area Income')
plt.legend()
plt.show()

plt.hist(housing_price['Avg. Area House Age'], bins = 100,
label ='Avg. Area House Age')
plt.legend()
plt.show()

plt.hist(housing_price['Avg. Area Number of Rooms'],
bins = 100, label = 'Avg. Area Number of Rooms')
plt.legend()
plt.show()

plt.hist(housing_
price['Avg. Area Number of Bedrooms'], bins = 100,
label = 'Avg. Area Number of Bedrooms')
plt.legend()
plt.show()

plt.hist(housing_price['Area Population'], bins = 100,
label = 'Area Population')
plt.legend()
plt.show()
```

Output:

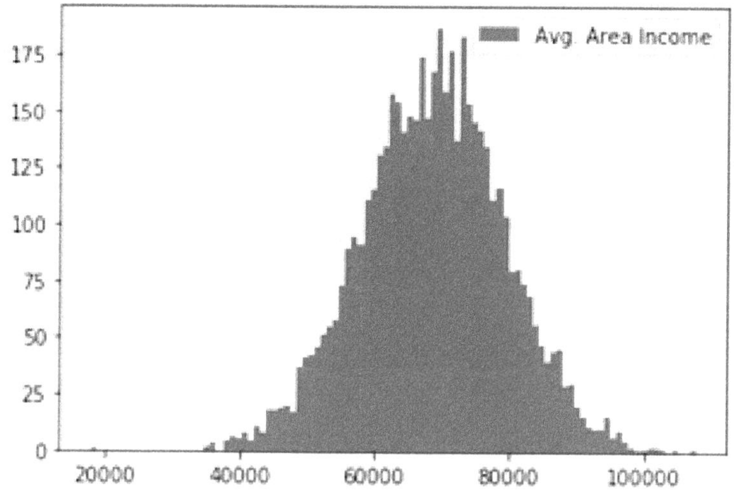
Avg. Area Income
175
150
125
100
75
50
25
0
20000
40000
60000
80000
100000

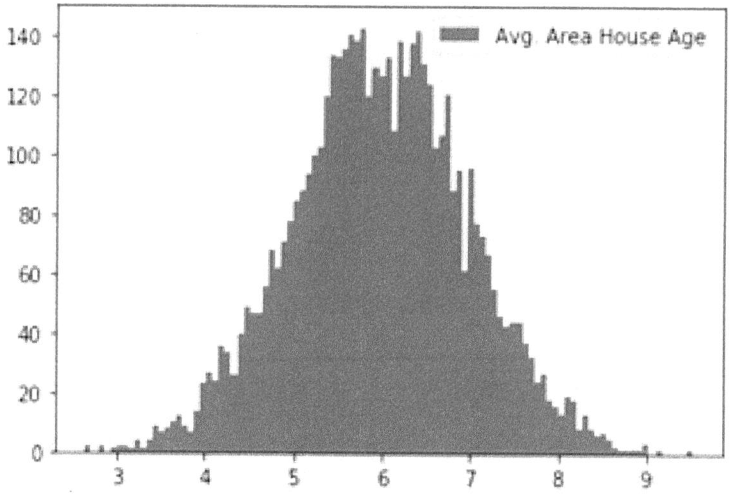
Avg. Area House Age
140
120
100
80
60
40
20
0
3
4
5
6
7
8
9

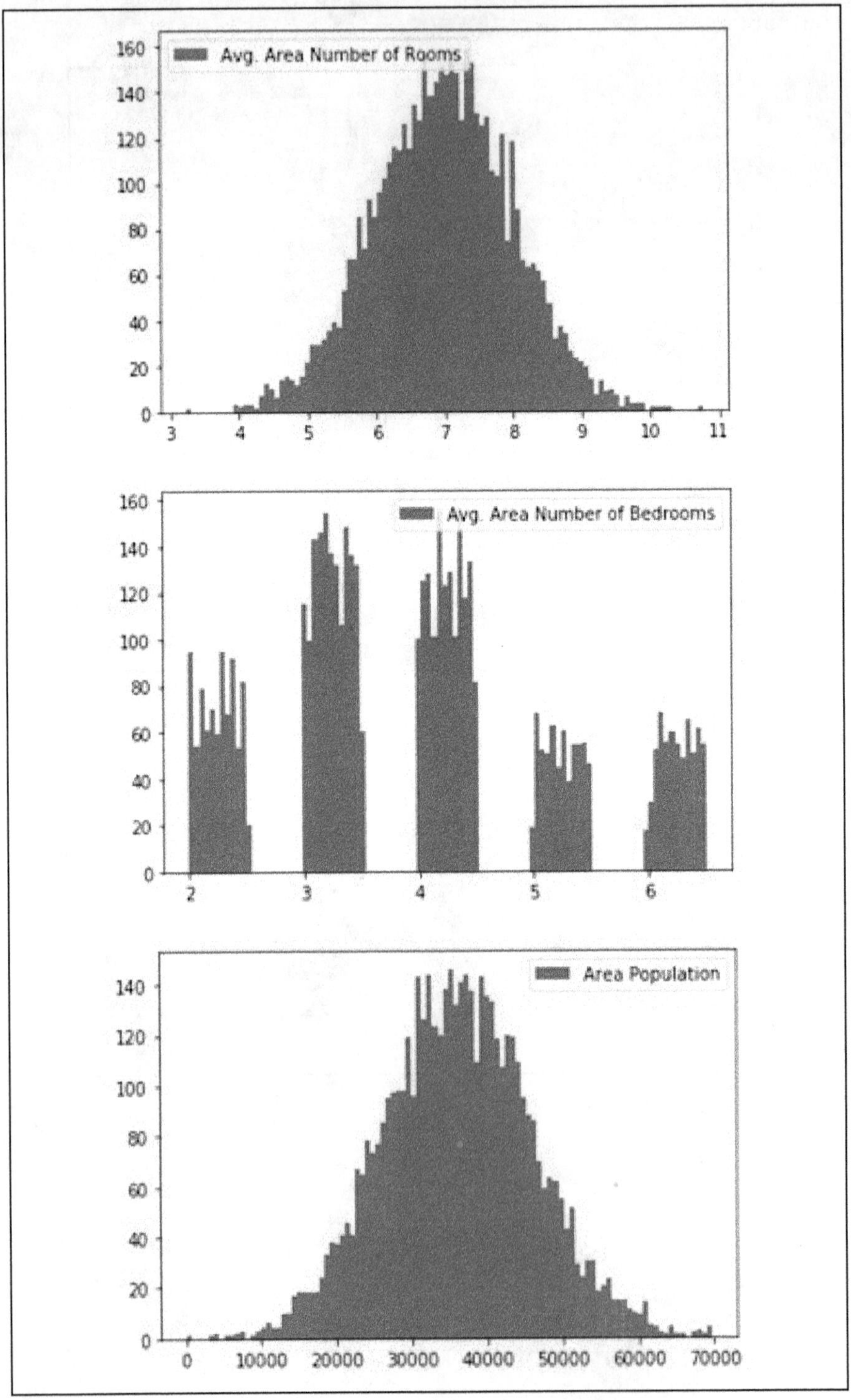
Avg. Area Number of Rooms
Avg. Area Number of Bedrooms
Area Population

§ Checking Independence of Features

We can also check if the features are independent of each other or not. One of the many possible ways is to draw a scatter plot of every pair of features. Another way is to draw a scatter matrix that is able to show histograms of every feature on its diagonal entries, and displays scatter plots of every pair of features on off-diagonal entries. We type the following to draw a scatter matrix.

```
1. from pandas.plotting import scatter_matrix
2. scatter_matrix(housing_
   price, figsize=(15, 15), diagonal='kde')
3. plt.show()
```

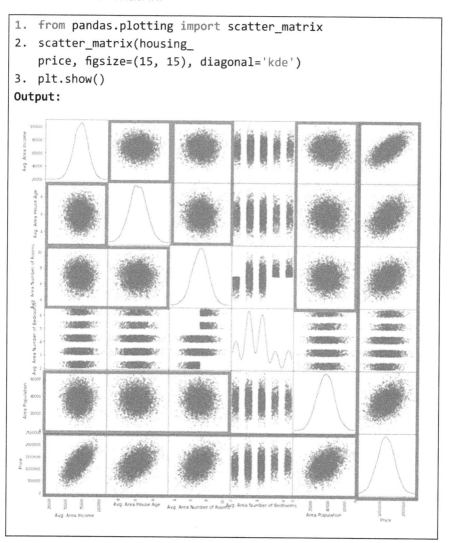

Output:

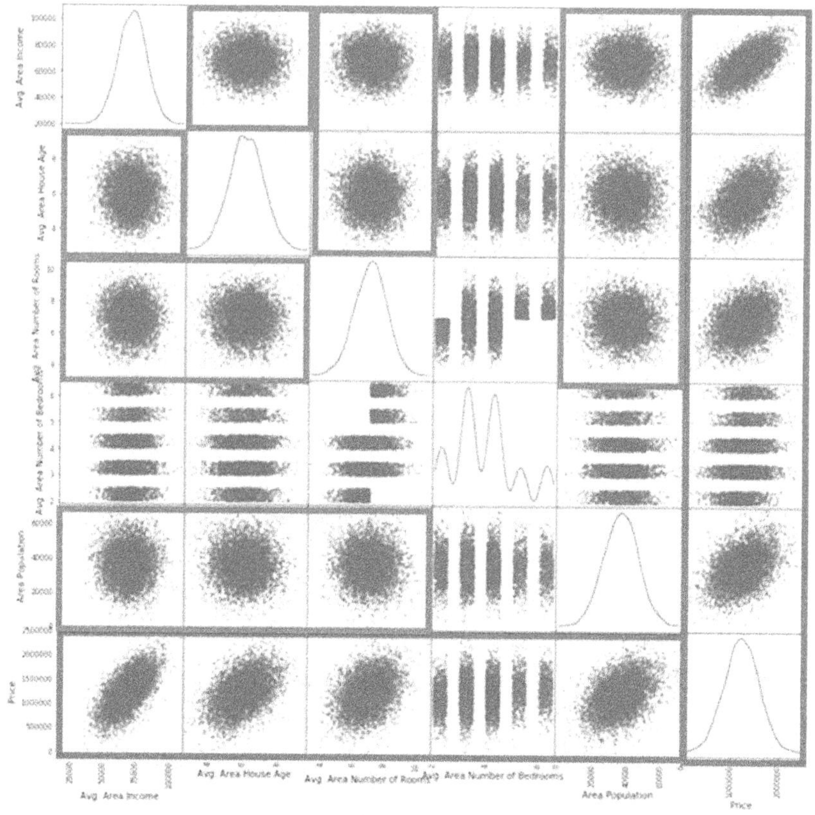

The option diagonal can be set to **kde**, kernel density estimation, that is closely related to the histogram, or it can be **hist**. If the points on a scatter plot are distributed such that they form a circle or approximately a circle, we say that the features are independent or approximately independent of each other.

A close inspection of this plot reveals that most features, enclosed in green rectangles, are independent of each other. If the points on a scatter plot are distributed such that they form an angled oval, we say that the features are dependent. A close inspection of this plot reveals that the target variable price depends upon:

- Avg. Area Income,
- Avg. Area House Age,
- Avg. Area Number of Rooms, and
- Area Population.

These dependencies are shown in red rectangles in this scatter plot.

6.5. Selecting Important Features/ Variables

In order to lessen the computational load and to achieve better accuracy, we have to identify the most relevant features from a set of data and remove the irrelevant or less important features which do not provide value to the target variable.

Feature selection is a core concept that impacts the performance of a machine learning model. The process of feature selection picks up those features which contribute most to the target variable or output. Though there are many statistical and machine learning-based methods to select important features/ variables from a dataset, here we describe a basic method based on the correlation between features. The correlation is a statistical term that measures the dependency between two features as a number ranging from −1 to 1.

If one variable increases, the other increases, and vice versa. We say that the correlation between these two variables is positive. However, if one variable increases, the other decreases, and vice versa, we say that the correlation between these two variables is negative.

To find the correlation, we use the method corr (). To plot the correlation matrix, we import the Seaborn library as sns.

```
import seaborn as sns
corrmat = housing_price.corr()
feature_ind = corrmat.index

plt.figure(figsize=(12,12))

#Plotting correlation matrix as an sns heat map
sns.heatmap(housing_price[feature_ind].
corr(),annot=True, cmap="RdYlGn")
plt.show()
```

Output:

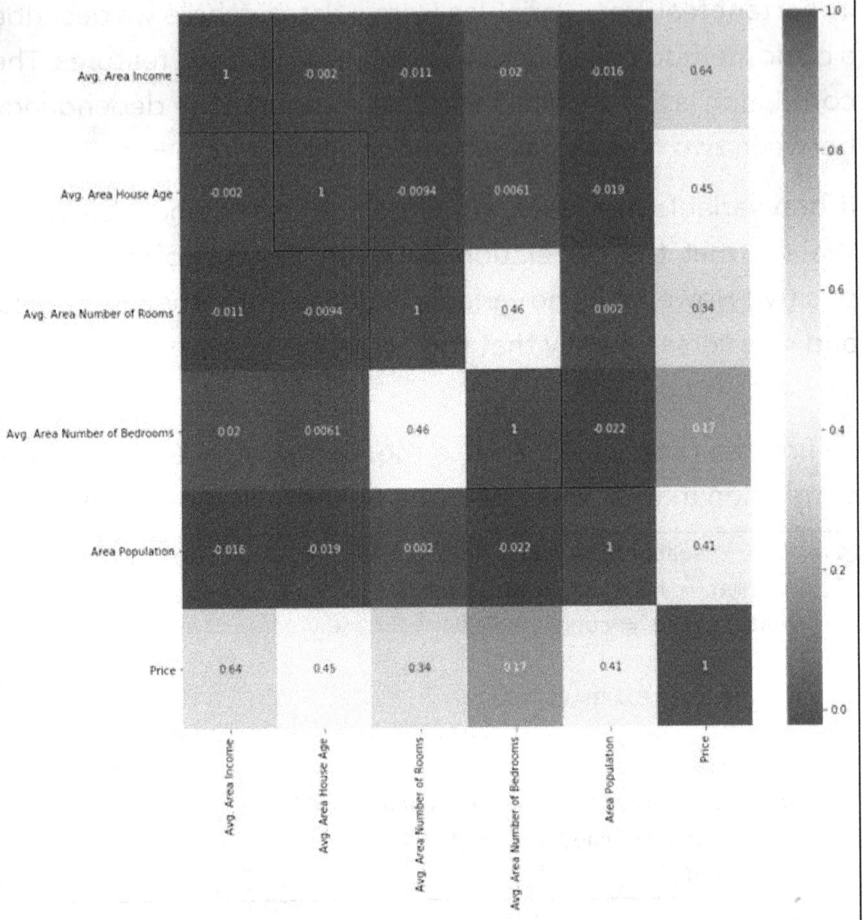

The *annot* and *cmap* options display the value of the correlation coefficient within the square boxes, and the color map to display the figure, respectively.

The values closer to zero in the red boxes indicate that these features are nearly independent of each other. However, larger values such as 0.64 between Price and Avg. Area Income indicates that the house prices are strongly correlated with the average income of residents of a particular area. Features having a small value of correlation with the target variable can be neglected. For example, the variable Avg. Area Number of Bedrooms has a correlation of 0.17 with the Price that can be neglected.

We have seen a basic method for feature selection. Advanced machine learning based methods can be employed for feature selection and extraction.

Hands-on Time - Exercise

To check your understanding of the basic data plotting and visualization with Matplotlib, complete the following exercise questions. The answers to the questions are given at the end of the book.

6.6. Exercise Questions

Question 1: To create a legend in a line plot, we specify the value of which of the following parameters?

A. axis
B. label
C. title
D. Any of the above

Question 2: Increasing the number of bins, ____________ the histogram.

A. Expands
B. Contracts
C. Smooths
D. roughens

Question 3: plt.plot() generates a ______________

A. Scatter plot

B. Line plot

C. Pie plot

D. Any of the above

Question 4: To check the frequency distribution or shape of a dataset, we generate a ______________

A. Bar plot

B. Pie plot

C. Histogram

D. Any of the above

Question 5: Which plot can be used for multivariate visualization?

A. Line plot

B. Scatter plot

C. Scatter matrix

D. All of the above

7

Data Modeling and Evaluation using Machine Learning

7.1. Introduction

In the previous chapter, we have performed Exploratory Data Analysis (EDA) to get familiar with the structure of a dataset. Various methods were presented to discover patterns in the data. Once we have explored the important features of the data, we choose suitable machine learning (ML) algorithms to model the data. Future instances of the data can make use of ML models to predict the output.

The field of machine learning is concerned with programming computers to optimize a performance criterion using example or training data. There are, however, several tasks that do not require machine learning. For example, to calculate the payroll of employees of a company, there is no need to learn because we may use some simple mathematical formulae to calculate payroll.

Machine learning is required when human skills are not available, or humans are not able to explain their skills, such as face and speech recognition. Learning may also be required when the solution to a problem changes over time-based upon the available data. For instance, routing algorithms working on a computer network may require previous data to perform better routing.

Several real-world problems such as customer relationship management in a retail business, fraud detection in financial transactions, robotics and control in the manufacturing industry, diagnosis in the field of medicine, spam detection and filtering in communications, and search engines in web mining are just a few of a vast majority of application areas of machine learning.

7.2. Important Statistics for Data Science

Statistics is widely used in data science. It is impossible for a data scientist to avoid statistics. A **statistic** is a numerical value that summarizes our dataset or a part of the dataset. Some well-known statistics are given below.

- The mean or the average value. For a list of numbers: [3, 8, 1, 3, 6, 21, −4]

  Mean = [3, 8, 1, 3, 6, 21, −4]/7 = 5.43

- The median or the middle value. To find the median of numeric data, we sort the numbers from smallest to largest. When we have an odd number of data points, the median is found as **(number of data points // 2) +1**, where // represents the floor division. Thus, out of 7 sorted values, the median would be the 4th value.

Median =[−4, 1 , 3, 3, 6, 8, 21]=3

If there are an even number of values, there is no middle number. In this case, the median of the list will be the mean of the middle two values within the list.

- The mode is the value that occurs the most. If no number in the list is repeated, then there is no mode for the list.

Mode =[−4, 1 , 3, 3, 6, 8, 21]= 3

- The range of a list of numbers is just the difference between the largest and smallest values.

Range = 21− (−4) = 25

- The standard deviation is a measure of the variability within a dataset around the mean value:

$$SD = Mean\ [\ (x\text{-}x\_avg)^2],$$

where x represents a data point, x_avg is the mean of the data points, and Mean is the average taken over the squared difference of all the data points from x_avg.

- The variance is the square of the standard deviation.

$$Var = SD^2$$

- The covariance is used to find the relationship between two variables. It is defined as,

COV(x,y) = Mean [(x-x_avg) (y-y_avg)]

- The correlation is obtained by normalizing the covariance. It is obtained by dividing the covariance by the product of individual standard deviations of the variables.

To find these quantities, we may write the following Python script.

```
from statistics import mode
toy_data = [3, 8, 1, 3, 6,  21, -4]

# Calculating statistics
mymean = np.mean(toy_data)
mymedian = np.median(toy_data)
mymode = mode(toy_data)
myrange = np.max(toy_data)-np.min(toy_data)
mystd=  np.std(toy_data)
myvar = np.var(toy_data)

# Printing the results
print('The mean is = %.2f' %mymean, '\nThe median is =',mymedian, '\nThe mode is =',mymode,
      '\nThe range is =',myrange, '\nThe standard deviation is = %.2f'%mystd,
      '\nThe variance is = %.2f'%myvar)
```

Output:

```
The mean is = 5.43
The median is = 3.0
The mode is = 3
The range is = 25
The standard deviation is = 7.27
The variance is = 52.82
```

To find the covariance and the correlation between two different features, we may use the following code:

```
1. mycov = np.cov([1, 2, 3], [1.0, 2.5, 7.5])
2. mycov

Output:
array([[ 1.        ,  3.25      ],
       [ 3.25      , 11.58333333]])

1. mycorr = np.corrcoef([1, 2, 3], [1.0, 2.5, 7.5])
2. mycorr

Output:
array([[1.        , 0.95491911],
       [0.95491911, 1.        ]])
```

7.3. Data Distributions

In statistics, a probability distribution or simply a data distribution gives the probabilities of occurrence of different values present in the dataset. A data distribution shows how the data points are spread. There are numerous continuous and discrete-valued distributions. In this section, we give details of some of the distributions commonly encountered and used by data scientists.

§ Bernoulli Distribution

A Bernoulli distribution has only two possible values, outputs, or outcomes, namely 0 for failure and 1 for success. This distribution assumes only one trial of the experiment that generates 0 or 1. Thus, the variable, also known as a random variable, that follows a Bernoulli distribution can take on the value 1 (success), or the value 0 (failure).

Let the probability of success = p and the probability of failure= q or 1-p.

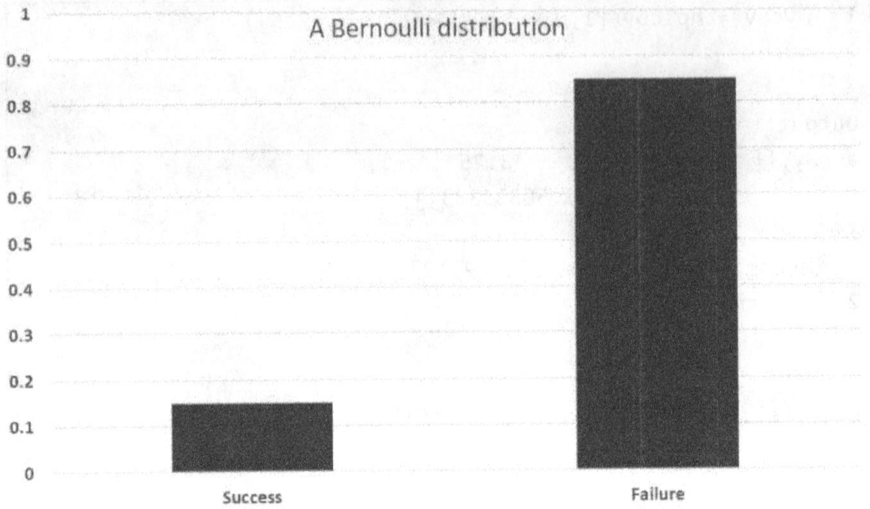

Figure 7.1: A Bernoulli distribution.

Here, the probability of success = p = 0.15 and probability of failure = q = 0.85. The expected value is the mean of all the data values in the distribution.

§ Uniform Distribution

A uniform distribution is for the continuous-valued data. It has a single value, 1/(b-a), which occurs in a certain range [a,b], whereas everything is zero outside that range. We can think of it as an indication of a categorical variable with two categories: 0 or the value. The categorical variable may have multiple values in a continuous range between some numbers a and b.

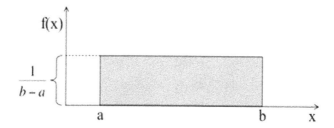

Figure 7.2: A Uniform distribution.

§ Gaussian Distribution

A Normal or Gaussian Distribution is defined by its mean and standard deviation. The data values are spread around the mean value, and the standard deviation controls the spread. A Gaussian distribution has most data values around the mean or center value. A smaller value of standard deviation indicates that data is highly concentrated and vice versa.

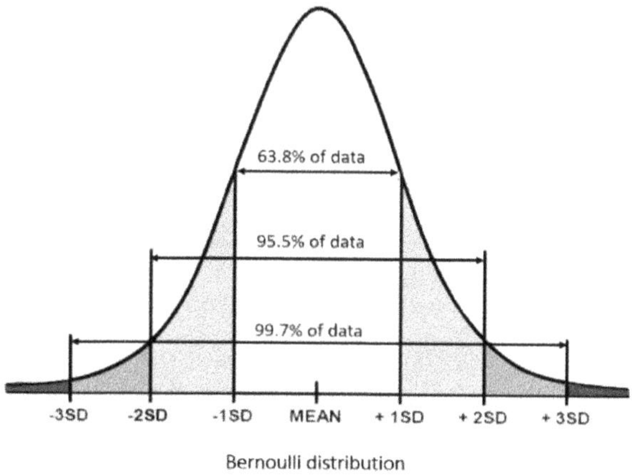

Figure 7.3: A Gaussian distribution.

In figure 7.3, a Normal or Gaussian distribution is shown that is centered at MEAN. Note that 68.3 percent of the samples of Normally distributed data lie within 1 standard deviation, −1SD to +1SD, on either side of the MEAN.

§ Poisson Distribution

A Poisson Distribution is similar to the Normal distribution but with some *skewness*. A Poisson distribution has relatively uniform spread in all directions, just like the Normal distribution; however, the spread becomes non-uniform for increasing values of skewness.

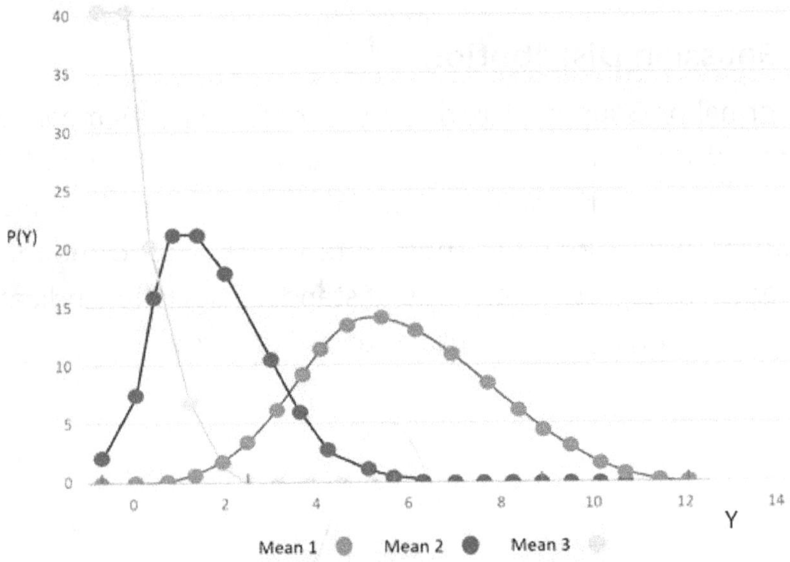

Figure 7.4: Poisson distributions with different values of the mean.

A Poisson distribution with a low mean is highly skewed. The tail of the data extends to the right. However, if the mean is larger, the distribution spreads out, tends to be more symmetric, and becomes more like the Gaussian distribution.

7.4. Basic Machine Learning Terminology

The specialty of machine learning can be subdivided into three major categories:

1. Supervised learning,

2. Unsupervised learning, and
3. Reinforcement learning.

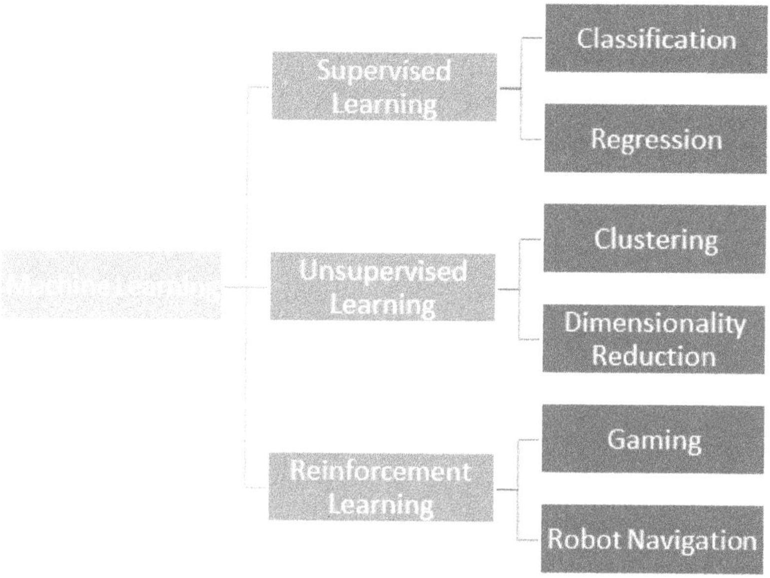

Figure 7.5: Three main types of machine learning.

The examples of these categories are shown in figure 7.5. We discuss supervised and unsupervised learning algorithms in the following sections.

7.4.1. Supervised and Unsupervised Learning

Supervised learning is a type of machine learning where we use the data having labeled outputs. For example, in the USA_Housing dataset, we have been given the prices of houses. Furthermore, in the Iris dataset, the name of three distinct species are provided to us as labels against each observation of the data. When we use the labels in our machine learning model, we deal with the supervised learning problem. There are two chief types of supervised learning algorithms: classification and regression. If the output labels have a continuous range of values, it is a regression problem (house prices). On the other hand, when the output has discrete values, it is a classification problem (Iris species).

Unsupervised learning is a type of machine learning where we have the data without any output labels. Here, the goal is to identify meaningful patterns in the data. To this end, the machine learning algorithm learns from an unlabeled dataset. Thus, the model has no clues to categorize the data and must infer its own rules for doing so.

For example, if we have been given some plant leaves without knowing the name of the plants, we do not know the output labels. In this case, the employed machine learning algorithm should be able to differentiate between the different types of leaves, even though we do not provide it with the labels to differentiate between examples of one type from another.

The two main tasks of unsupervised learning are clustering and dimensionality reduction. In the former, we group the data based upon input features, whereas, in the latter, we reduce the dimensions of the data to come up with only the most salient features.

Reinforcement Learning (RL) is the third main branch of machine learning that differs from the other two types of ML. In RL, we do not gather example data with labels. The main objective in RL is to maximize some kind of reward over a series or sequence of steps. Imagine, we are going to design a computer game that plays chess. In this case, the output of the system is a sequence of actions. A single action may not be important. It is the policy (or sequence of actions) that is important to reach the goal, i.e., winning the game. Such type of learning of a policy is the main task in reinforcement learning.

We shall not go into the details of reinforcement learning as it is beyond the scope of this book. However, we will go into the details of supervised and unsupervised learning in the subsequent parts of this chapter.

7.4.2. Training and Test Data

A **model** is a mathematical description or formula that is used to describe a dataset. To model a dataset, we usually divide our dataset into a training set and a test set. The former is used to build a machine learning model, while the latter is used to validate the built model. Data points in the training set are omitted from the test set and vice versa.

In machine learning, we try to generalize the prediction capabilities of the built model. To test the generalization power of the model, we select the data from the dataset, which is not used in the creation of the model. This left out data is called a test set. Thus, we use the training data to learn or fit the model and testing data to assess its performance.

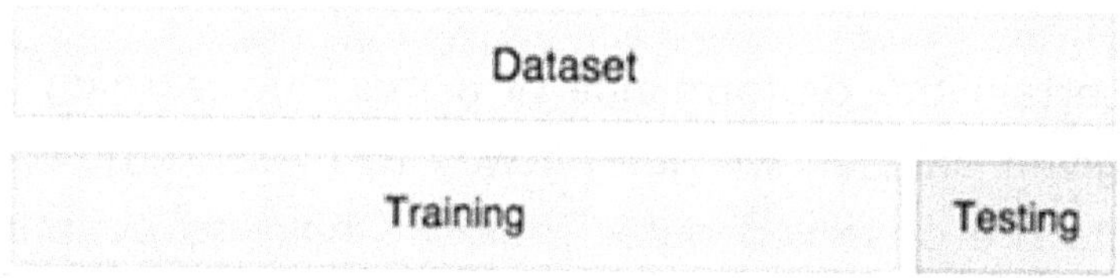

Figure 7.6: Division of a dataset into training and test sets.

The proportion to be divided is usually such that nearly 70 percent of the data is set aside for the training set and 30 percent for the test set. However, this division depends upon the task at hand and on the dataset being used.

For example, if we train our model on 50 percent data and test it on the remaining 50 percent, its performance will be different from training it on 70 percent and testing on the remaining 30 percent. As a rule of thumb, in machine learning, the bigger the dataset to train, the better is the trained model and its generalization power.

7.4.3. Cross-Validation

Generally, we split our dataset into training and test datasets. Sometimes, we keep aside the test set, and choose some percentage of the training set to train the model, and use the remaining part of the training set to validate the model. This reserved portion of the training set is called the **validation set.**

The model is iteratively trained and validated on these different sets generated randomly from the training set. When we perform this process iteratively, it is commonly known as **cross-validation (CV).** We explain CV in detail in Section 7.8, where the methods to evaluate a trained machine learning model are discussed.

7.4.4. Error, Loss Function, and Cost Function

To ascertain the performance of a machine learning model on a given dataset, we need a way to measure how well it predicts the observed data. Thus, we have to quantify the predicted response for a given observation to the true label for that observation. In the supervised learning where we have the labeled data, a commonly used cost function is the mean squared error (MSE), given by

$$\mathrm{MSE} = \frac{1}{n}\sum_{n}(f(x) - y)^2$$

where *n, f(x),* and *y* represent the number of observations, the assumed model possibly a linear one, and the actual labels of the data points, respectively.

The terms loss function and cost function are both based upon difference or error between the model and actual labels. These terms are used interchangeably; however, the loss function is defined for one data point, and a cost function is the average of all loss functions. Thus, MSE is a cost function, and the term $(f(x) - y)^2$ can be considered as a loss function.

Normally, a suitable loss function is defined, and a cost function is constructed from the defined loss function. The model is trained such that the cost function is minimized. In other words, the difference between all the labels of the training examples and the predictions by our trained model should be minimum. In figure 7.7, a pair of data points (X,Y) are shown. We assume a linear model. The error between the data points and the model is shown as vertical lines.

A linear model is also shown as a line that passes through the given data points. The model is chosen so that the average error between all the data points and the model is minimum, i.e., the cost function is minimum.

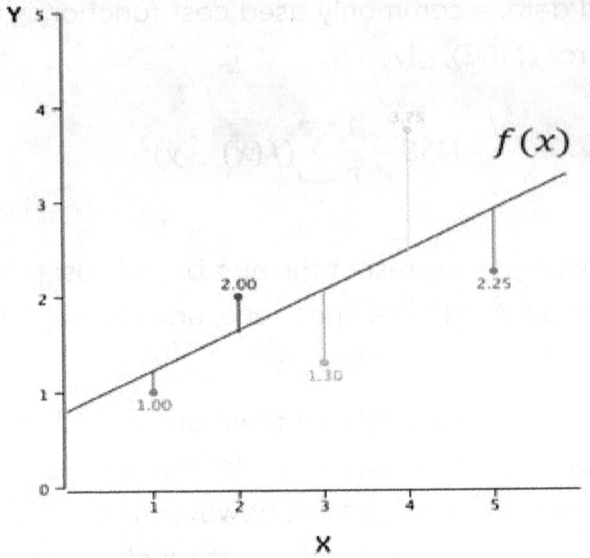

Figure 7.7: The pair of data points (X,Y) are shown as dots in colors. The model is assumed to be a line that approximates the data points.

7.4.5. Learning Parameters of a Model

Once we assume a model, the next important task is to find its parameters. Many features in a given dataset approximately have a linear relationship with the target variable. In this case, it is safe to assume that the model to be learned is a linear model.

If we have only one input variable, the linear model can be mathematically described by the equation of a line.

$$f(x) = mx + c$$

The parameter *m* is the slope of the line, and the parameter c is the intercept on the vertical axis. These two parameters of the linear model have to be learned to find the optimal line that passes through the data points such that the error between the line and the data points is minimum.

Even when we have multiple input features *x1, x2, x3, ...,* and all of them have a linear relationship with the target variable *y*, a linear model can still be employed.

$$f(x) = m_1 x_1 + m_2 x_2 + m_3 x_3 + \cdots + c.$$

In this case, the parameters to be learned are *c, m1, m2, m3 ...* In this case, there are multiple features; thus, it is a multivariate parameter learning problem.

7.4.6. Feature Selection and Extraction

The process of feature selection removes unnecessary features from the dataset. In the previous chapter, we have seen a method based on correlations between features to select relevant features. Advanced machine learning-based methods are sometimes used for feature selection.

The success of a machine learning algorithm depends on many factors, such as selecting a suitable model and a good set of features to train the model. The process to obtain good features is called feature engineering, which involves feature selection and feature extraction & transformation.

Feature selection: selecting the most relevant and useful features to train the model.

Feature extraction & transformation: combining existing features to produce better features. In this case, dimensionality reduction algorithms help, which are discussed later in this chapter.

7.4.7. Underfitting and Overfitting

Model underfitting and overfitting are amongst the primary causes for the poor performance of machine learning algorithms. The main objective of a good machine learning model is to generalize from the training data to the unseen test data to make predictions.

The term *generalization* refers to the capability of a model to perform well on those examples that were not used at the time of training/learning.

If a model is too simple to capture the real trend of data, we say that the model underfits the data. On the other hand, if a model is complex such that it captures the noise in the data along with the actual trend, the model overfits the data.

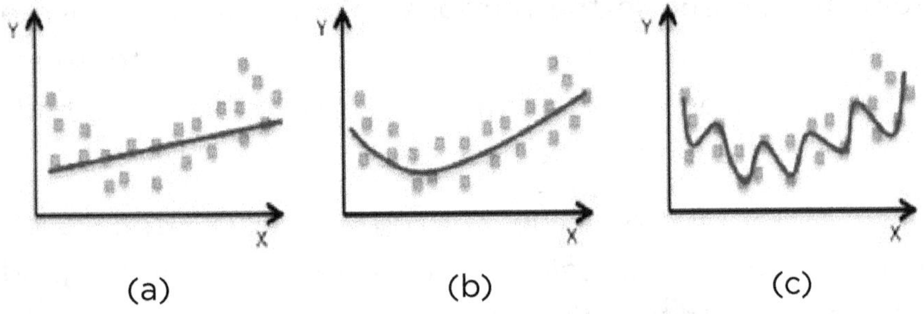

Figure 7.8: (a) An underfit, (b) an optimal, and (c) an overfit model.

Figure 7.8 shows examples of model underfitting and overfitting, along with an optimal model. An underfit model shown as a line in figure 7.8 (a) is too simple to capture the real trend of the data. An optimal model is more complex than an underfit model to explain the relationship between the input feature x and output variable y. However, an overfit model, as shown in figure 7.8 (c), is too complex to correctly explain the underlying trend of the data. This model captures the noise present in the data. Due to this, both underfit and overfit models fail to generalize well on the test data.

7.5. Supervised Learning: Regression

As mentioned earlier in this chapter, there are two main types of supervised learning: classification and regression. If the output labels have a continuous range of values, it is a regression problem (house prices problem).

If the relationship between the input features and the output target variable is assumed to be linear, the regression would be linear. Otherwise, it would be non-linear. Here, we discuss linear regression that is more prevalent than its non-linear counterpart.

The primary objective of a linear regression model is to determine a relationship between one or more independent input features and a continuous target variable that is dependent upon the input features. When there is only one feature, it is called *univariate* or simple linear regression, whereas the case of multiple input features is known as *multiple* linear regression. The following equation represents the linear regression model:

$$f(x) = \theta_1 x_1 + \theta_2 x_2 + \theta_3 x_3 + \cdots + \theta_0,$$

where $f(x)$ is the predicted value, θ_0 is the bias term, $[\theta_1 \theta_2 \theta_3 \ldots]$ are model parameters, and $[x_1 x_2 x_3 \ldots]$ are the features. This regression model can be compactly represented as

$$f(x) = \theta^{\mathrm{T}}\mathbf{x}$$

where $\Theta^T=[\theta_1\theta_2\theta_3 \ldots]$ is the vector that contains all the parameters of the model, and $\mathbf{x} = [x_1x_2x_3 \ldots]$ is the vector of features. If we have more than one input feature, as in the aforementioned model, the concept of a line is extended in more than two dimensions. The line in more than two dimensions is known as a plane or a hyper-plane.

To implement linear regression in Python, we first import the libraries and packages.

```
# Importing the required libraries.
import numpy as np
import matplotlib.pyplot as plt
import sklearn as sk
from sklearn.linear_model import LinearRegression
from sklearn.metrics import mean_squared_error
```

To generate and prepare the data for linear regression, we type the following Python script:

```
# Generate random data of 100 samples
x = np.random.rand(100, 1)
# Randomly generated samples are shifted to have a mean
of 5 and a standard deviation of -3.
y = - 3 * x + 5 + np.random.rand(100, 1)
```

We initialize the linear regression model and use it for training by specifying input and output variables as follows.

```
# Linear regression model initialization
regress_model = LinearRegression()

# Fit the data (train the model)
regress_model.fit(x, y)
```

To predict the output values from the input x, and to evaluate the performance of the trained model, we use the following Python commands.

```
# Predict output values from the input x.
y_predicted = regress_model.predict(x)

# Model evaluation by calculating root mean squared error
rmse = np.sqrt(mean_squared_error(y, y_predicted))
```

The following section of the code displays the results, such as learned parameters. It also plots the learned model.

```
# Printing values of the learned model
print('Slope:' ,regress_model.coef_)
print('Intercept:', regress_model.intercept_)
print('Root mean squared error: ', rmse)
# plotting data points
plt.scatter(x, y, color='r'), plt.xlabel('x'), plt.
ylabel('y')
# plotting predicted values
plt.plot(x, y_predicted, color='b'), plt.show()
```

Output:

```
Slope: [[-3.10115181]]
Intercept: [5.54571968]
Root mean squared error:  0.2684135372229655
```

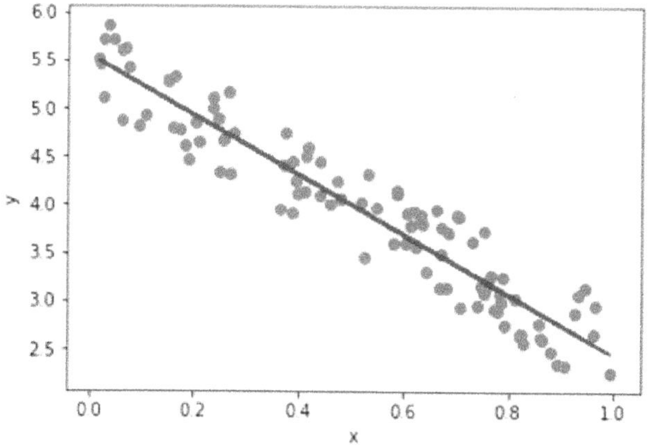

The regression model, **regress_model**, has **coef_** and **intercept_** attributes for the slope and the intercept. These attributes and the related help on our model can be found by just typing "**regress_model?**" in the Jupyter Notebook.

The red points in the aforementioned plot show the data points, whereas the blue line represents the linear model obtained by applying regression on the given data.

The widely used metrics to assess the performance of regression problems are the mean squared error (MSE), the root mean squared error (RMSE), and the mean absolute error (MAE). We have also calculated the root mean squared error (RMSE) of our model, which is 0.2684 for the generated data points.

Advantages and Applicability: Linear regression is easy to implement and efficient to train. It performs well when the actual relationship between input features and the output variable is linear. In the aforementioned example, where we applied linear regression, the relationship between the input and the output variable is almost linear. Thus, we get a small value of MSE.

Limitations: The main limitation of linear regression is the assumption of linearity between the dependent variable and the independent variables. In the real world, features may not be linearly related to the output variable. In this case, we have to use non-linear regression to model our dataset. Linear regression performs poorly when there are outliers in the data. Outliers should be removed from the dataset before applying linear regression.

7.6. Supervised Learning: Classification

In addition to the regression, the second most common supervised learning problem is a classification that works when the output labels have a discrete set of values. Plant species prediction, spam email detection, face recognition, and human emotion recognition are classic examples of classification problems where we have a small set of classes or discrete labels to predict. The commonly used classification algorithms are described below.

7.6.1. Logistic Regression

Logistic regression, contrasting to its name, is a classification method. It is a type of **linear classifier** that bears similarities with **linear regression**. This method of classification uses a logistic or sigmoid function which is given as

$$f(x) = \frac{1}{1 + e^{-x}}$$

The plot of the sigmoid function, given in figure 7.9, reveals that it varies between 0 and 1. The sigmoid function, across most of its domain, has values close to either 0 or 1. This fact makes it perfect for application in classification methods. It is used for binary or two-class classification problems. However, it can also be applied to multi-class problems.

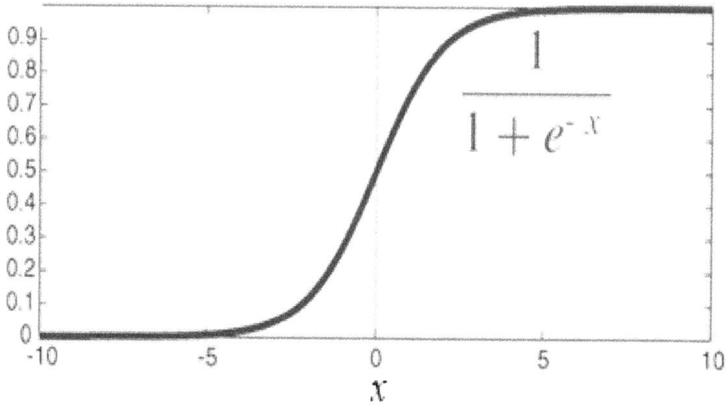

Figure 7.9: A sigmoid function that varies between 0 and 1.

Classification of output variables based on logistic regression is fast, and its results are easy to interpret.

To implement the logistic regression in Python, we first import libraries and packages.

```
1. import matplotlib.pyplot as plt
2. import numpy as np
3. from sklearn.linear_model import LogisticRegression
4. from sklearn.metrics import classification_
   report, confusion_matrix
```

We may write the following script to generate data for classification.

```
1. x = np.arange(10).reshape(-1, 1)
2. y = np.array([0, 0, 0, 0, 1, 1, 1, 1, 1, 1])
```

We initialize the logistic regression model and use it for training by specifying input and output variables as follows.

```
1. model = LogisticRegression(solver='liblinear', random_
   state=0)
2. model.fit(x, y)
Output:
LogisticRegression(C=1.0, class_weight=None, dual=False, fit_intercept=True,
                   intercept_scaling=1, l1_ratio=None, max_iter=100,
                   multi_class='warn', n_jobs=None, penalty='l2',
                   random_state=0, solver='liblinear', tol=0.0001, verbose=0,
                   warm_start=False)
```

The output shows the details of the logistic regression model. For example, the solver *liblinear* is used to solve large-scale linear classification problems, and the parameter *max_iter* tells that the algorithm takes a maximum of 100 iterations to solve for the parameters of the model.

To print various attributes of the model, we may write the following script.

```
#the attribute.classes_ represents the array of distinct values that y takes.
print(model.classes_)
print(model.intercept_)
print(model.coef_)
print(model.predict(x))
print(model.score(x, y))
print(classification_report(y, model.predict(x)))
```

Output:

```
[0 1]
[-1.04608067]
[[0.51491375]]
[0 0 0 1 1 1 1 1 1 1]
0.9
              precision    recall  f1-score   support

           0       1.00      0.75      0.86         4
           1       0.86      1.00      0.92         6

    accuracy                           0.90        10
   macro avg       0.93      0.88      0.89        10
weighted avg       0.91      0.90      0.90        10
```

We have used the "**classification_report**" from **sklearn.metrics** to get the details of the performance of the logistic regression model. We discuss these details in Chapter 8.

To visualize the output, we plot the *confusion matrix* that summarizes the performance of the model to classify various observations belonging to different classes.

```
from sklearn import metrics

cm = metrics.confusion_matrix(y, model.predict(x))
score = model.score(x, y)

plt.figure(figsize=(9,9))
sns.heatmap(cm, annot=True, fmt=".3f", linewidths=.5,
square = True, cmap = 'YlGnBu');
plt.ylabel('Actual label');
plt.xlabel('Predicted label');
all_sample_title = 'Accuracy Score: {0}'.format(score)
plt.title(all_sample_title, size = 15);
```

Output:

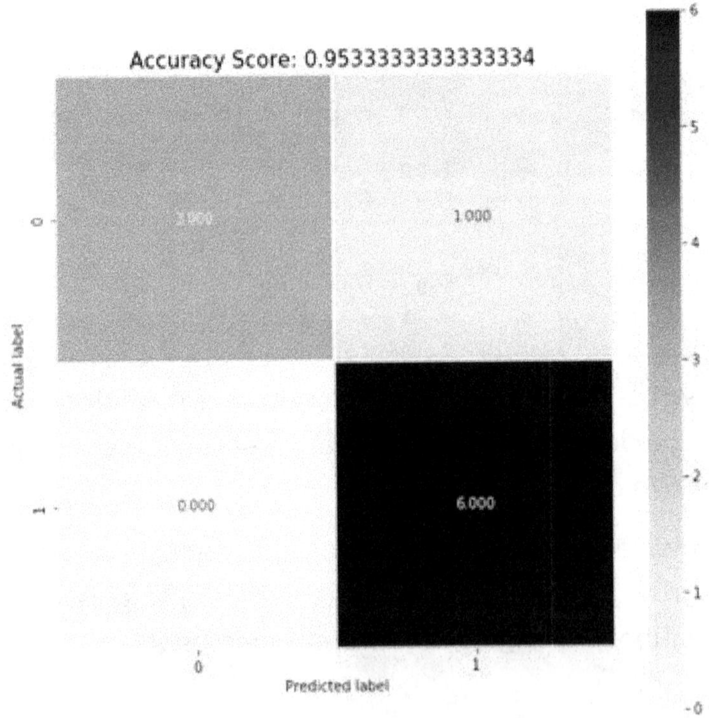

The entries on the diagonal of the confusion matrix indicate correct predictions. For example, in the previous output, 3 class 0 examples and 6 class 1 examples are correctly predicted by the logistic regression model. However, one example of class 0, shown in the top right of the confusion matrix, is incorrectly predicted as a class 1 example by the model.

Advantages and Applicability: Logistic regression is easy to implement and interpret. It is used to predict the dependent output variable when it is categorical instead of continuous. Since logistic regression is based upon linear regression, it generates a linear boundary between classes. Thus, it performs well when the classes are linearly separable. Since logistic regression is fast and easy to implement, it is usually used as a benchmark model.

The output of a logistic function varies between 0 and 1. Thus, the output of a logistic regression model can be considered as a probability that gives us confidence about the predicted class.

Limitations: The main limitation of the logistic regression model is the assumption of linearly separable classes. It performs poorly when the classes are not linearly separable. A non-linear function may be used in the exponent of the logistic function to cope with this situation.

Logistic regression requires the features to be independent of each other. It performs poorly when two or more features have a high correlation. Dimensionality reduction techniques discussed later in this chapter can be used to remove/transform the dependent features to get independent features.

7.6.2. Nearest Neighbor Classification

Nearest neighbor (NN) classification is a non-parametric and a slow learning algorithm. Since it uses no assumption for the underlying data, it is a non-parametric method.

The structure of the model is determined directly from the dataset. This is helpful in those real-world datasets which do not follow simple assumptions. It learns slowly because it does not need any training data points for the creation of the model. It uses all of the training data in the testing phase. This makes the testing phase slower and memory consuming.

The most used algorithm of this family of classifiers is called k-nearest neighbor (KNN), where K represents the number of nearest neighbors to consider for classification. K is usually taken as a small odd number.

For instance, in a two-class problem given in figure 7.10, we want to predict the label for the test point with the question marks, ?. If we take K = 1, we have to find one training example closest to this test point. To classify, we assign the label of this nearest point to the test point.

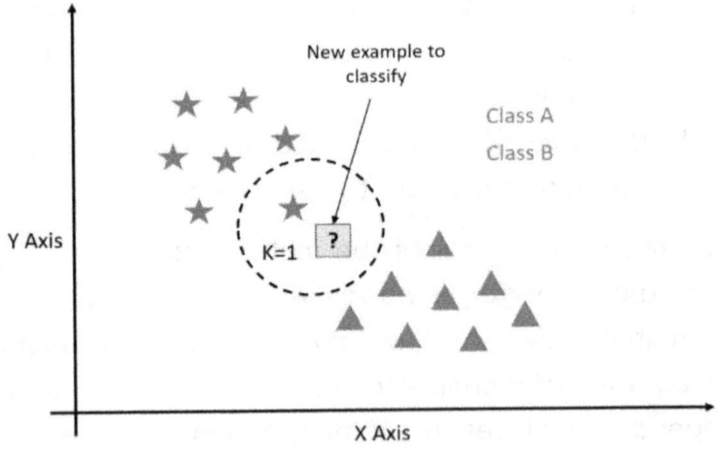

Figure 7.10: KNN for K=1 in a binary classification problem.

For any other arbitrary value of K, we find the K closest point to the test point, and then classify the test point by a majority vote of its K neighbors. Each training point in the K closest points votes for its class. The class with the most votes in the neighborhood is taken as the predicted class for the test point. To find points closest or similar to the test point, we find the distance between points. The steps to classify a test point by KNN are as follows:

- Calculate distance
- Find closest neighbors
- Vote for labels

To implement a KNN classifier in Python, we first import the libraries and packages.

```
from sklearn.datasets import load_digits
from sklearn.model_selection import train_test_split
from sklearn.neighbors import KNeighborsClassifier
from sklearn import metrics
```

We load the Digits dataset and split it into test and training sets using the following script.

```
digits = load_digits()
# Train the model using the training sets
x_train, x_test, y_train, y_test = train_test_split(digits.data, digits.target, test_size=0.25)
```

Note that we split our dataset into a ratio of 75:25 for training:test sets. We use the KNN model for training by specifying the input and output variables of the training set as follows.

```
model = KNeighborsClassifier(n_neighbors=3)
model.fit(x_train,y_train)
```

To predict the output values from the test input x_test, and to evaluate the performance of the trained model, we use the following Python commands.

```
#Predict Output
cm = metrics.confusion_matrix(y_test, model.predict(x_test))
score = model.score(x_test, y_test)
```

The following section of the code displays the results using the confusion matrix.

```
plt.figure(figsize=(9,9))
sns.heatmap(cm, annot=True, fmt=".3f", linewidths=.5,
square = True, cmap = 'YlGnBu')
plt.ylabel('Actual label');
plt.xlabel('Predicted label');
all_sample_title = 'Accuracy Score: {0}'.format(score)
plt.title(all_sample_title, size = 15);
```

Output:

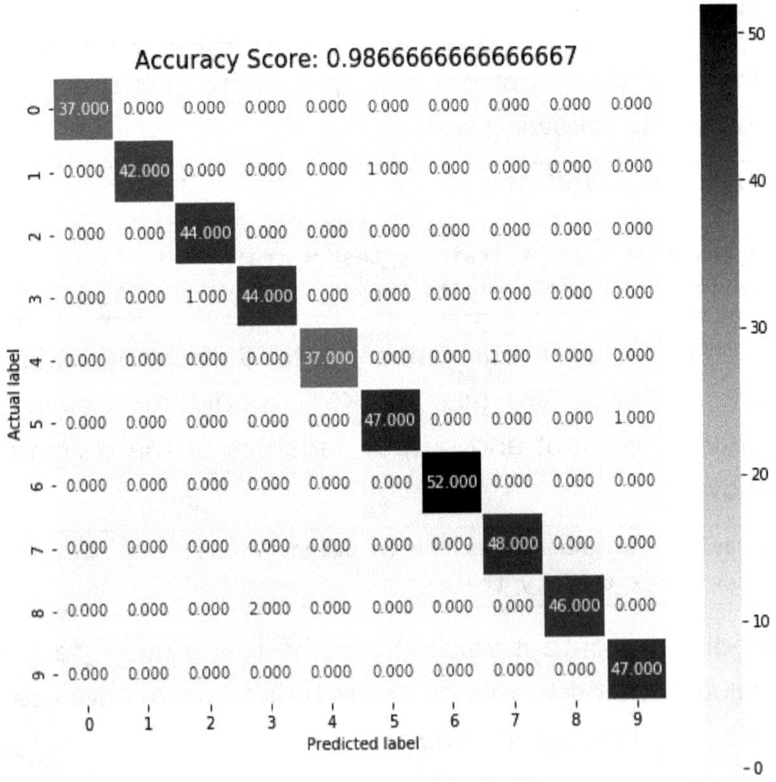

The predicted and actual labels are shown on the x and y-axis of the confusion matrix, respectively. The diagonal entries on the confusion matrix represent correct classification results. It can be observed that most digits are correctly classified by the model. However, occasional misclassified results are shown on the off-diagonal entries of the matrix. The output of the model shows an accuracy of 98.67 percent.

Advantages and Applicability: Nearest neighbor classification is very easy to implement by just specifying the value of neighbors and a suitable distance function, e.g., Euclidean distance.

The nearest neighbor classifier does not learn anything in the training period. This is referred to as instance-based learning. Classification using the nearest neighbor is accomplished by storing the whole training dataset. This makes nearest neighbor classifiers much faster than logistic regression and other classification models. Since no training is required before making predictions, new data can be added easily to the algorithm without affecting its accuracy.

Limitations: It is very slow in the testing phase; thus, it is not suitable for large datasets because calculating the distance between the test point and each training point takes a large amount of time for large datasets.

Furthermore, algorithms based on the nearest neighbor are sensitive to noise, outliers, and missing feature values. We have to remove outliers and impute missing values before applying this class of algorithms to our dataset.

7.6.3. Naïve Bayes' Classification

Naive Bayes is one of the most fundamental classification algorithms. It is based on Bayes' Theorem of probability. A basic assumption used by a Naive Bayes' classifier is the independence of features. This assumption is considered naïve, which simplifies computations. In terms of probability, this assumption is called class conditional independence.

To understand Bayes' theorem, we describe the conditional probability that is defined as the likelihood of occurrence of an event based on the occurrence of a previous event. Conditional probability is calculated by multiplying the probability of the preceding event by the updated probability of the conditional event. For example, let us define events A and B:

- **Event A:** It is raining outside, and let it has a 0.4 (40 percent) chance of raining today. The probability of event A is P(A) = 0.4.
- **Event B:** A person needs to go outside, and let it has a probability P(B) = 0.3 (30 percent).

Joint probability: Let the probability that both events happen simultaneously is 0.2 or 20 percent. It is written as P(A and B) or P(A∩B) and is known as the joint probability of A and B. The symbol ∩ is for the intersection of the events.

Conditional probability: Now, we are interested to know the probability or chances of occurrence of rain given the person has come out. The probability of rain given the person went out is the conditional probability P(A|B) that can be given as,

$$P(A|B) = P(A \cap B)/P(B) = 0.2/0.3 = 0.66 = 66.6\%.$$

Besides P(A|B), there is another conditional probability related to the event: the probability of occurrence of event B given A has already occurred, P(B|A). **Bayes' theorem** converts one conditional probability to the other conditional probability. It is given as

$$P(B|A) = (P(A|B)\ P(B))/(P(A))$$

$$= (0.66)(0.3)/0.4 = 0.495 = 49.5\%.$$

It is evident from this example that generally, P(A|B) is not equal to P(B|A).

Some terminology related to Bayes' theorem is given as follows.

- P(B): the probability of hypothesis B being true, regardless of the data. This is known as the **prior** probability of B or the unconditional probability.
- P(A): the probability of the data, regardless of the hypothesis. This is known as the **evidence**.
- P(B|A): the probability of hypothesis B given the data A. This is known as **posterior** probability. Usually, we are interested in finding this probability.
- P(A|B): the probability of data A given that hypothesis B is true. This is known as the **likelihood** of data A conditional on the hypothesis B.

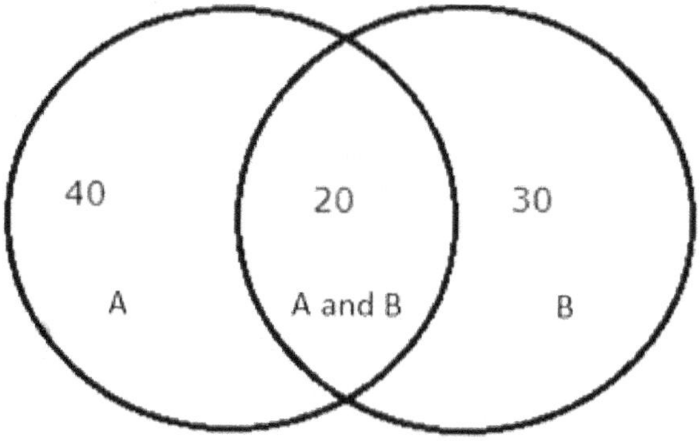

Figure 7.11: Explanation of the joint and conditional probability.

To implement the Naïve Bayes' algorithm in Python, we may write the following script.

```
#Import Gaussian Naive Bayes model
from sklearn.naive_bayes import GaussianNB
from sklearn import preprocessing
```

Suppose we want to predict whether we should play based on weather conditions and temperature readings. Weather and temperature become our features, and the decision to play becomes the target variable or the output. We assign features and label variables as follows.

```
weather=['Sunny','Sunny','Overcast','Rainy','Rainy','Rainy',
'Overcast','Sunny','Sunny','Rainy','Sunny','Overcast',
'Overcast','Rainy']

temp=['Hot','Hot','Hot','Mild','Cool','Cool','Cool','Mild',
'Cool','Mild','Mild','Mild','Hot','Mild']

play=['No','No','Yes','Yes','Yes','No','Yes','No','Yes','Yes',
'Yes','Yes','Yes','No']
```

Since weather and temperature are given as strings, it is difficult to train our model on strings. We transform our features and the target variable to numeric data as follows.

```
weather_encoded=le.fit_transform(weather)
#creating label Encoder
le = preprocessing.LabelEncoder()

# Converting string labels into numbers.
weather_encoded=le.fit_transform(weather)
print ("Weather:",weather_encoded)

# Encode temp and play columns to convert string labels into numbers
temp_encoded=le.fit_transform(temp)
label=le.fit_transform(play)
print ("Temp:",temp_encoded)
print ("Play:",label)
```

```
#Combining features weather and temp in a single variable (list of tuples).
features=np.column_stack((weather_encoded,temp_encoded))
print ("Combined feature:",features)

Output:
Weather: [2 2 0 1 1 1 0 2 2 1 2 0 0 1]
Temp: [1 1 1 2 0 0 0 2 0 2 2 2 1 2]
Play: [0 0 1 1 1 0 1 0 1 1 1 1 1 0]
Combined feature: [[2 1]
 [2 1]
 [0 1]
 [1 2]
 [1 0]
 [1 0]
 [0 0]
 [2 2]
 [2 0]
 [1 2]
 [2 2]
 [0 2]
 [0 1]
 [1 2]]
```

We convert string feature values and output labels into integers using label encoding method **preprocessing.LabelEncoder()**. The function **fit_transform (weather)** converts string labels for weather conditions into numbers.

We generate a model using Naive Bayes' classifier by the following steps:

1. Create naive Bayes' classifier
2. Fit the dataset on classifier
3. Perform prediction.

```
#Create a Gaussian Classifier
model = GaussianNB()
# Train the model using the training sets
model.fit(features,label)
#Predict Output for input 0:Overcast, 2:Mild
predicted= model.predict([[0,2]])
print ("Predicted Value:", predicted)

Output:
Predicted Value: [1]
```

To predict a test point, we have used the function predict ().

Advantages and Applicability: Naïve Bayes' is easy to implement and interpret. It performs better compared to other similar models when the input features are independent of each other. A small amount of training data is sufficient for this model to estimate the test data.

Limitations: The main limitation of Naïve Baye' is the assumption of independence between the independent variables. If features are dependent, this algorithm cannot be applied. Dimensionality reduction techniques can be used to transform the features into a set of independent features before applying the Naïve Bayes' classifier.

> **Further Reading**
>
> Further reading related to the nearest neighbor and K-means can be found at
>
> https://bit.ly/3hURUIp

7.6.4. Decision Trees

A decision tree is similar to a flowchart in which the nodes represent features, the branches represent a decision rule, and each leaf node represents the result or outcome of applying the rules on these features. In a decision tree, the topmost node is known as the root or parent node.

The learning in decision trees is accomplished by partitioning at each internal node on the basis of the values of features. The visualization of a tree as a flowchart mimics human thinking. Thus, decision trees are easy to understand and interpret. The paths from the root to the leaf represent classification rules. Decision trees are mostly used for classification; however, these can also be utilized for regression.

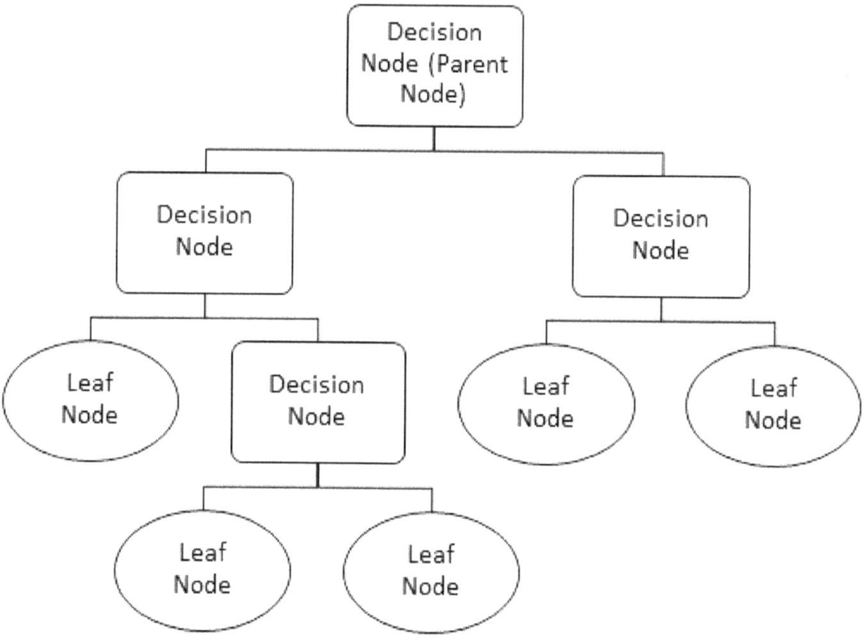

Figure 7.12: A decision tree showing decision and leaf nodes.

Decision trees learn from data with a set of if-then-else rules. The decision tree is a non-parametric method that does not depend upon the assumptions of probability distributions. The basic point behind any decision tree algorithm is along these lines:

- Select the best feature at each node using some kind of feature selection measure to split the observations given in the data. The best feature is the one that best separates the given data.
- This feature becomes a decision node, and we break the dataset into smaller subsets at this node.
- Start building a tree by repeating this process recursively for each child node until either there are no more remaining features or there are no more observations.

Let us assume we want to play tennis on a particular day. How do we decide whether to play or not? We check the weather if it is hot or cold, check the speed of the wind and humidity. We take all these factors into account to decide if we shall play or not.

We gather data for temperature, wind, and humidity for a few days and make a decision tree similar to the one shown in figure 7.13. All possible paths from the root to the leaf nodes represent a set of rules that lead to the final decision of playing or not playing tennis.

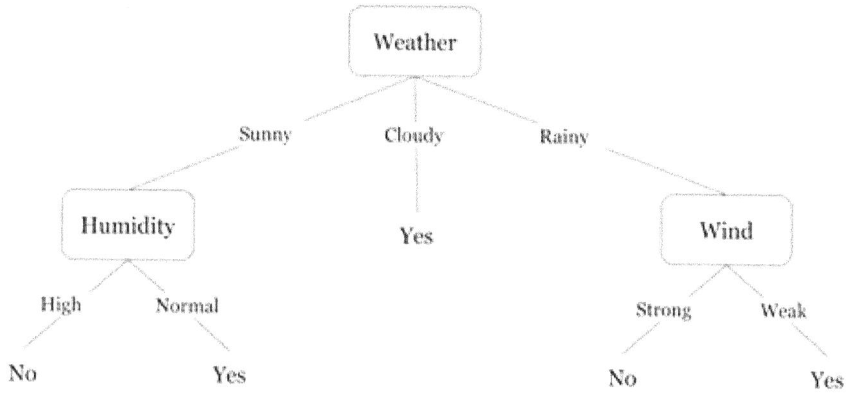

Figure 7.13: A decision tree for playing tennis or not.

As an example, consider the leftmost path from the root Weather all the way down to No. The decision rule in this path says that if Weather is Sunny and the Humidity is High, we shall not play.

To implement the decision tree algorithm for classification in Python, we may write the following script.

```
# code for decision tree based classification
from sklearn import datasets
#Loading the iris data
iris_data = datasets.load_iris()
print('Classes to predict: ', iris_data.target_names)

Output:
Classes to predict:  ['setosa' 'versicolor' 'virginica']
```

We extract data attributes and target/ class labels as follows.

```
X = iris_data.data
y = iris_data.target

print('Number of examples in the data:', X.shape[0])

Output:
Number of examples in the data: 150
```

We split our dataset into test and training sets using train_test_split.

```
X_train, X_test, y_train, y_test = train_test_
    split(X, y, random_state = 47, test_size = 0.25)
```

Next, we import the decision tree classifier from the sklearn library and use it to train the model.

```
from sklearn.tree import DecisionTreeClassifier
clf = DecisionTreeClassifier(criterion = 'entropy')

#Training the decision tree classifier.
clf.fit(X_train, y_train)
Output:
DecisionTreeClassifier(ccp_alpha=0.0, class_weight=None,
    criterion='entropy',max_depth=None, max_features=None, max_
    leaf_nodes=None,min_impurity_decrease=0.0, min_impurity_
    split=None,min_samples_leaf=1, min_samples_split=2,
    min_weight_fraction_leaf=0.0, presort='deprecated',random_
    state=None, splitter='best')
```

We use the trained model to predict the output labels and assess the performance of the model.

```
# Predicting labels on the test set.
y_pred =  clf.predict(X_test)

# Importing the accuracy metric
from sklearn.metrics import accuracy_score

# Printing the accuracy score
print('Accuracy Score on train data: ', accuracy_score(y_
    true=y_train, y_pred=clf.predict(X_train)))
print('Accuracy Score on test data: ', accuracy_score(y_
    true=y_test, y_pred=y_pred))
Output:
Accuracy Score on train data:  1.0
Accuracy Score on test data:  0.9473684210526315
```

The output indicates that the model performs 100 percent on the training data. However, its generalization power to predict test points decreases to about 95 percent. This accuracy is usually considered acceptable because the model generalizes well to unseen examples.

Ensemble methods: The predicting power of decision trees can be enhanced by growing multiple trees on a slightly different version of the training data. The resulting class of methods is known as ensemble methods. To predict the output or class for a particular test example, each grown tree present in the model votes. The class with majority votes wins, and the test example is assigned to that class.

Advantages and Applicability: Decision tree models are intuitive and easy to explain because these are based upon if-else conditions. These algorithms do not require much data preprocessing because they do not make any assumptions about the distribution of data. This fact makes them very useful in identifying the hidden pattern in the dataset. Decision trees do not require normalization and scaling of the dataset. These algorithms require a small amount of training data to estimate the test data.

Limitations: Small changes in the dataset can cause the structure of the decision tree to change considerably, causing instability. The training time of decision trees is often higher than relatively simpler models such as logistic regression and Naïve Bayes'.

7.7. Unsupervised Learning

Unsupervised learning is a category of machine learning techniques used to find patterns in the given data. In these techniques, the input data is not labeled, i.e., the input variables or features are provided with no corresponding output labels. The algorithms based on the unsupervised learning aim to discover patterns and structures within the data.

Figure 7.14 depicts the difference between supervised learning and unsupervised learning. In supervised learning, two-dimensional data points are drawn along with the classes they belong to: red and blue. The learning is done to find the best separator, such as a line between these two classes. However, in unsupervised learning, the same two-dimensional data points are drawn that do not have any label associated with them. The aim of the unsupervised algorithm would be to find patterns present in the data based on the similarity between data points. In this example, two different clusters, shown as circles, are detected.

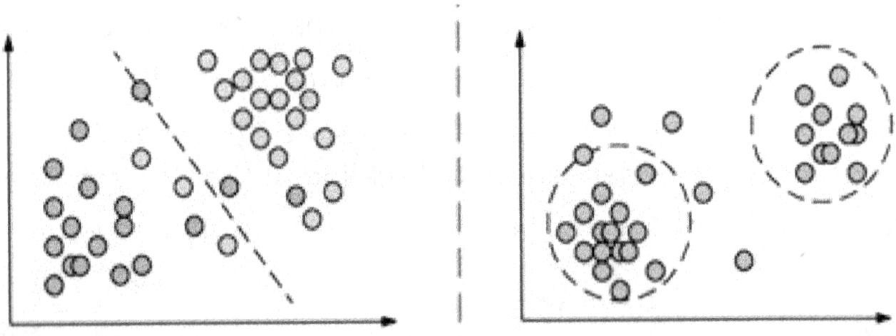

Figure 7.14: Supervised (left) vs. unsupervised (right) learning.

There are two major types of unsupervised learning:

- Clustering (grouping of the data), and
- Dimensionality reduction.

We go into the details of these two in the following sections.

7.7.1. Clustering

The aim of clustering is to divide or group the given data into several categories based on their similarities. Let us assume we have only two features in a given dataset. The labels of the data are not given to us. We plot this data, and it looks like the plot given in figure 7.15. The left side of figure 7.15 shows the data without labels, and the right side presents the clustered data based on the similarities between the data points.

To test an unsupervised learning algorithm such as clustering, we give an input that is to be predicted. The learned or trained model checks the test input against every cluster. The input test observation is assigned to the cluster that the point is most similar to.

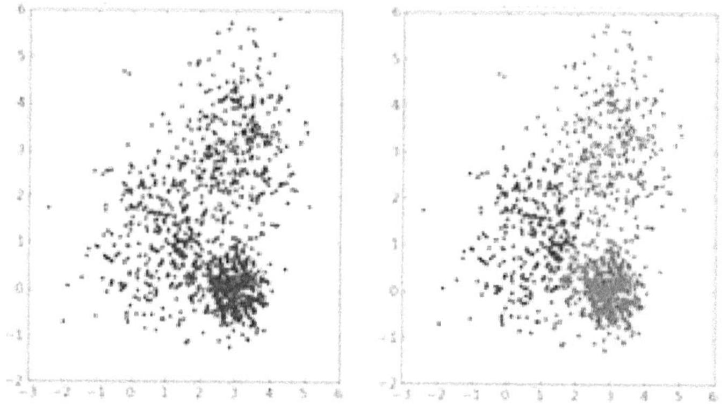

Figure 7.15: The data without labels (left), and the clustered data shown as three groups.

In the following section, we give details of K-means clustering, one of the most widely used clustering algorithms.

§ K-Means Clustering

K-means clustering is the most popular clustering algorithm. It is an iterative algorithm that aims to find the best cluster for each observation in each iteration. The basic process followed by the K-means algorithm is as follows.

- First, we choose the desired number of clusters, the value of K, and input this number K to the algorithm as an argument.
- Second, K input data points are assigned randomly to K clusters. These K points become the centroids or center points of the clusters.
- Third, the distance of each data point is calculated from all K centroids. Every data point is assigned to that cluster whose centroid is closest to it.
- Fourth, the centroids are re-computed for all the clusters because the data points are re-assigned to the clusters.

To implement the K means algorithm, we import the k means model from Scikit-Learn, library fit the features, and make predictions on the test points.

```
1. # K Means Clustering
2. # Importing required datasets and modules
3. from sklearn.cluster import KMeans
4. from sklearn.metrics import accuracy_score
5.
6. iris_data = pd.read_csv(r'I:/Data science books/
   Data science datasets and notebooks/iris_data.csv')
7. iris_data.head()
```

Output:

	Id	SepalLengthCm	SepalWidthCm	PetalLengthCm	PetalWidthCm	Species
0	1	5.1	3.5	1.4	0.2	Iris-setosa
1	2	4.9	3.0	1.4	0.2	Iris-setosa
2	3	4.7	3.2	1.3	0.2	Iris-setosa
3	4	4.6	3.1	1.5	0.2	Iris-setosa
4	5	5.0	3.6	1.4	0.2	Iris-setosa

To find the optimum number of clusters for classification, we implement a widely used technique called the elbow method on the Iris dataset.

```
from sklearn.cluster import KMeans

# WCSS = Within Cluster Sum of Squares
WCSS = []

# Getting length and width of the input features
# iloc indexer for a Dataframe is used for integer location-based selection of data
x = iris_data.iloc[:, [1, 2, 3, 4]].values


# Trying different number of clusters and recording WCSS or inertia of clustering
for i in range(1, 6):
    kmeans = KMeans(n_clusters = i)
    kmeans.fit(x)
    WCSS.append(kmeans.inertia_)
```

Next, we plot the Within Cluster Sum of Squares (WCSS) against the number of clusters onto a line graph, allowing us to observe 'The elbow' of the graph.

```
plt.plot(range(1, 6), WCSS)
plt.title('The elbow method')
plt.xlabel('Number of clusters')
plt.ylabel('WCSS') #within cluster sum of squares
plt.show()
```

Output:

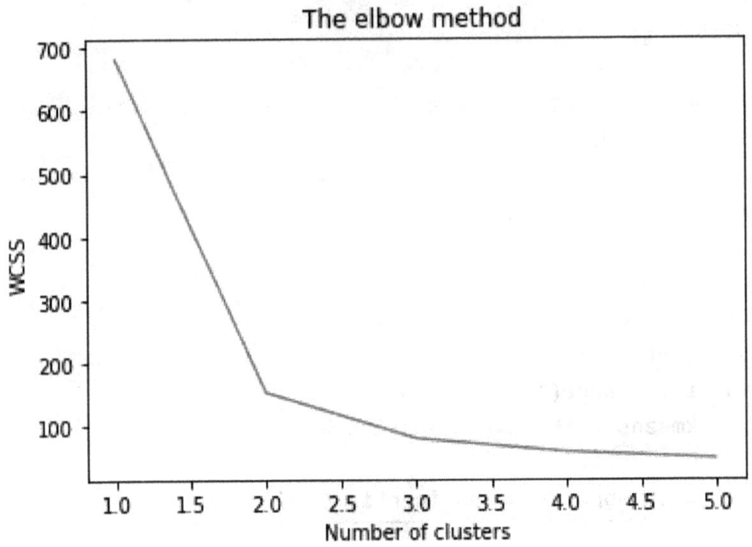

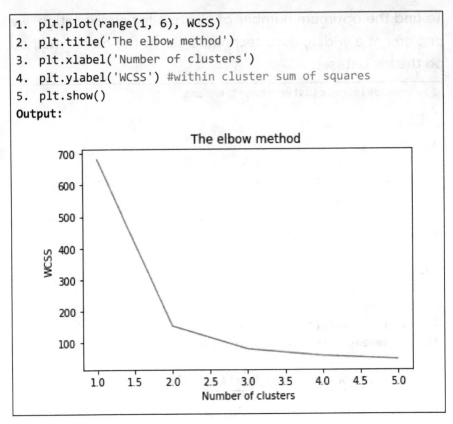

The graph given above shows 'the elbow method' that gives us the optimum number of clusters where the elbow occurs on the plot. This is the point after which WCSS does not decrease significantly with an increasing number of clusters. It is evident from the graph that the optimum number of clusters is three, which confirms the actual number of species/classes in the Iris dataset. We can apply the K-means clustering algorithm to the Iris dataset after getting the optimum number of clusters from the elbow method.

```
# Creating and applying kmeans classifier to the dataset

kmeans = KMeans(n_clusters = 3, init = 'k-means++', max_iter = 300, n_init = 10, random_state = 0)
y_kmeans = kmeans.fit_predict(x)

#Visualising the clusters 2 and 3, PetalLengthCm vs PetalWidthCm

plt.scatter(x[y_kmeans == 0, 2], x[y_kmeans == 0, 3], s = 30, c = 'red', label = 'Iris-first')

plt.scatter(x[y_kmeans == 1, 2], x[y_kmeans == 1, 3], s = 30, c = 'green', label = 'Iris-second')

plt.scatter(x[y_kmeans == 2, 2], x[y_kmeans == 2, 3], s = 30, c = 'blue', label = 'Iris-third')

#Plotting the centroids of the clusters
plt.scatter(kmeans.cluster_centers_[:, 2], kmeans.cluster_centers_[:,3], s = 30, c = 'yellow',

# Showing the results of the plot
label = 'Centroids')
plt.xlabel('Petal length (cm)')
plt.ylabel('Petal width (cm)')
plt.title('Iris dataset: Petal length vs Petal width')
plt.legend()
plt.show()
```

Output:

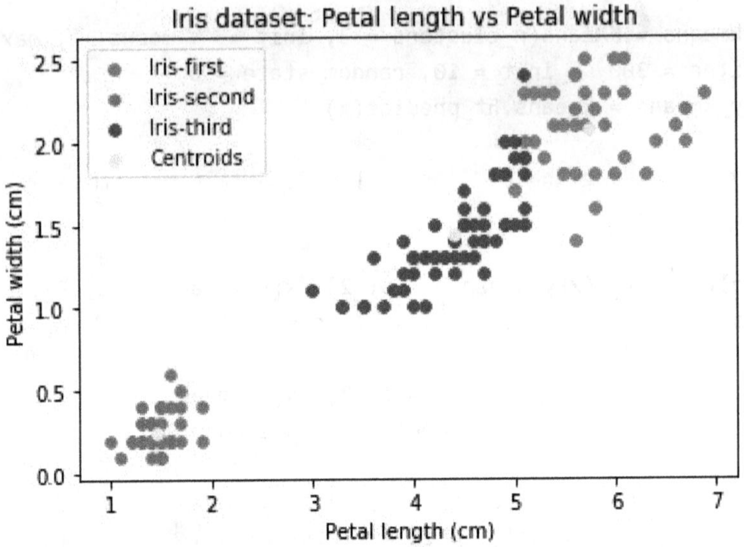

It can be observed that the K-Means algorithm has created three clusters. One of the clusters that we arbitrarily name **Iris-second** is linearly separable from **Iris-first** and **Iris-third** when we plot Petal length vs. Petal width. Since we are using just the features without output labels, we do not know the labels of the Iris species yet.

To visually assess the clustering capability of K-Means, we draw a scatter plot of Petal length vs. Petal width for all three classes of the dataset using their given labels.

```
# Selecting all 3 classes
setosa_selection = iris_data.Species == 'Iris-setosa'
versicolor_selection = iris_data.Species == 'Iris-
versicolor'
virginica_selection = iris_data.Species == 'Iris-
virginica'

# Getting examples of all 3 classes
setosa_examples= iris_data[setosa_selection]
```

```
versicolor_examples= iris_data[versicolor_selection]
virginica_examples= iris_data[virginica_selection]

# Plotting the examples of all 3 classes on a single plot
plt.scatter(setosa_examples['PetalLengthCm'],setosa_examples['PetalWidthCm'],c='red', label='Iris-setosa')
plt.scatter(versicolor_examples['PetalLengthCm'], versicolor_examples['PetalWidthCm'], c='green', label='Iris-versicolor')
plt.scatter(virginica_examples['PetalLengthCm'], virginica_examples['PetalWidthCm'], c='blue', label='Iris-virginica')

# Giving title and labels to the plot
plt.xlabel('Petal length (cm)')
plt.ylabel('Petal width (cm)')
plt.title('Iris dataset: Petal length vs Petal width')
plt.legend(loc='lower right')
plt.show()
```

Output:

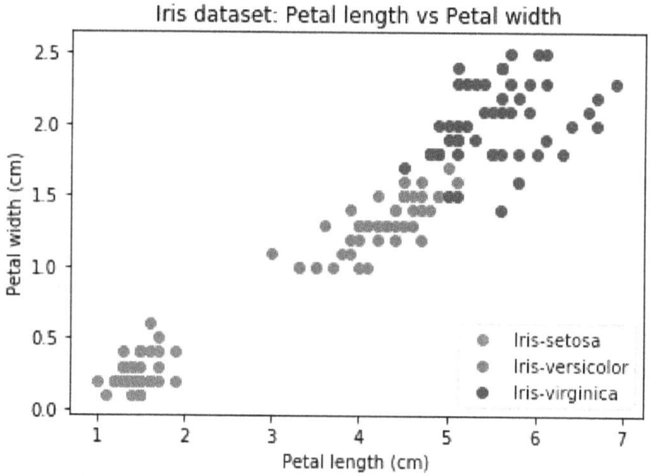

Conclusion: A visual comparison of the aforementioned plot with the plot we got from K-Means clustering reveals that Iris-setosa corresponds to the Iris-second and is linearly separable from the other two species of the dataset. Furthermore, Iris-versicolor and Iris-virginica are not separable in this plot. Thus, the output of the clustering shows some example points erroneously assigned to the wrong clusters because the training examples of two of the three classes are mixed with each other. Thus, it can be concluded when the examples of different classes are mixed together, the result of clustering shows errors.

7.7.2. Dimensionality Reduction

The techniques for *dimensionality reduction* aim to reduce the number of dimensions in a given dataset. In data science, the dimensionality corresponds to the number of feature variables. The lesser the important and distinct features we have, the lesser computations we shall have to perform to train and test our machine learning model. The key benefits of applying dimensionality reduction techniques to a dataset include the following.

- Computer memory required to store the data is reduced when the number of dimensions is reduced.
- Fewer computations, and fast training and testing are possible on a smaller number of dimensions.
- Visualizing data in higher dimensions is very difficult; hence, reducing the dimensions to just 2D or 3D allows us to plot and observe patterns.

Dimensionality reduction methods remove redundant features by paying attention to the dependency and correlation of features. For example, if we have two variables: *time spent on the treadmill in minutes* and *the calories burnt*. These two variables are highly correlated as the more time we spend on a treadmill, the more calories we burn. Thus, there is no need to store both variables, working with one of them is sufficient.

Applying a dimensionality reduction technique, to a dataset of three features only, may *project* the 3D data onto a 2D plane. This effectively reduces the number of points and the number of computations.

Dimensionality reduction can be done in two different ways:

- Just select the most relevant features from the original dataset. This technique is called **feature selection,** which we have already covered earlier in this chapter.
- Find a smaller set of new variables as combinations of the input features. This technique is called **feature extraction**.

One of the most common techniques used for dimensionality reduction is **Principal Component Analysis (PCA)** that creates new features by linearly combining the existing features. These newly extracted features are known as principal components, which aim to retain the maximum variance in the given dataset.

The principal components are extracted in such a way that the first principal component explains maximum variance in the dataset. The second principal component explains the remaining variance in the dataset and is uncorrelated to the first principal component. The third principal component explains the variance, which is not explained by the first two principal components, and so on.

To implement the PCA algorithm, we import its model from the Scikit-Learn library. We also lead the training data from the MNIST handwritten digit recognition dataset.

```
from sklearn.decomposition import PCA

# Give the complete path of your train.csv file
train = pd.read_csv("C:/…/mnist_train.csv")
df = pd.DataFrame(train)
df['label'] = train['label']

# Applying PCA to the training data by specifying number of PCA components.
pca = PCA(n_components=50)
pca_result = pca.fit_transform(df.values)

# Showing the results.
plt.plot(range(50), pca.explained_variance_ratio_)
plt.plot(range(50), np.cumsum(pca.explained_variance_ratio_))
plt.title("Component-wise and Cumulative Explained Variance")
```

Output:

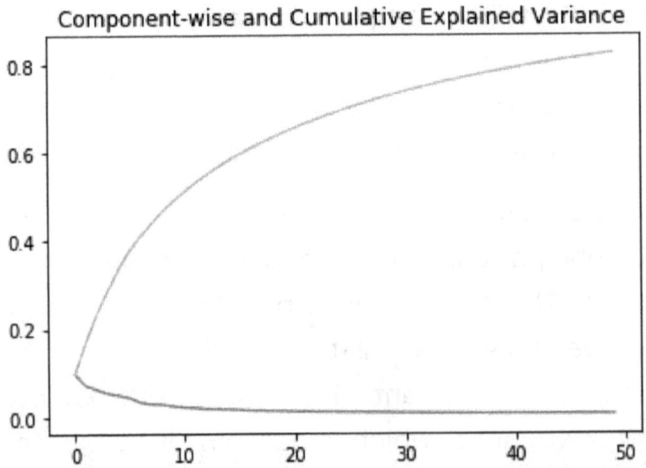

Conclusion: The handwritten digit recognition dataset MNIST has 60,000 observations of 785 features. In the graph given above, the blue line represents component-wise explained variance, whereas the orange line represents the cumulative explained variance.

We are able to explain around 50 percent variance in the dataset using just 10 components. If we use 50 PCA components, we get about 80 percent of the variance. This implies that instead of using 785 features, if we transform them using PCA, and use 50 new features, i.e., principal components, we get about 80 percent of the variance in the dataset.

The use of 50 features instead of 785 means we use about $50/785 \approx 6.4$ percent of the data that saves us about 93.6 percent of the computations.

7.8. Evaluating Performance of the Trained Model

The model evaluation aims to estimate the generalization accuracy of a machine learning model on future unseen test data. The methods for assessing the performance of a model are divided into two main categories: holdout and cross-validation (CV).

Both methods use a test set to evaluate model performance. It is not a good practice to use the training data to evaluate the built model because the model remembers the training set and performs well on this set. However, it may not generalize to unseen test sets. We discuss the aforementioned techniques in the following sections.

§ Holdout

In the holdout method, the dataset is *randomly* divided into three subsets.

- **The training set** is used to prepare models.
- **The validation set** is used to assess the performance of

the model built in the training phase. By validating our model, we can fine-tune the parameters of the model.

- **The test set** is also used to assess the future performance of a model.

The holdout approach is simple and flexible. However, differences in the training and test dataset can result in changes in the estimate of model accuracy.

§ Cross-Validation

As discussed earlier, often, we choose a percentage of the training set to train the model and use the remaining part of the training set to validate the model. If the model is iteratively trained and validated on different validation sets generated randomly from the training set, the process is commonly referred to as cross-validation (CV).

One of the most common cross-validation techniques is k-fold cross-validation, where the original dataset is partitioned into k equal-sized subsets or folds. A typical value of the user-specified number k is between 5 to 10. This process is repeated k times, such that each time one of the k subsets is used as the validation set and the other k-1 subsets are put together to form a training set. The error estimates are averaged over all k runs to get the total error of our model.

In the first iteration of the process, CV uses the training set to generate a validation set. In the next iteration, CV generates another validation set from the same training set, and the process continues. CV increases the robustness of the trained model and is used to tune the parameters of the model. This helps us get the most optimized model.

Figure 7.16 shows the process of cross-validation. The top part of the figure shows that the dataset is split into training and testing. The training set is further divided into 10 parts. In the process of cross- validation, we repeatedly train our model on 9 out of 10 parts of the training set and test the model on the left-out part. This process is repeated 10 times to cover all 10 combinations of the 90:10 ratio of the training:validating sets. The bottom part of the figure shows that validation is performed first before the final testing.

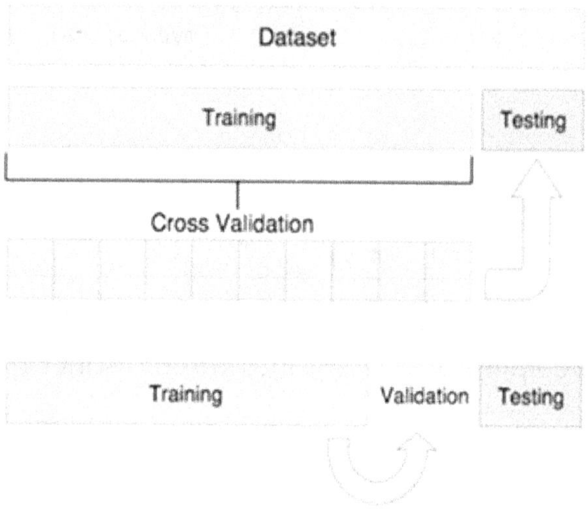

Figure 7.16: Cross-validation performed on the training data. The final testing is performed once we have cross-validated our dataset.

The procedure of cross-validation has a single parameter k that represents the number of groups the data is to be split into. Thus, this process is called k-fold cross-validation. For a specific value of k, such as 10, it becomes 10-fold cross-validation.

To perform cross-validation, we may write the following Python script.

```
# scikit-learn k-fold cross-validation
from numpy import array
from sklearn.model_selection import KFold

# Generation of sample data
mydata = array([1, 2, 3, 4, 5, 6])

# prepare cross-validation
kfold = KFold(3, True, 1)

# enumerate splits
for train, test in kfold.split(mydata):
    print('train: %s, test: %s' % (mydata[train], mydata[test]))

Output:
train: [1 4 5 6], test: [2 3]
train: [2 3 4 6], test: [1 5]
train: [1 2 3 5], test: [4 6]
```

The output of the aforementioned Python script demonstrates that we have split our dataset into three distinct training and test sets.

We can train a machine learning model of our choice in these three training sets. The performance of all three trained models is assessed, and an average is taken at the end to report a summary of the model performance.

§ Model Evaluation Metrics

Metrics are required to quantify the performance of a trained model. These evaluation metrics depend on the given task, such as classification, regression, and clustering. Classification and regression are mostly used in common machine learning applications. Some of the metrics used in classification problems are as follows:

- Classification Accuracy,
- Confusion matrix,
- Precision recall curve, and
- Receiver operating characteristic (ROC) curve.

§ Classification Accuracy

Accuracy is the commonly accepted evaluation metric for classification problems. It is defined as the number of correct predictions made as a ratio of all predictions made.

§ Confusion Matrix

A confusion matrix offers a detailed breakdown of correct and incorrect classifications for each class. A sample confusion matrix is shown in figure 7.17.

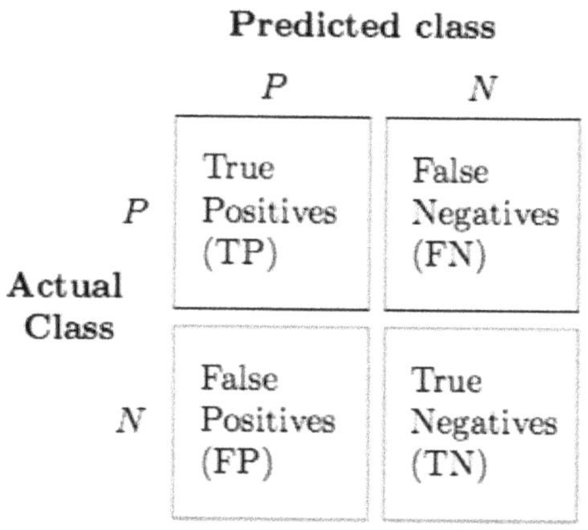

Figure 7.17: A confusion matrix showing the relationship between true and predicted classes.

In a confusion matrix, the diagonal elements indicate the number of points for which the predicted label is equal to the true label, while off-diagonal entries are misclassified or wrongly labeled by our classifier model. Thus, the higher the diagonal values in a confusion matrix, the better, which indicates many correct predictions. We go into the details of the confusion matrix in the next chapter.

§ Area Under the Curve (AUC)

The area under the curve (AUC) measures the discriminatory ability of a binary classifier to differentiate between positive (1) and negative (0) classes.

```
AUC - Test Set: 79.55%
```

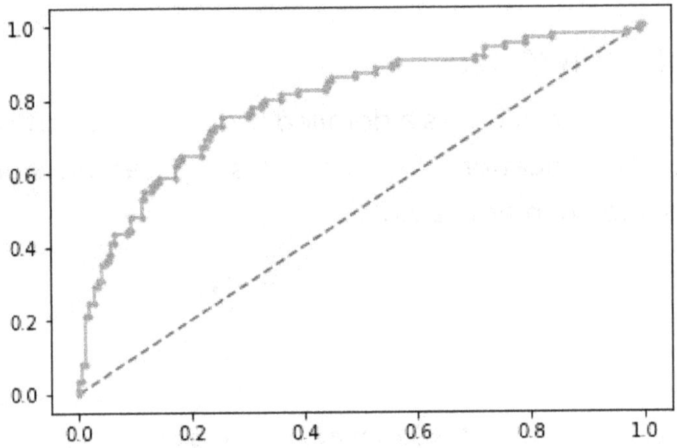

Figure 7.18: Area under the curve (AUC).

In the example above, the AUC of the orange curve is greater than 0.5 and close to 1. A perfect classifier will have a 100 percent area under the curve. The performance of the classifier decreases as the area under its curve decreases. Details of AUC are given in Chapter 8.

§ Regression Metrics

The two most common metrics to assess the performance of regression models are the mean absolute error (MAE) and the mean squared error (MSE). The MAE is the sum of the absolute differences between predictions and actual values, whereas MSE is the average squared difference between prediction and actual observation.

The root mean squared error (RMSE) is the square root of the MSE. We go into the details of these metrics in Chapter 8 of the book.

Hands-on Time

It is time to check your understanding of this chapter through the exercise questions given in Section 7.9. The answers to these questions are given at the end of the book.

7.9. Exercise Questions

Question 1. What is the minimum number of variables/ features required to perform clustering?

A. 0

B. 1

C. 2

D. 3

Question 2. What is the median of the following data [−3, 1, 4, −3, 6, 2, −4]?

A. 2

B. −3

C. −4

D. 1

Question 3. What is the mode of the following data [−3, 1, 4, −3, 6, 2, −4]?

A. 2

B. −3

C. −4

D. 1

Question 4. What is the median of the following data [−3, 1, 4, −4]?

A. −1

B. −3

C. Undefined

D. Not given

Question 5. Which one of the following is a discrete probability distribution?

A. Normal distribution

B. Poisson distribution

C. Uniform distribution

D. Bernoulli distribution

Question 6. We have been given a dataset containing heights and weights of female and male sportspersons. We are required to tell the gender of an unseen person based upon his/her height and weight. This is an example of ______________

A. Unsupervised learning

B. Supervised learning

C. Either supervised or unsupervised learning

D. Reinforcement learning

Question 7. In successive iterations of the K-Means algorithm, do observations always change clusters during the assignment step?

A. Yes

B. No

C. Cannot tell

D. None of these

Question 8. Suppose we want to predict the income of a person based upon some features related to his/her lifestyle. This is an example of _________________.

A. Classification

B. Regression

C. Either Classification or Regression

D. Clustering

Question 9. In Naïve Bayes' classification, the naïve assumption is related to the ____________

A. Dependency between features

B. Independence of features

C. Bayes' rule of probability

D. Conditional probability

Question 10. ________________ is used to perform classification based on if-then-else rules?

A. Naïve Bayes'

B. Logistic Regression

C. Decision Tree

D. Nearest Neighbor

8

Interpretation and Reporting of Findings

8.1. Introduction

All the hard work behind data preprocessing, analysis, and modeling is of little value unless we interpret the results and explain the important findings to the stakeholders. At the end of a data science project, we should interpret the results using suitable mathematical and visualization tools, and explain our results to technical and non-technical stakeholders.

An important but undervalued step in the data science pipeline is to learn how to explain the findings through communication. In this chapter, we present some of the widely used tools that summarize the findings of a data science project.

8.2. Confusion Matrix

In a binary classification problem, we call one class positive and the other class negative. There are four types of outcomes that could occur when we perform predictions in this classification problem.

1. A true positive (TP) is an outcome when the model correctly predicts the positive class.
2. A true negative (TN) is an outcome when the model correctly predicts the negative class.
3. A false positive (FP) is an outcome when the model incorrectly predicts the positive class. It is also called a Type I error in statistics.
4. A false negative (FN) is an outcome when the model incorrectly predicts the negative class. It is also called a Type II error in statistics.

These four outcomes are usually plotted in a matrix called a **confusion matrix**. For instance, in Aesop's fable: *The Boy Who Cried Wolf*, let us make the following definitions:

- Shepherd says, "wolf" = **positive class**.
- Shepherd says, "no wolf" = **negative class**.

We summarize this prediction model using a 2x2 confusion matrix that describes all four possible outcomes as follows.

True Positive (TP): · Reality: A wolf came. · Shepherd said: Wolf.	**False Positive (FP):** · Reality: No wolf came. · Shepherd said: Wolf.
False Negative (FN): · Reality: A wolf came. · Shepherd said: No wolf.	**True Negative (TN):** · Reality: No wolf came. · Shepherd said: No wolf.

Figure 8.1: A 2x2 confusion matrix showing all four possible outcomes.

An example confusion matrix for the case of binary classification is given in figure 8.1. This matrix is generated after we make predictions on the test data and then identify each prediction as one of the four possible outcomes defined above.

n=165	Predicted: NO	Predicted: YES	
Actual: NO	TN = 50	FP = 10	60
Actual: YES	FN = 5	TP = 100	105
	55	110	

Figure 8.2: An example of a confusion matrix for a binary classification problem.

Suppose we apply a classifier to n=165 examples. We have 105 instances of the positive class and 60 instances of the negative class. Our classifier predicts 100 positive and 50 negative examples correctly, whereas it predicts 5 positive and 10 negative examples incorrectly. Figure 8.2 shows the details of this outcome in a confusion matrix.

Based on figure 8.2, we define and calculate some important metrics to measure the performance of a classifier.

Accuracy of a classifier model is a measure of how often it classifies correctly. It can be computed from the confusion matrix as

Accuracy = (TP+TN)/Total observations

= (100+50)/(100+50+5+10)

= 150/165 = 90.9%.

An important metric of a classifier is **misclassification** or **error rate** that describes how often the prediction of a classifier is wrong.

Misclassification Rate = (FP+FN)/ Total observations.

Misclassification rate for the example given in figure 8.2 is given as:

Misclassification Rate = (10+5)/ (100+50+5+10)

=15/165

= 9.1%

To generate a confusion matrix in Python, we implement a logistic regression classifier using the following script.

```
# Import libraries and packages
import numpy as np
import pandas as pd
import matplotlib.pyplot as plt
import seaborn as sns
import sklearn as sk

from sklearn.linear_model import LogisticRegression
from sklearn import metrics
from sklearn.metrics import classification_report, confusion_matrix

# Data generation
x = np.arange(10).reshape(-1, 1)
# reshape(-1, 1) arranges the Numpy array in a format suitable for model fitting
y = np.array([0, 0, 0, 0, 1, 1, 1, 1, 1, 1])

# Applying logistic regression model on generated data
model = LogisticRegression(solver='liblinear', random_state=0)
model.fit(x, y)
```

```

# Calculating confusion matrix and accuracy
cm = metrics.confusion_matrix(y, model.predict(x))
score = model.score(x, y)

# Plotting the results
sns.heatmap(cm, annot=True, fmt=".3f", linewidths=.5,
    square = True, cmap = 'YlGnBu');

plt.ylabel('Actual label');
plt.xlabel('Predicted label');
all_sample_title = 'Accuracy Score: {0}'.format(score)
plt.title(all_sample_title, size = 15);
```

Output:

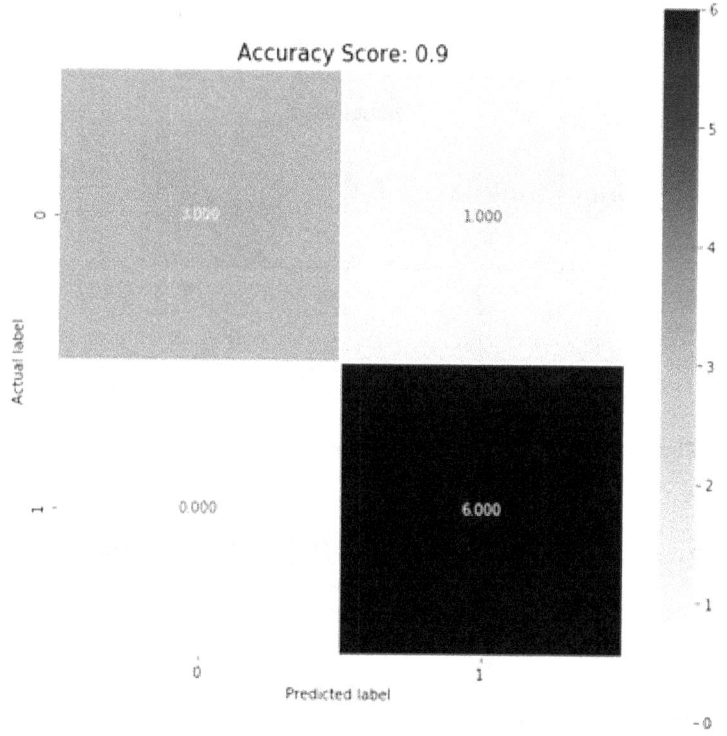

Note that the confusion matrix shows the accuracy score of 0.9 at its top in this output. The confusion matrix shows that out of a total of 10 observations, 9 are correctly predicted with 3 true positives and 6 true negatives. There is only one mislabeled observation in which our model misclassified a point from the actual negative class as a positive (false positive).

It is possible to extend a confusion matrix to plot multi-class classification predictions. An example confusion matrix for classifying observations from the Iris dataset is given below.

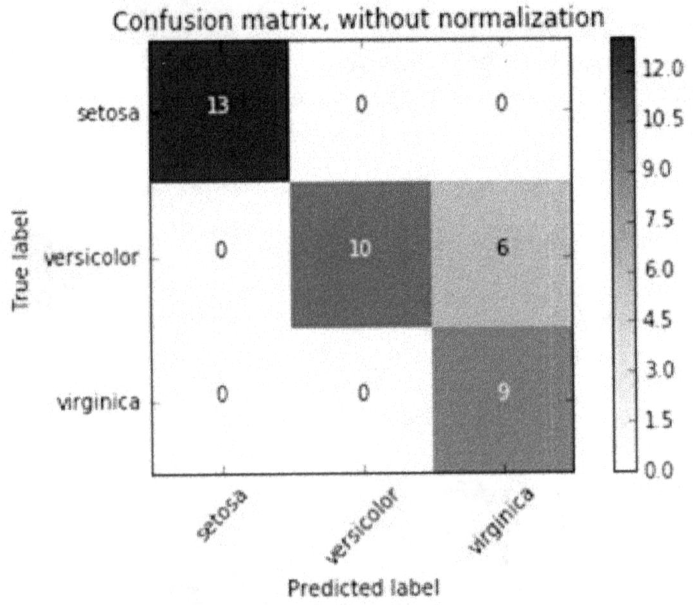

Figure 8.3: A confusion matrix for a 3-class problem.

8.3. Receiver Operating Characteristics (ROC) Curve

A receiver operating characteristic (ROC) curve is a plot that demonstrates the ability of a binary classifier to predict classes when its threshold is varied. To understand the ROC curve, we first define the true positive rate (TPR) and the false positive rate (FPR).

True positive rate (TPR), also called recall, sensitivity, or probability of detection measures the proportion of actual positives that are correctly identified, e.g., the percentage of sick people who are correctly identified as having the disease.

TPR (recall) = True positives / total positives

= TP /P

= TP / (TP + FN)

= 100/105

= 0.95 (for figure 8.2)

The FPR is known as the probability of false alarm and can be calculated as the ratio between the number of negative events wrongly categorized as positive (false positives) and the total number of actual negative events.

FPR = False positives / total negatives

= FP / N

= FP / (FP+TN)

FPR = 10/60 = 0.17 (for figure 8.2)

The ROC curve is generated when we plot the true positive rate (TPR) against the false positive rate (FPR) at various thresholds.

Besides TPR and FPR, we have the true negative rate (TNR), also called the specificity or selectivity of a classifier model. TNR measures the proportion of actual negatives that are correctly identified as such (e.g., the percentage of healthy people who are correctly identified as not having the disease).

TNR = TN / N

= TN / (FP+TN)

= 1 - FPR

= 50/60

= 0.83 (for figure 8.2)

The false negative rate (FNR), also called the miss rate, measures the chance or probability that a true positive is missed. It is given as:

FNR = FN/P

= FN/(FN+TP)

= 5/(5+100)

= 0.048

where (FN+TP) are the total number of positives.

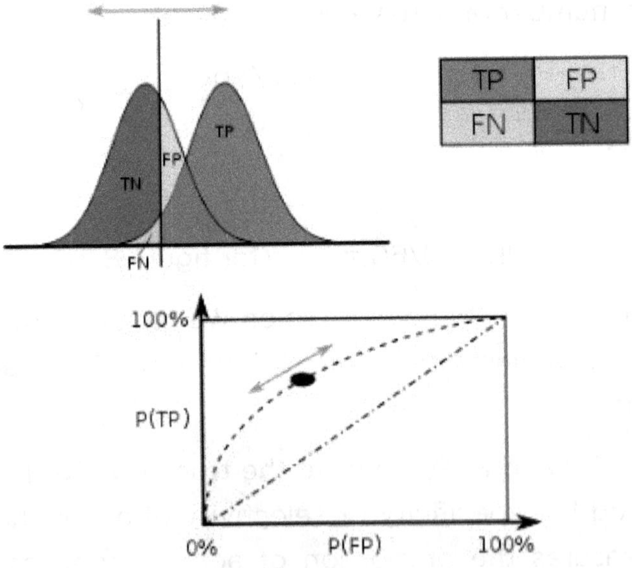

Figure 8.4: A Receiver Operating Characteristic (ROC) curve.

On the upper left side of figure 8.4, negative and positive classes are shown in blue and red, respectively. A black vertical line shows the threshold. Every example on the right of the threshold is predicted as positive, and each example on the left is taken as negative. It can be observed that if the threshold is moved toward the left, we get a lot of positives. On the other hand, if the threshold is moved toward the right, we get a lot of negatives. The optimal value of the threshold is somewhat in the middle of two classes.

This threshold is varied to generate a set of TPR and FPR values. The ROC curve is generated using these pairs of TPR-FPR values.

To generate a ROC curve in Python, we first load the libraries and packages.

```
# Importing libraries and packages
from sklearn.metrics import roc_curve
from sklearn.metrics import roc_auc_score
from sklearn.datasets import make_classification
from sklearn.model_selection import train_test_split
from sklearn.linear_model import LogisticRegression
```

We type the following script to generate the data for a 2-class dataset and split it into training and test sets of equal sizes.

```
x2, y2 = make_classification(n_samples=1000, n_
classes=2, random_state=1)

# split into train/test sets
trainx, testx, trainy, testy = train_test_
split(x2, y2, test_size=0.5, random_state=2)
```

We fit the logistic regression model to our dataset specified by trainx and trainy. Furthermore, the accuracy score of the trained model is also calculated.

```
model = LogisticRegression(solver='lbfgs')
model.fit(trainx, trainy)

# generate a no skill prediction (always predicts the majority class)
ns_probs = [0 for i in range(len(testy))]

# predict probabilities for logistic regression
lr_probs = model.predict_proba(testx)

# keep probabilities for the positive outcome only
lr_probs = lr_probs[:, 1]

# calculate scores
ns_auc = roc_auc_score(testy, ns_probs)
lr_auc = roc_auc_score(testy, lr_probs)

# summarize scores
print('No Skill: ROC AUC=%.3f' % (ns_auc))
print('Logistic: ROC AUC=%.3f' % (lr_auc))

Output:
No Skill: ROC AUC=0.500
Logistic: ROC AUC=0.903
```

We calculate ROC curves for the logistic regression classifier and a no-skill classifier that makes a random guess. Furthermore, we draw these ROC curves on the same plot.

```
ns_fpr, ns_tpr, _ = roc_curve(testy, ns_probs)
lr_fpr, lr_tpr, _ = roc_curve(testy, lr_probs)

# plot the ROC curves for both the model
plt.plot(ns_fpr, ns_tpr, linestyle='--', label='No Skill')
plt.plot(lr_fpr, lr_tpr, marker='.', label='Logistic')

plt.xlabel('False Positive Rate')
plt.ylabel('True Positive Rate')
plt.legend()
plt.show()
```

Output:

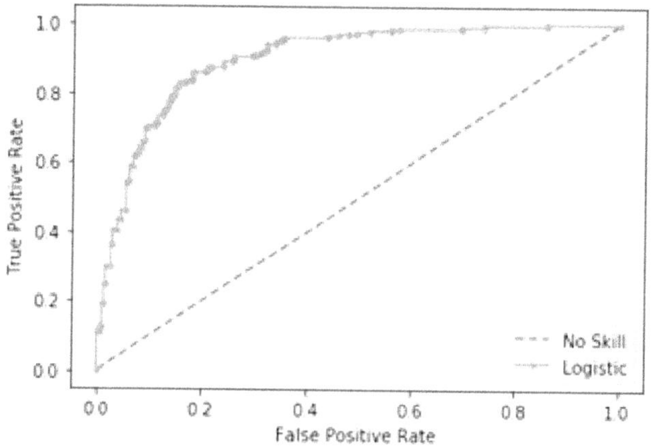

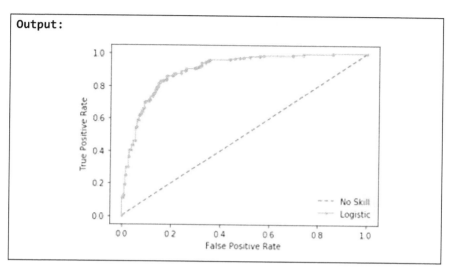

The leftmost side of the ROC curve corresponds to the case when our threshold given in figure 8.4 is toward the rightmost. In this case, all examples will be predicted as instances of the negative class. Thus, no instance will be predicted to belong to the positive class. TPR and FPR both would be zero.

Similarly, the rightmost side of the ROC curve corresponds to the case when our threshold given in figure 8.4 is toward the leftmost. In this case, all examples will be predicted as instances of the positive class. Thus, no instance will be predicted to belong to the negative class. TPR and FPR both would be 1 or 100 percent.

The generated ROC curves from the previous Python script show that the area under the curve for the logistic regression classifier and a majority class classifier is about 90.3 percent and 50 percent, respectively. A classifier that is even better than the logistic regression will have AUC more than 90.3 percent. Thus, plotting the ROC of multiple classifiers on the same plot is a good way to compare the performances of the classifiers.

8.4. Precision-Recall Curve

Precision (P) is defined as the number of true positives (TP) divided by the number of true positives (TP) plus the number of false positives (FP).

$$\text{Precision (P)} = TP/(TP+FP)$$

$$= 100/110$$

$$= 0.91 \text{ (for figure 8.2)}$$

Recall (R) or TPR is defined as the number of true positives (TP) divided by the number of true positives (TP) plus the number of false negatives (FN).

$$R = TPR = TP/(TP+FN)$$

These quantities are also related to the **F1-score**, which is defined as the harmonic mean of precision and recall.

$$F1 = 2(P \times R)/(P+R)$$

The precision of a classifier may or may not decrease with recall. Lowering the threshold of a classifier may increase the denominator of the precision formula because more positives will be returned. If the threshold was previously set too high, the new results may all be true positives, which will increase precision. If the previous threshold was about right or too low, further lowering the threshold will introduce false positives, decreasing precision.

In the recall formula, the denominator (TP+FN) does not depend on the classifier threshold. This means that lowering the classifier threshold may increase recall by increasing the number of true positive results.

The relationship between recall and precision can be observed on a curve called the precision-recall (PR) curve that is a plot with precision on the y-axis and recall on the x-axis. In other words, the PR curve contains TP/(TP+FN) on the y-axis and TP/(TP+FP) on the x-axis.

Average precision (AP) is a one-number summary of a PR curve. AP is the weighted mean of precisions achieved at each threshold, with the increase in recall from the previous threshold used as the weight.

$$AP = \sum_n (R_n - R_{n-1})Pn$$

where P_n and R_n are the precision and recall at the nth threshold, and $(R_n - R_{n-1})$ is the increase in the recall. To generate a PR curve in Python, we first load the libraries, packages, and train our model.

```
import matplotlib.pyplot as plt
from sklearn.metrics import precision_recall_curve
from sklearn.metrics import plot_precision_recall_curve
from sklearn.metrics import average_precision_score
from sklearn.model_selection import train_test_split
from sklearn.linear_model import LogisticRegression

# Here, we use the same LogisticRegression model that was
  used to generate a ROC curve in the previous program.

model = LogisticRegression(solver='lbfgs')
model.fit(trainx, trainy)
```

After training the model, we generate the PR curve by using the following script.

```
scorey = model.decision_function(testx)
average_precision = average_precision_score(testy, scorey)

disp = plot_precision_recall_curve(model, testx, testy)
disp.ax_.set_title('2-class Precision-Recall curve: '
                   'AP={0:0.2f}'.format(average_precision))
```

Output:

```
Text (0.5, 1.0, '2-class Precision-Recall curve: AP=0.90')
```

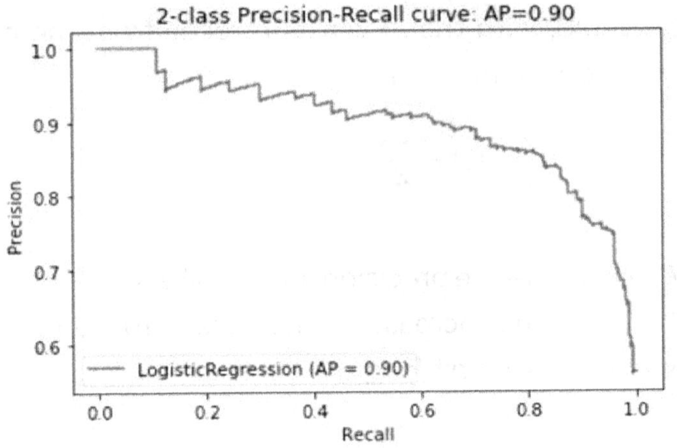

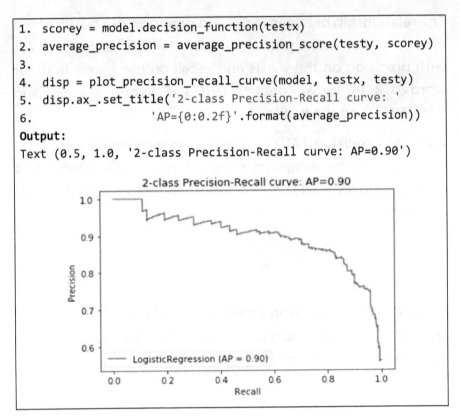

This precision-recall curve shows that our classifier gives an average precision of 0.9 or 90%. The more the PR curve is toward the upper right corner, the more is the area under the curve, and, hence, the average precision. Similar to a ROC, the PR curve can also be used to compare the performances of various classifiers by plotting them on the same plot.

8.5. Regression Metrics

The most common metrics for evaluating the performance of regression models are the mean absolute error (MAE), the mean squared error (MSE), and the root mean squared error (RMSE). The MAE is the sum of the absolute differences between predictions and actual values.

$$\text{MAE} = \frac{1}{n}\sum_{n} |y_{\text{true}} - y_{\text{pred}}|$$

where y_{true} is the actual value of the output variable, y_{pred} is the predicted output value, and || represents the mode or absolute value. The MSE is the average squared difference between prediction and actual observation.

$$\text{MSE} = \frac{1}{n}\sum (y_{\text{true}} - y_{\text{pred}})^2$$

The RMSE is the square root of MSE.

$$\text{RMSE} = \sqrt{\frac{1}{n}(\sum_{n} (y_{\text{true}} - y_{\text{pred}})^2}$$

To calculate MAE, MSE, and RMSE in Python, we may type the following commands:

```
from sklearn.linear_model import LinearRegression
from sklearn.metrics import mean_absolute_error
from sklearn.metrics import mean_squared_error

# Linear regression
x = np.random.rand(100, 1)  # generate random data of 100
samples
y = - 3 * x + 5 + np.random.rand(100, 1)   # randomly
generated samples are offset and multiplied

# Linear Regression Model initialization
regress_model = LinearRegression()

# Fit the data(train the model)
regress_model.fit(x, y)

# Predict
y_pred = regress_model.predict(x)

mae = mean_absolute_error(y, y_pred)
mse = mean_squared_error(y, y_pred)
rmse = np.sqrt(mse)

print('The MAE is: %f,:' % mae)
print('The MSE is: %f,:' % mse)
print('The RMSE is: %f,:' % rmse)
```

Hands-on Time

It is time to check your understanding of the topic of this chapter through the exercise questions given in Section 8.6. The answers to these questions are given at the end of the book.

8.6. Exercise Questions

Question 1: In a 2x2 confusion matrix [[15 3] ,[1 20]], what is the value of False Negatives?

A. 15

B. 3

C. 1

D. 20

Question 2: In a 2x2 confusion matrix [[15 3] ,[1 20]], what is the value of True Negative?

A. 15

B. 3

C. 1

D. 20

Question 3: For a 10-class supervised learning problem, the number of entries in the confusion matrix would be?

A. 10

B. 20

C. 100

D. 2x2

Question 4: The accuracy of the classifier from the 2x2 confusion matrix [[15 3] ,[1 20]], would be?

A. 35/39

B. 15/35

C. 20/35

D. 4/39

9

Data Science Projects

This chapter presents three data science projects to give the reader a better understanding of the concepts introduced in previous chapters.

The first project is to perform weather forecasting. It is a regression problem because we predict the temperature of the next day based on measurements of weather variables from the previous days.

The second project deals with the task of accent recognition of people from English-speaking countries. The third project builds a model to recognize human faces. The last two projects solve classification problems because there is a discrete set of output labels in both accent recognition and face recognition tasks. We give details of these projects in the following sections.

9.1. Regression

This project forecasts temperature using a numerical prediction model with an advanced technique known as **bias correction**. The dataset used for this project is publicly available at the UCI Machine Learning Repository:

https://archive.ics.uci.edu/ml/datasets/Bias+correction+of+numerical+prediction+model+temperature+forecast#

We import the required packages, and read the csv file of the project as follows:

```
import pandas as pd
import numpy as np
df = pd.read_csv('temperature.csv')
df.drop('Date',axis=1,inplace=True)
df.head()
```

Output:

	station	Present_Tmax	Present_Tmin	LDAPS_RHmin	LDAPS_RHmax	LDAPS_Tmax_lapse	LDAPS_Tmin_lapse	LDAPS_WS
0	1.0	28.7	21.4	58.255688	91.116364	28.074101	23.006936	6.818887
1	2.0	31.9	21.6	52.263397	90.604721	29.850689	24.035009	5.691890
2	3.0	31.6	23.3	48.690479	83.973587	30.091292	24.565633	6.138224
3	4.0	32.0	23.4	58.239788	96.483688	29.704629	23.326177	5.650050
4	5.0	31.4	21.9	56.174095	90.155128	29.113934	23.486480	5.735004

5 rows × 24 columns

To show the features and observations, we may type:

```
df.describe
```

Output:

```
<bound method NDFrame.describe of       station  Present_Tmax
   Present_Tmin  LDAPS_RHmin  LDAPS_RHmax  \
0        1.0         28.7        21.4    58.255688    91.116364
1        2.0         31.9        21.6    52.263397    90.604721
2        3.0         31.6        23.3    48.690479    83.973587
3        4.0         32.0        23.4    58.239788    96.483688
4        5.0         31.4        21.9    56.174095    90.155128
...      ...          ...         ...          ...          ...
7747   23.0         23.3        17.1    26.741310    78.869858
7748   24.0         23.3        17.7    24.040634    77.294975
7749   25.0         23.2        17.4    22.933014    77.243744
7750    NaN         20.0        11.3    19.794666    58.936283
7751    NaN         37.6        29.9    98.524734   100.000153
```

```
  LDAPS_Tmax_lapse  LDAPS_Tmin_lapse   LDAPS_WS    LDAPS_LH  LDAPS_CC1 \
0       28.074101      23.006936   6.818887   69.451805   0.233947
1       29.850689      24.035009   5.691890   51.937448   0.225508
2       30.091292      24.565633   6.138224   20.573050   0.209344
3       29.704629      23.326177   5.650050   65.727144   0.216372
4       29.113934      23.486480   5.735004  107.965535   0.151407
...           ...            ...        ...         ...        ...
7747    26.352081      18.775678   6.148918   72.058294   0.030034
7748    27.010193      18.733519   6.542819   47.241457   0.035874
7749    27.939516      18.522965   7.289264    9.090034   0.048954
7750    17.624954      14.272646   2.882580  -13.603212   0.000000
7751    38.542255      29.619342  21.857621  213.414006   0.967277

       ...  LDAPS_PPT2  LDAPS_PPT3  LDAPS_PPT4       lat
    lon        DEM  \
0      ...   0.000000    0.000000    0.000000  37.6046
   126.991  212.3350
1      ...   0.000000    0.000000    0.000000  37.6046
   127.032   44.7624
2      ...   0.000000    0.000000    0.000000  37.5776
   127.058   33.3068
3      ...   0.000000    0.000000    0.000000  37.6450
   127.022   45.7160
4      ...   0.000000    0.000000    0.000000  37.5507
   127.135   35.0380
...  ...        ...         ...         ...      ...
   ...        ...
7747 ...   0.000000    0.000000    0.000000  37.5372
   126.891   15.5876
7748 ...   0.000000    0.000000    0.000000  37.5237
   126.909   17.2956
7749 ...   0.000000    0.000000    0.000000  37.5237
   126.970   19.5844
7750 ...   0.000000    0.000000    0.000000  37.4562
   126.826   12.3700
7751 ...  21.621661   15.841235   16.655469  37.6450
   127.135  212.3350
```

```
       Slope  Solar radiation  Next_Tmax  Next_Tmin
0     2.785000      5992.895996       29.1       21.2
1     0.514100      5869.312500       30.5       22.5
2     0.266100      5863.555664       31.1       23.9
3     2.534800      5856.964844       31.7       24.3
4     0.505500      5859.552246       31.2       22.5
...        ...              ...        ...        ...
7747  0.155400      4443.313965       28.3       18.1
7748  0.222300      4438.373535       28.6       18.8
7749  0.271300      4451.345215       27.8       17.4
7750  0.098475      4329.520508       17.4       11.3
7751  5.178230      5992.895996       38.9       29.8

[7752 rows x 24 columns]>
```

It shows that the DataFrame *df* that contains our dataset has 23 input features and one output variable Next_Tmax.

To convert a list or a tuple into an array suitable for machine learning models, we use np.asarray(). To replace NaN values with 0s, we use np.nan_to_num(). Finally, we check the total number of NaN values by using np.isnan().sum() as follows:

```
y = np.asarray(df.Next_Tmax)
X = np.asarray(df.drop('Next_Tmax',axis=1))
X = np.nan_to_num(X)
y = np.nan_to_num(y)
print(np.isnan(X).sum())
print(np.isnan(X).sum())

Output:
0
0
```

We observe that NaN values have been removed. **StandardScaler** from **sklearn.preprocessing** transforms our data such that its distribution has a mean value 0 and standard deviation 1. This process is known as normalization of feature vectors and is required for many machine learning algorithms to perform better. We normalize our features as follows.

```
from sklearn.preprocessing import StandardScaler
s = StandardScaler()
X = s.fit_transform(X)
X.shape
```

Output:

```
(7752, 23)
```

Before applying a machine learning model, let us determine the strength of the relationship between different feature vectors. We can, for example, find the correlation between the feature vectors as follows.

```
import seaborn as sns
plt.figure(figsize=(22,22))
sns.heatmap(df.corr(), annot=True, annot_kws={"size": 10})
plt.show()
```

Output:

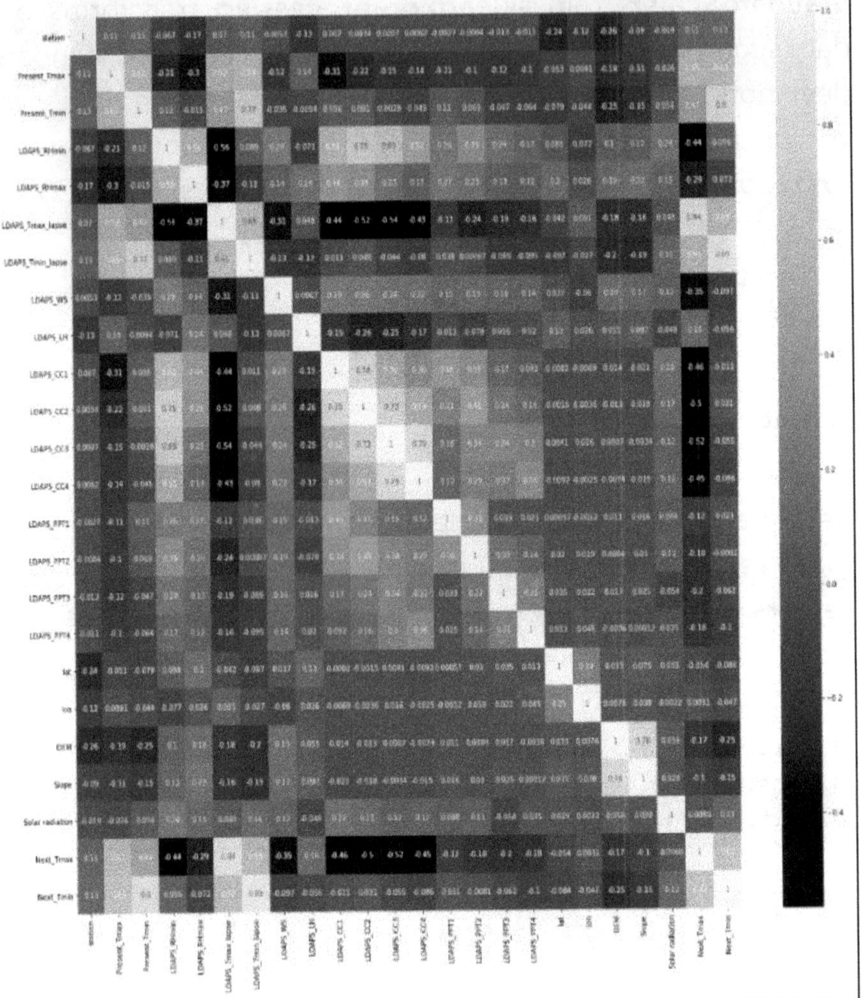

The light color boxes in the aforementioned plot indicate a strong positive correlation between features. The dark-colored boxes represent strong, negatively correlated features. However, the purple color is an indication of features almost independent of each other.

To apply a linear regression model to the training data, we import necessary libraries and packages. We also find and display the MAE and the MSE of the result to assess the performance of the method.

```
from sklearn.model_selection import train_test_split
Xtrain,Xtest,ytrain,ytest = train_test_split(X,y,test_
size=0.2)
from sklearn.linear_model import LinearRegression
m = LinearRegression()
m.fit(Xtrain,ytrain)
y_pred = m.predict(Xtest)
print('Absolute Error: %0.3f'%float(np.abs(ytest-y_pred).
sum()/ len(y_pred)))
```

Output:

```
Absolute Error:  1.181
```

```
from sklearn.metrics import mean_squared_error
print('Mean Squared Error: %0.3f'% mean_squared_
error(ytest, y_pred))
```

Output:

```
Mean Squared Error: 2.325
```

MAE = 1.181 and MSE = 2.325 may be acceptable, depending upon the problem to be solved. However, these errors are an indication that the output variable does not have a perfect linear relationship with the input features.

Furthermore, the correlation of variables in the confusion matrix shows that some features are strongly dependent upon other features. This is considered not suitable for a linear regression model because the independence of features is assumed in a linear regression model.

To cope with feature dependency, we may use PCA to extract new independent features from the dataset. If the output variable is almost linearly related to the feature vectors, the error of the linear regression model would be even less than what is reported above. To increase the performance, we may replace the linear model with a non-linear one such as non-linear regression, at the cost of computations.

9.2. Classification

This project aims to detect and recognize different English language accents. We use the Speaker Accent Recognition dataset from the UCI Machine Learning Repository.

https://archive.ics.uci.edu/ml/datasets/Speaker+Accent+Recognition#

This dataset contains single English words read by speakers from six different countries. This is a classification problem because we want to predict from six different accents/classes. We import the required libraries and the dataset as follows.

```
# import libraries
import numpy as np
import pandas as pd
import seaborn as sns
import matplotlib.pyplot as plt
# default seaborn settings
sns.set()
df = pd.read_csv('accent-mfcc-data-1.csv')
df.head()
```

Output:

	language	X1	X2	X3	X4	X5	X6	X7	X8	X9	X10	
0	ES	7.071476	-6.512900	7.650800	11.150783	-7.657312	12.484021	-11.709772	3.426596	1.462715	-2.812753	0.86
1	ES	10.982967	-5.157445	3.952060	11.529381	-7.638047	12.136098	-12.036247	3.491943	0.595441	-4.508811	2.33
2	ES	7.827108	-5.477472	7.816257	9.187592	-7.172511	11.715299	-13.847214	4.574075	-1.687559	-7.204041	-0.01
3	ES	6.744083	-5.688920	6.546789	9.000183	-6.924963	11.710766	-12.374388	6.169879	-0.544747	-6.019237	1.35
4	ES	5.836843	-5.326557	7.472265	8.847440	-6.773244	12.677218	-12.315061	4.416344	0.193500	-3.644812	2.15

To show the features and observations, we may type:

```
1. df.describe
```

Output:

```
<bound method NDFrame.describe of     language          X1          X2          X3          X4          X5          X6
0          ES   7.071476 -6.512900  7.650800  11.150783 -7.657312  12.484021
1          ES  10.982967 -5.157445  3.952060  11.529381 -7.638047  12.136098
2          ES   7.827108 -5.477472  7.816257   9.187592 -7.172511  11.715299
3          ES   6.744083 -5.688920  6.546789   9.000183 -6.924963  11.710766
4          ES   5.836843 -5.326557  7.472265   8.847440 -6.773244  12.677218
..        ...        ...       ...       ...        ...       ...        ...
324        US  -0.525273 -3.868338  3.548304   1.496249  3.490753   5.849887
325        US  -2.094001 -1.073113  1.217397  -0.550790  2.666547   7.449942
326        US   2.116909 -4.441482  5.350392   3.675396  2.715876   3.682670
327        US   0.299616  0.324844  3.299919   2.044040  3.634828   6.693840
328        US   3.214254 -3.135152  1.122691   4.712444  5.926518   6.915566

            X7         X8         X9        X10       X11       X12
0   -11.709772   3.426596   1.462715  -2.812753  0.866538 -5.244274
1   -12.036247   3.491943   0.595441  -4.508811  2.332147 -6.221857
2   -13.847214   4.574075  -1.687559  -7.204041 -0.011847 -6.463144
3   -12.374388   6.169879  -0.544747  -6.019237  1.358559 -6.356441
4   -12.315061   4.416344   0.193500  -3.644812  2.151239 -6.816310
..         ...        ...        ...        ...       ...       ...
324  -7.747027   9.738836 -11.754543   7.129909  0.209947 -1.946914
325  -6.418064  10.907098 -11.134323   6.728373  2.461446 -0.026113
326  -4.500850  11.798565 -12.031005   7.566142 -0.606010 -2.245129
327  -5.676224  12.000518 -11.912901   4.664406  1.197789 -2.230275
328  -5.799727  10.858532 -11.659845  10.605734  0.349482 -5.983281

[329 rows x 13 columns]>
```

We find 12 numerical features and 1 output categorical variable describing the classes. To find the correlation between features, use the following Python script:

```
import seaborn as sns
plt.figure(figsize=(22,22))
ax = sns.heatmap(df.corr(), annot=True, annot_
kws={"size": 20})
col_ax = plt.gcf().axes[-1]
col_ax.tick_params(labelsize=20)
plt.show()
```

Output:

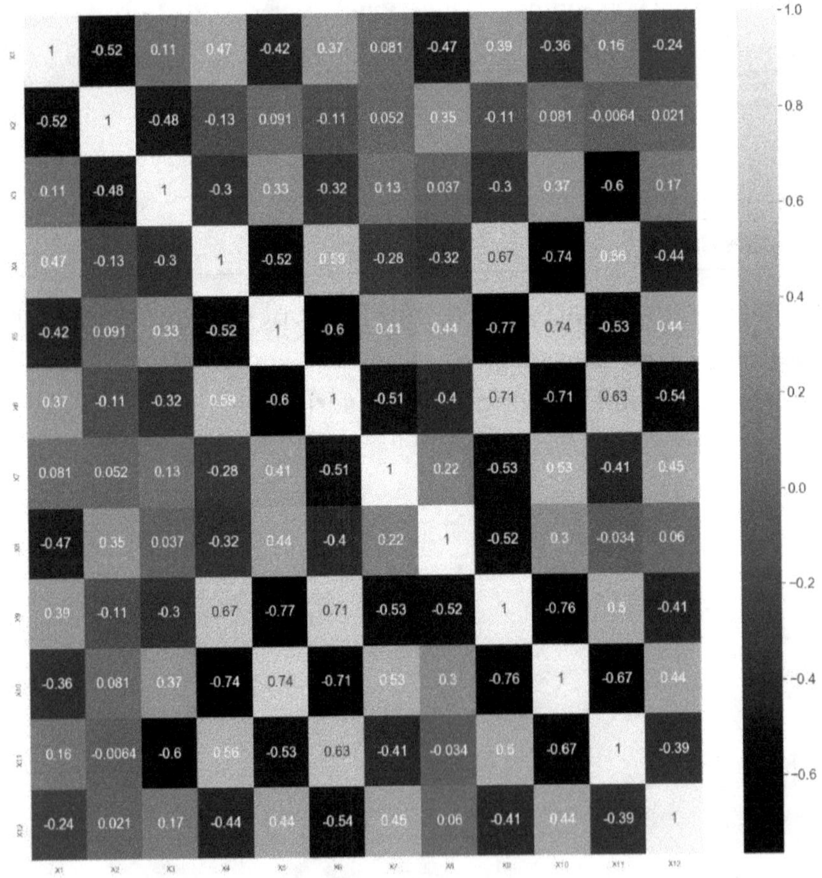

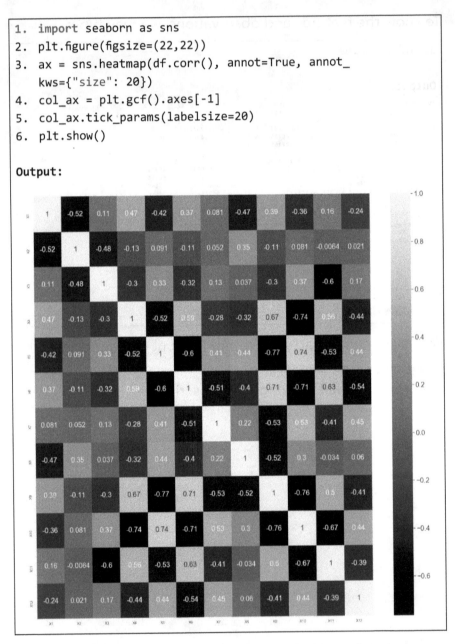

It can be observed that a strong correlation exists between features. Next, we explore whether classes are overlapping or not. To this end, we apply PCA to the features to get the first two principal components. Next, we encode string output labels to numbers to display the scatter plot of all six classes. We may type the following Python script:

```
from sklearn.decomposition import PCA
from sklearn import preprocessing
y = np.asarray(df.language)

# Creating label encoder to convert string labels to
numbers
le = preprocessing.LabelEncoder()
y_encoded=le.fit_transform(y)

# Applying PCA to extract first 2 principal components
pca = PCA(n_components=2)
X = np.asarray(df.drop('language',axis=1))
proj = pca.fit_transform(X)

# Plotting the first two principal components.
plt.scatter(proj[:, 0], proj[:, 1], c=y_encoded,
cmap='rainbow_r')
plt.colorbar()
plt.show()
```

Output:

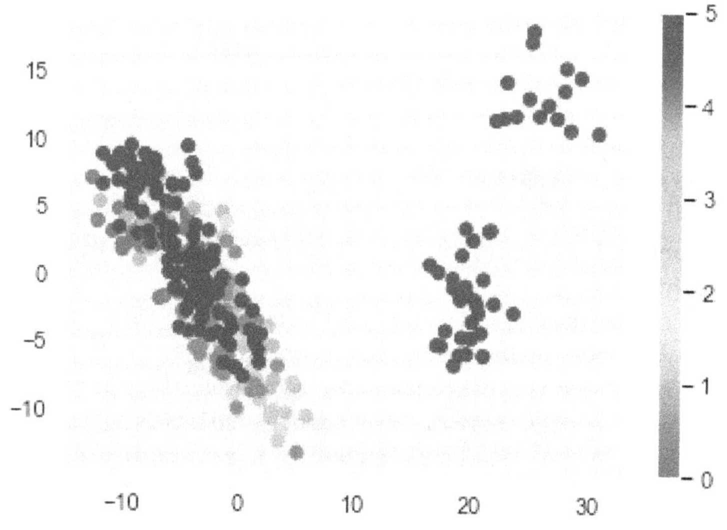

The classes are shown in six distinct colors. We observe a big overlap between classes. Due to this overlap, a learned classifier may not be able to distinguish between the instances of the classes.

To apply a machine learning model, we import the required libraries and packages. Moreover, we extract the target **language** in variable y and input features in Numpy array X.

```
from sklearn.model_selection import train_test_split
Xtrain,Xtest,ytrain,ytest = train_test_split(X,y,test_size=0.3)
from sklearn.ensemble import RandomForestClassifier
# Extraction of target variable and features, and storing them in Numpy arrays using asarray ( )
y = np.asarray(df.language)
X = np.asarray(df.drop('language',axis=1))
```

We apply a decision tree-based classifier known as a *random forest classifier*. This classifier is regarded as an ensemble method, in which we grow multiple trees on slightly different versions of the same dataset to predict the output class. We specify 100 estimators for a random forest classifier and use it to fit the training data.

```
M = RandomForestClassifier(100)

# Training the RandomForestClassifier
M.fit(Xtrain,ytrain)
Output:
RandomForestClassifier(bootstrap=True, ccp_alpha=0.0, class_weight=None,
        criterion='gini', max_depth=None, max_features='auto',
        max_leaf_nodes=None, max_samples=None,
        min_impurity_decrease=0.0, min_impurity_split=None,
        min_samples_leaf=1, min_samples_split=2,
        min_weight_fraction_leaf=0.0, n_estimators=100,
        n_jobs=None, oob_score=False, random_state=None,
        verbose=0, warm_start=False)
```

Note that we use test_size=0.3. That means 30 percent of the examples are assigned to the test set. Growing multiple trees allows us to predict the output class using all the grown trees of a random forest classifier. Each tree votes for the class it predicts. Finally, we choose the class by the majority vote. We have used 100 estimators, i.e., the number of trees in the random forest classifier. Thus, for each test point, the class that gets the maximum number of votes out of 100 votes is assigned to that test point.

Now, we make predictions and display the classification report.

```
1. y_pred = M.predict(Xtest)
2. from sklearn.metrics import classification_report
3. print(classification_report(ytest,y_pred,target_names=df.
   language.unique()))
```

Output:

```
              precision    recall  f1-score   support

          ES       0.80      0.44      0.57         9
          FR       1.00      0.57      0.73         7
          GE       1.00      0.50      0.67        10
          IT       0.56      0.62      0.59         8
          UK       0.91      0.77      0.83        13
          US       0.75      0.94      0.84        52

    accuracy                           0.78        99
   macro avg       0.84      0.64      0.70        99
weighted avg       0.80      0.78      0.77        99
```

We observe that an accuracy of 74 percent is reported by the random forest classifier. One of the main reasons for not getting accuracy close to 100 percent is the presence of overlapping classes, as observed in the plot of principal components. The accuracy of the model can be improved if we separate the classes as much as possible.

To draw the confusion matrix, we type the following commands:

```
from sklearn.metrics import confusion_matrix

mat = confusion_matrix(ytest,y_pred)
sns.heatmap(mat.T,square=True,annot=True,fmt='d',
cbar=False,xticklabels=df.language.unique(),
yticklabels=df.language.unique())

plt.xlabel("True label")
plt.ylabel("predicted label")
```

Output:

```
Text(89.18, 0.5, 'predicted label')
```

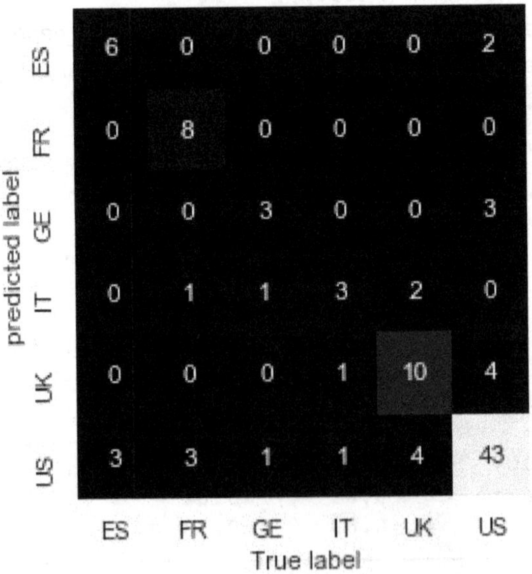

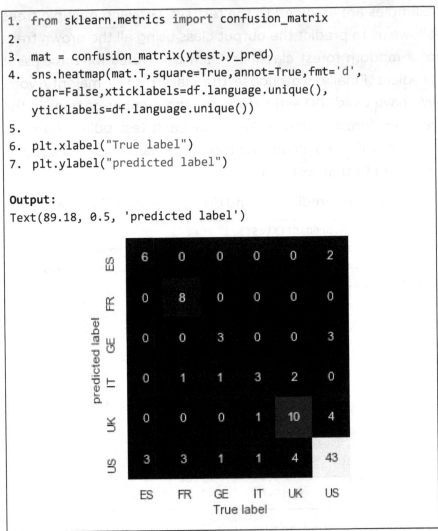

The entries on the diagonal of the confusion matrix indicate correct predictions. However, there are some misclassified points, as well. For example, four UK accents are wrongly classified as US accents, and four US accents are misclassified as UK accents. Note that we have randomly split the dataset into training and test sets. When we run the same Python script again, we may get slightly different results because of the random assignment of the dataset examples to training and test sets.

9.3. Face Recognition

Our third project is on Face Recognition, which deals with the problem: given the picture of a face, find the name of the person given in a training set. For this project, we use **Labeled Faces in the Wild (LFW)** people dataset. This dataset is a collection of JPEG pictures of famous people collected on the internet; the details of this dataset are available on the official website:

http://vis-www.cs.umass.edu/lfw/

In this dataset, each color picture is centered on a single face. Each pixel of the color image is encoded by a float in the range 0.0 - 1.0. We import the libraries and download the dataset.

```
# Importing libraries and packages
from sklearn.datasets import fetch_lfw_people
import numpy as np
import matplotlib.pyplot as plt
import seaborn as sns

# Settings default settings of sns library
sns.set()

# requires internet connection to download data for the
first time
faces = fetch_lfw_people(min_faces_per_person=50)    ]
```

Output:

```
Downloading LFW metadata: https://ndownloader.figshare.com/files/5976012
Downloading LFW metadata: https://ndownloader.figshare.com/files/5976009
Downloading LFW metadata: https://ndownloader.figshare.com/files/5976006
Downloading LFW data (~200MB): https://ndownloader.figshare.com/files/5976015
```

When we run this code, the dataset starts to download. It may take a while to download the dataset depending upon the speed of the internet connection. We start exploring the dataset. To check the number of rows and column of the dataset, we may type:

```
faces.data.shape

Output:
(1560, 2914)
```

There are 1,560 images, each having a total of 2914 pixels. To check the shape of an individual image, we may type the following command.

```
faces.images[0].shape

Output:
(62, 47)
```

It shows that each image has a pixel grid of 62 rows and 47 columns. We display the names of the persons whose images are present in the dataset.

```
faces.target_names

Output:
array(['Ariel Sharon', 'Colin Powell', 'Donald Rumsfeld', 'George W Bush',
       'Gerhard Schroeder', 'Hugo Chavez', 'Jacques Chirac',
       'Jean Chretien', 'John Ashcroft', 'Junichiro Koizumi',
       'Serena Williams', 'Tony Blair'], dtype='<U17')


faces.target_names.size

Output:
12

np.unique(faces.target)

Output:
array([ 0,  1,  2,  3,  4,  5,  6,  7,  8,  9, 10, 11],
    dtype=int64)
```

We can also display the names of the images by typing the following command.

```
faces.target_names[4]

Output:
'Gerhard Schroeder'
```

To show one image or many images together, we type the following command.

```
plt.imshow(faces.images[0])

Output:
<matplotlib.image.AxesImage at 0x2b9c8a12588>
```

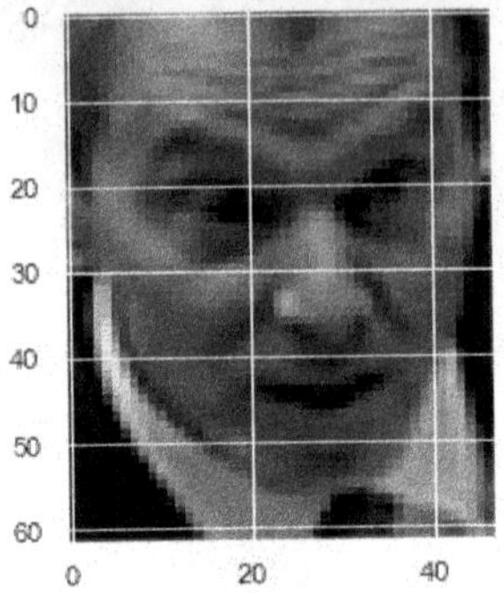

We can also plot multiple images together as follows:

```
fig , ax = plt.subplots(2,4)
for idx,axidx in enumerate(ax.flat):
    axidx.imshow(faces.images[idx],cmap='bone')
    axidx.set(xticks=[],yticks=[],xlabel=faces.target_
names[faces.target[idx]])

Output:
```

To model our dataset, we import the required machine learning libraries and packages such as support vector classifier (SVC) and PCA.

```
from sklearn.svm import SVC
from sklearn.decomposition import PCA
from sklearn.pipeline import make_pipeline
```

Note that we have also imported make_pipelie a utility that allows us to specify the sequence of steps such as preprocessing to be taken to apply a machine learning model.

Since neighboring pixels in any image are highly correlated and cannot be used directly into a machine learning algorithm, we transform our images using principal component analysis.

```
pcaModel = PCA(n_components=150,whiten=True)

#Support vector machine with radial basis function (rbf)
svmModel = SVC(kernel='rbf',class_weight='balanced')

mdl = make_pipeline(pcaModel,svmModel)
```

We have used 150 PCA components to transform the images of the dataset. The option whiten ensures that outputs have unit component-wise variances.

We split our dataset into training and test images.

```
from sklearn.model_selection import train_test_split
Xtrain,Xtest,ytrain,ytest = train_test_split(faces.
data,faces.target,test_size=0.2)
```

A support vector classifier uses hyper-parameters whose values affect the prediction accuracy of the learned classifier. These parameters have to be estimated, and their optimal values should be used for better accuracy of the model.

In Scikit-Learn, the parameters are passed as arguments to the constructor of the estimator classes. It is possible and recommended to search the hyper-parameter space for the best cross-validation score.

Grid search is a technique that is used to estimate the optimal value of the hyper-parameters. Thus, we import and use GridSearchCV for the best cross-validation score.

```
from sklearn.model_selection import GridSearchCV
param_grid = {'svc__C':[1,5,15,30],'svc__
gamma':[0.00001,0.00005,0.0001,0.005]}
grid = GridSearchCV(mdl,param_grid)

grid.fit(Xtrain,ytrain)
```

Output:

```
GridSearchCV(cv='warn', error_score='raise-deprecating',
             estimator=Pipeline(memory=None,
                                steps=[('pca',
                                        PCA(copy=True, iterated_power='auto',
                                            n_components=150, random_state=None,
                                            svd_solver='auto', tol=0.0,
                                            whiten=True)),
                                       ('svc',
                                        SVC(C=1.0, cache_size=200,
                                            class_weight='balanced', coef0=0.0,
                                            decision_function_shape='ovr',
                                            degree=3, gamma='auto_deprecated',
                                            kernel='rbf', max_iter=-1,
                                            probability=False,
                                            random_state=None, shrinking=True,
                                            tol=0.001, verbose=False))],
                                verbose=False),
             iid='warn', n_jobs=None,
             param_grid={'svc__C': [1, 5, 15, 30],
                         'svc__gamma': [1e-05, 5e-05, 0.0001, 0.005]},
             pre_dispatch='2*n_jobs', refit=True, return_train_score=False,
             scoring=None, verbose=0)
```

```
print(grid.best_params_)
```

Output:

```
{'svc__C': 1, 'svc__gamma': 0.005}
```

To make predictions, we type the following Python script.

```
mdl = grid.best_estimator_
y_pred = mdl.predict(Xtest)
fig,ax = plt.subplots(5,7)

for idx , axidx in enumerate(ax.flat):
    axidx.imshow(Xtest[idx].reshape(62,47),cmap='bone')
    axidx.set(xticks=[],yticks=[])
    axidx.set_ylabel(faces.target_names[y_pred[idx]].
split()[-
    1],color='green' if y_pred[idx]==ytest[idx] else 'red')

    plt.figure(figsize=(15,15))
    fig.suptitle('Wrong are in red',size=14)
```

Output:

To assess the performance of the proposed support vector classifier, we generate the classification report as follows.

```
1. from sklearn.metrics import classification_report
2. print(classification_report(ytest,y_pred,target_
   names=faces.target_names))
```

Output:

```
                   precision    recall  f1-score   support

     Ariel Sharon       0.82      0.90      0.86        20
     Colin Powell       0.84      0.90      0.87        51
  Donald Rumsfeld       0.81      0.74      0.77        23
    George W Bush       0.89      0.90      0.89       107
Gerhard Schroeder       0.68      0.89      0.77        19
      Hugo Chavez       0.91      0.77      0.83        13
   Jacques Chirac       0.90      0.82      0.86        11
    Jean Chretien       1.00      0.82      0.90        11
    John Ashcroft       0.89      0.73      0.80        11
Junichiro Koizumi       0.80      0.67      0.73         6
  Serena Williams       0.92      0.75      0.83        16
       Tony Blair       0.92      0.92      0.92        24

         accuracy                           0.86       312
        macro avg       0.86      0.82      0.84       312
     weighted avg       0.86      0.86      0.86       312
```

It is evident from the report that we get an accuracy score of 83 percent. To check the performance of the method on individual classes, we plot the confusion matrix as follows.

```
from sklearn.metrics import confusion_matrix
mat = confusion_matrix(ytest,y_pred)

# heatmap with format fmt as decimal, colorbar is off
sns.heatmap(mat.T,square=True,annot=True,fmt='d',
cbar=False,xticklabels=faces.target_
names,yticklabels=faces.target_names)


plt.xlabel("True label")
plt.ylabel("predicted label")
```

Output:

```
Text(89.18, 0.5, 'predicted label')
```

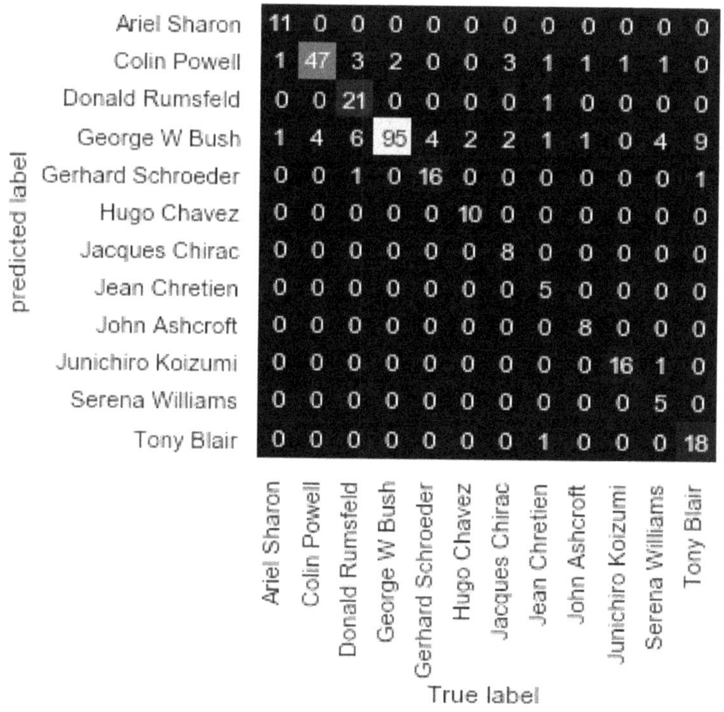

The true and predicted labels are shown on the x and y-axis of the confusion matrix, respectively. The diagonal entries on the confusion matrix represent correct classification results. It can be observed that most images are correctly classified by the model. However, occasional misclassified results are shown on the off-diagonal entries of the matrix. For example, *Tony Blair* is misclassified as *George W Bush* nine times, and *Donald Rumsfeld* is wrongly predicted as *George W Bush* six times.

One of the many possible reasons to get an accuracy score less than 100 percent is due to the fact that we are using a small set of images, 1,560, for the training set as compared to the dimensions, 2914 pixels in each image of the input images.

When we use a large dataset with a sufficient number of training examples of each class, the model learns better because it sees a whole lot of features of each class. State-of-the-art results have been obtained by different machine learning algorithms to recognize human faces when people used a training set containing millions of images.

10

Key Insights and Further Avenues

This book gives a good deal of introductory material on data science and Python to the beginners. However, it is noteworthy to realize that this book is just the tip of the iceberg. Obviously, data science is a vast topic, and there is a lot more information on data science and Python available online and offline. The following sections introduce the reader to ample amounts of data science resources that the reader can explore and use.

The aim of this chapter is to conclude the book and provide the reader with a number of promising avenues that will, hopefully, help in further developing the knowledge and skills of Python for data science.

10.1. Key Insights

Data science applies scientific methods and algorithms to extract knowledge and insights by processing and analyzing data. It is a multidisciplinary field that makes use of machine learning algorithms and statistical methods to train the computer to make predictions and get insights from the data.

Every occupation can be considered a complicated system with many facets. Even experienced personnel do not have a 100 percent understanding of how the occupation works. Any data we gather about the business describes some characteristics of the behavior of this complex system.

The data science process starts with the right questions related to real-world business problems. For example, a new company, trying to find its place in a market, may ask the question: How can we increase our sales? How can we fulfill the demands and requests of our clients?

After having a clear picture of the problem to be solved, we collect the data from various sources. We ask ourselves, *Is the collected data is useful? If not, what more data do we need?*

Next, we process the data to remove errors in the corrupt records of the collected data and to handle missing values in the data. At this stage, we clean the data to convert it in a form that is suitable to analyze.

To understand the information contained in a dataset, we explore the cleaned preprocessed data. Here, we ask questions such as:

- What are the trends and correlations in the data?
- What are the significant characteristics/ features of the data?
- What are the distributions of key features/ variables?
- What relationships between features do we expect to observe?
- What are the assumptions about the features?

Next, we apply machine learning/statistical algorithms to come up with a model that describes the relationship between the input and the output. This step reveals the insights and the trained model at this stage used in making predictions on the unseen test data.

Finally, we communicate the results of our findings to the stakeholders using visualizations that summarize the results.

10.2. Data Science Resources

There is a wealth of information available online on data science and Python. In this section, we furnish the reader with some of the popular resources.

To explore data science resources, articles, interviews, and data science newsletters, you are encouraged to visit:

https://www.datascienceweekly.org/.

KDnuggets is a popular learning resource that provides a step by step guide to learn data science. You can also find links to other online resources. The resources on this website can make your learning process easier.

https://www.kdnuggets.com/

Data science central is a platform to get social interaction, forum-based support, and the latest information on technology, tools, trends, and careers.

https://www.datasciencecentral.com/

Fivethirtyeight or 538 is a website that focuses on opinion poll analysis, politics, economics, and sports blogging. It also provides public datasets for data scientists to work on.

https://fivethirtyeight.com/

Flowing Data is a useful website that is a collection of data science projects, tutorials, courses, and newsletters. However, most of the data on this website is in R, a popular programming language for statistics and data science.

https://flowingdata.com/

University of California Irvine (UCI) maintains datasets specifically for the machine learning and data science community.

https://archive.ics.uci.edu/ml/index.php

10.3. Challenges

If you want to access tons of public datasets, learn from the examples by top data scientists, and even start competing, Kaggle is an obvious place for you.

https://www.kaggle.com/competitions

Topcoder connects data scientists throughout the world via contests, tasks, and talent pools to deliver insights and solutions.

https://www.topcoder.com/community/data-science/

For advanced competitions, DrivenData hosts online challenges, usually lasting 2–3 months, where a global community of data scientists has to compete to present best models for real-world problems.

https://www.drivendata.org/

To discover ongoing machine learning and data science contests across Kaggle, DrivenData, etc., visit:

https://mlcontests.com/

Conclusions

A huge amount of data is being generated at an unprecedented rate by individual users and companies. If this data is not processed and analyzed at the same or comparable rate, the value associated with this data reduces. Thus, it is of utmost importance to extract knowledge from the data.

This book employed Python to demonstrate to the readers how the knowledge could be extracted, and practical insights are generated from the data. Python, an open-source language, has a simple syntax, and it makes data science tasks easy and doable.

Numerous useful libraries offered by Python are used extensively in this book to perform all the tedious tasks in the background. The libraries employed in this book for data processing, analysis, modeling, and visualization include Numpy, Pandas, Scikit-Learn, and Matplotlib. The book also establishes how machine learning algorithms could be used to perform a variety of real-world data science tasks.

The book provides readers with the necessary tools and packages to kick-start data science projects to solve problems of practical nature. Considerable time is spent on the main stages of a data science pipeline that include data acquisition, data preparation, exploratory data analysis, data modeling, evaluation, and interpretation of the results.

In each chapter, the theoretical background behind numerous techniques has been provided, and practical examples have been furnished to explain the working of these techniques. As a final note, the readers are encouraged to explore the online data science resources given in this chapter.

Answers to Exercise Questions

Chapter 1

Question 1: C

Question 2: D

Question 3: D

Question 4: C

Chapter 2

Question 1: B

Question 2: B

Question 3: C

Question 4: C

Question 5: D

Chapter 3

Question 1: A

Question 2: C

Question 3: B

Question 4: A

Question 5: B

Question 6: C

Question 7: B

Question 8: C

Question 9: C

Question 10: C

Chapter 4

Question 1: B

Question 2: A

Question 3: D

Question 4: B

Question 5: C

Chapter 5

Question 1: A

Question 2: B

Question 3: C

Question 4: B

Question 5: A

Chapter 6

Question 1: B

Question 2: C

Question 3: B

Question 4: C

Question 5: D

Chapter 7

Question 1: B

Question 2: D

Question 3: B

Question 4: A

Question 5: D

Question 6: B

Question 7: B

Question 8: B

Question 9: B

Question 10: C

Chapter 8

Question 1: C

Question 2: D

Question 3: C

Question 4: A

From the Same Publisher

Python Machine Learning
https://bit.ly/3gcb2iG

Python Deep Learning
https://bit.ly/3gci9Ys

Python Data Visualization
https://bit.ly/3wXqDJl

Python for Data Analysis
https://bit.ly/3wPYEM2

Python Data Preprocessing

https://bit.ly/3fLV3ci

Python for NLP

https://bit.ly/3chlTqm

10 ML Projects Explained from Scratch

https://bit.ly/34KFsDk

Python Scikit-Learn for Beginners

https://bit.ly/3fPbtRf

Data Science with Python

https://bit.ly/3wVQ5iN

Statistics with Python

https://bit.ly/3z27KHt